MW00773592

EVOLVING HAMLET

Cognitive Studies in Literature and Performance

Literature, Science, and a New Humanities
  Jonathan Gottschall

Engaging Audiences
  Bruce McConachie

The Public Intellectualism of Ralph Waldo Emerson and W.E.B. Du Bois
  Ryan Schneider

Performance, Cognitive Theory, and Devotional Culture
  Jill Stevenson

Shakespearean Neuroplay
  Amy Cook

Evolving Hamlet
  Angus Fletcher

Evolving Hamlet

Seventeenth-Century English Tragedy and the Ethics of Natural Selection

Angus Fletcher

EVOLVING HAMLET
Copyright © Angus Fletcher, 2011.

First published in 2011 by
PALGRAVE MACMILLAN®
in the United States—a division of St. Martin's Press LLC,
175 Fifth Avenue, New York, NY 10010.

Where this book is distributed in the UK, Europe and the rest of the world,
this is by Palgrave Macmillan, a division of Macmillan Publishers Limited,
registered in England, company number 785998, of Houndmills,
Basingstoke, Hampshire RG21 6XS.

Palgrave Macmillan is the global academic imprint of the above companies
and has companies and representatives throughout the world.

Palgrave® and Macmillan® are registered trademarks in the United States,
the United Kingdom, Europe and other countries.

ISBN: 978–0–230–11168–4

Library of Congress Cataloging-in-Publication Data

Fletcher, Angus, 1930–
    Evolving Hamlet : seventeenth-century English tragedy and the ethics
of natural selection / Angus Fletcher.
        p. cm.—(Cognitive studies in literature and performance)
        ISBN 978–0–230–11168–4 (hardback)
        1. English drama (Tragedy)—History and criticism. 2. English drama—
17th century—History and criticism. 3. Philosophy of mind in literature.
4. Natural selection—Philosophy. 5. Evolution (Biology)—Philosophy.
6. Philosophy of mind. 7. Science and literature. I. Title.

PR678.T7F54 2011
822'.05120936—dc22   2010035290

A catalogue record of the book is available from the British Library.

Design by Newgen Imaging Systems (P) Ltd., Chennai, India.

First edition: March 2011

10 9 8 7 6 5 4 3 2 1

Printed in the United States of America.

What's this war in the heart of nature?
—The Thin Red Line

Contents

Acknowledgments   ix

Preface   xi

Introduction: The Descent of Ethics   1

1   Faustus, Macbeth, and the Riddle of Tomorrow   15

2   Partial Belief in *Julius Caesar* and *Hamlet*   39

3   *Othello* and the Subject of Ocular Proof   67

4   *The Indian Emperour* and the Reason of
    New World Conflict   85

5   Cartesian Generosity and the New Shakespeare   101

6   *King Lear* and the Endurance of Tragedy   123

7   The Progress of Ethics   135

Conclusion   147

Notes   151

Index   185

Acknowledgments

In writing this book, I have incurred many debts. I owe Edward Stuenkel for opening the toolkit of neuroscience; David Quint for reading closely; Giles Gunn for pragmatism; Victoria Kahn for encouraging chances; Michael Della Rocca for philosophy as history; Joseph Roach for the matter of performance; Blakey Vermeule for courage; Mike Benveniste, Daniel Breen, and Vanessa Ryan for comradeship; and Madeline Puzo for the gift of theater. I owe Sarah and my sisters, Ashley, Katrina, and Joanna, for a glimpse of the good life. And I owe Lawrence Manley for his patient care and his infinite stores; I owe Seth Lerer for his genius and his generosity; and I owe Thomas Habinek for his spirit and support—*inveniet viam aut faciet.* I hope that in some small way, this book repays the confidence that you have shown in me.

Preface

This is an eclectic book with a narrow purpose: to suggest that *Hamlet* and the other tragedies of the English seventeenth century can help address the challenge posed to ethics by the theory of natural selection. Put in such naked terms, this must seem a rather fanciful enterprise—a roundabout solution to a problem that does not really exist. Old plays are not obviously suited to resolving the concerns of modern science, and anyway, Darwin's theory is not regarded as much of a moral menace anymore. Though his contemporaries fretted that it would "sink the human race,"[1] we have survived its existence so capably that even the Catholic Church has grown conciliatory, proposing recently that "biological evolution and creation are by no means mutually exclusive."[2] What has allowed this calming of fears, however, is not the integration of natural selection into ethics. Rather, it is the segregation of each into its own domain. Evolutionary biologists from Darwin to Richard Dawkins have spoken of the need to supplement natural selection with some outside notion of the good,[3] and in general, natural selection has been seen as a scientific theory, not an ethical one. In part, this preference for keeping natural selection out of ethics has been motivated by moral idealism, for Darwin's theory spells an end not only to providence, but to social justice, natural rights, and any other moral absolute. But the separation of Darwinism from ethics is also pragmatic. For having dispensed with idealism, natural selection appears no kinder to practical ethics. Because selection is a nonteleological process in which the criteria for survival are always changing, there is no way to anticipate what forms of life will prove durable in the future. So it is that our own sex cells are set up to randomize the transmission of genetic material, blindly hoping for a lucky strike. Even practices such as maximizing one's offspring are no guarantee, for having fewer (or even no) offspring can be the more effective way to keep one's genes alive.[4] In short, just as Darwinism denies a fixed hierarchy of species, so too does it preclude a fixed ranking of behaviors. And if this means that we need no longer fear that natural selection will authorize a descent into rape and murder, it also confronts us with the practical difficulty that natural selection does not seem to underwrite any particular actions at all.

Given how little Darwinism contributes to ethics, the decision to keep them apart can seem a sensible one. And yet far from resolving the difficulty raised by natural selection, this segregation only highlights it. For the real problem is not that Darwinism fails to generate a usable theory of ethics; the real problem is that this failure reveals a deep conflict within the nature of life itself. On the one hand, we are led by life to believe that there is a purpose to our existence. Although we may not be inherently moral in the idealistic sense of having a spark of timeless virtue implanted in our souls, we are—as Darwin's heirs in cognitive science have shown—inherently ethical in a more practical sense. Because we inhabit a world that brings us both reward and pain, our brains are hardwired to analyze the connection between our actions and their consequences, seeking a logic that leads to a more pleasurable state. Yet on the other hand, natural selection suggests that this biological drive is a fool's dream. There is no greater logic, only blind motion. Our subtly calculating brains, our hopes, our fears, our values—all of it springs from a process that is dull, insentient, utterly without design. In short, the grim riddle of Darwinism is not that it leaves us without direction. It is that it pits life against itself. Informing us that we are intentional beings in a nonintentional world, it asks us to accept that our nature is alien to the nature that conceived us.

That we have lived so long with this contradiction says something about the brute pragmatism of life. When we are pressed with worldly concerns, scrambling to keep our families sheltered and our tables full, questions about the ultimate purpose of it all recede into the background. We would like to know what it all means, of course, but we can take comfort in the knowledge that the answer will come in time. Whatever the end, we will find out when we get there. Until then, puzzles like the one posed by Darwinism seem like errands for the idle, excuses for those ivory towers that have been thrown high, raised low, and rebuilt a million times, all without offering a view above the clouds. And yet even as the paradox of Darwinism seems an invitation to irrelevance, it has deeply practical consequences. Because our brains relentlessly parse life into hypothetical narratives of cause-and-effect, we are naturally thrown into a hunt for first origins and ultimate ends. This is where we get our fear of death and it is also where we get our hunger for heaven and other distant utopias. In effect, the same narrative capacity that gives us a practical edge at navigating the problems of this world also burdens us with the anxieties that have encouraged the invention of the other worlds of religion and social idealism. These imaginary places, in turn, have become plot-points in real-world narratives, propelling us into martyrdom and revolution, imperialism and holy war, punishing human bodies in the service of fable. And this is why our ambivalence to Darwinism has proved unfortunate. For though the strict anti-idealism of Darwin's theory could remedy much of the cruelty that we author on ourselves, we have found it impossible to abandon our religious or social Shangri-Las for what amounts to a nonethics. To our story-telling brains, this is a cure that feels worse than the disease. However much we may want peace, we want purpose more, and so rather than embracing Darwinism for its humane potential, we have preferred our violent plots.[5]

It is here, I believe, that *Hamlet* can prove useful. Specifically, I believe that it can help us develop an intentional ethics that accepts the nonintentionality of life, allowing the practical benefits of a Darwinist worldview without placing an impossible demand on our psyches. In light of the situation described above, this confidence in the power of an antique drama might seem peculiar, even perverse. Even if we ignore the fact that *Hamlet* was written long before Darwin proposed his theory, the very form of Shakespeare's play seems inappropriate to the task at hand. After all, if a major part of the problem with ethics is our overattachment to narrative, then why would we turn to more stories for relief? As I hope to show in this book, however, the narrative aspect of *Hamlet* is precisely what makes it useful. To begin with, because *Hamlet* is a story, it speaks to us in a language that we are biologically built to understand. Where Darwin's theory asks us to change our nature, *Hamlet* works in concert with the way we already are. Moreover, *Hamlet* is not just any story—it is a tragedy. Since the time of Oedipus, tragedy has explored the problem of human action in a world driven by an inhuman logic, and as I will explain in the following chapter, there are a number of practical reasons (both physical and historical) for supposing that seventeenth-century English tragedy is a particularly promising resource for engaging with the question of intentional behavior in an unintentional cosmos. Unlike stories of better worlds, this tragedy faces the challenge of living in a universe that is set up on principles antithetical to our own habits of thought, and it does so not by fueling dreamy speculation, but by encouraging specific behaviors that work with our physical nature. *Hamlet*, in short, offers a practical remedy to a biological problem, one that rubbed against human life long before Darwin described it, and so though it may seem odd to seek a scientific ethics in the corridors of an old story, I hope to show that it is not such a fanciful enterprise after all. Rather, it is an experiment in practical ethics, and in the end, what matters is not its deductive self-evidence, but whether it fails or bears fruit.

That such an unlikely experiment could be launched at all is a reflection of the growing openness to biological approaches to literature. What was until recently unthinkable has become a vibrant subfield, yielding dozens of books and articles in less than a decade. And yet as is perhaps already obvious, this book will be rather different from previous efforts to find a convergence-point between biology and literature. In the main, these previous efforts—which I will refer to as "biological criticism"—have set out to use the tools of science to elucidate the function of literature. Sometimes they have searched for the cognitive capacities that allow the human brain to appreciate literature;[6] sometimes they have looked for the broader contexts of our physical evolution to explain our drive to generate and consume literary works;[7] and sometimes they have sought a scientific method for studying literary form.[8] Almost all of this work, moreover, has been written against the current of contemporary literary studies, treating science as a means to resolve longstanding scholarly disputes or to protect our primitive experience of reading from the killing fields of high theory. In place of the intractable and often unfathomable disagreements that have come to dominate the contemporary study of literature, biological criticism has offered a regularization of method, a validation of our impulse to read the minds of literary characters, and a declaration of the importance of poems, novels, and plays to human life.

I am grateful for the opportunities this work has opened, but because it is the place of a preface to distinguish a book as precisely as possible from other similar labors, I will confess why I have not joined the mainstream of biological criticism myself. Having spent four years working in a neuroscience lab, and having been heavily influenced by Karl Popper and other twentieth-century philosophers of science, I have come to view science not as a source of knowledge, but as a source of practical solutions to human problems. That is, I see science not as metaphysics, but as a handbook of jimmy-rigged responses to physical concerns. Science is happy, of course, to give us models and hypotheses that sketch out the laws of motion and the mechanisms of life; but what justifies these sketches is not their relationship to truth, but their ability to help us build bridges and devise medicines and predict the weather. To this end, it seems to me that there is something impractical about the interest that many biological critics have in using science to address the problems faced by contemporary literary studies. Literary studies is the way that it is because it has always made large room for the speculations of philosophers and social reformers. Driven by concerns about knowledge and justice, its students have debated the nature of humanity, the possibility of truth, and the way to a better world. In the end, these are not matters that science can give us final certainty about, and so when scholars have tried to use biology to resolve the speculations of literary studies, the results have been disappointing. Attempting to regularize the methods of literary criticism, they have inspired more quarreling; announcing themselves as allies in the old cause, they have been derided as tyrants; and most worrying of all, in trying to introduce literary critics to the wonders of science, they have diminished the vitality of scientific inquiry. For though scientific inquiry does not point us toward any set ideal, its reactive, problem-solving method gives it a progressive function. Like life itself, it may not be going anywhere particular, but it is always growing nonetheless. In contrast, because biological critics have focused on explaining why literature does what it does, their work has a distinctly self-congratulatory tone. It validates the way we already read, the way our brains already are, the way that literature already works.[9] In effect, it is a conservative enterprise, one that seems less matched to the quickness of the living than to the complacence of the doomed.

Instead of treating literature as the end product of evolution, my own preference has therefore been to approach it as a biological tool that has emerged in organic response to the problems of life. As such, it is useful without being an ordained necessity, and as I have been suggesting over the preceding pages, I believe that its particular usefulness lies not in the enrichment of knowledge, but in the practice of ethics. Following the standard view of biologists, I take the core problem of ethics to be the tension between the individual and society.[10] Out of physical necessity, we are more conscious of our own needs than of the needs of others. Since our brains are not materially continuous with the brains of others, our hunger, our fear, and our other mental states are vivid to us in a way that the mental states of others are not. This egoistic bias, moreover, is often a practical problem, for cooperative societies are usually better than lone individuals at overcoming the physical challenges of existence. There is therefore a biological incentive to address the problem of our isolated awareness, and so it is that many different forms of sentient life—from primates to rodents—have their brains hardwired to include "social" impulses such as generosity and a sense of fairness.[11] In humans, moreover, this social impulse has been lent an added dimension by our capacity for tool-use.[12] To help restrain our egoistic bias and allow room for others, we have developed moral codes, we have developed democracy, and perhaps most importantly, we have developed language.[13] Language is a form of restrained communication, a way to express ourselves without resorting to physical force, a means to articulate subtle differences and negotiate them. As an elaboration of the possibilities of language, literature is therefore at least in part a continuation of its function as an ethical tool,[14] and so whatever other uses literature may have, I am interested in its place in our ethical toolbox, in its value for generating social practices that help us survive the changing tides of life.

Where previous biological critics have focused on science as a means to resolve the problems raised by literature, the following chapters will therefore look to literature to resolve the problems raised by science. And while this is not a road much traveled at present, there are many examples, ancient and modern, of the horizons it can open. Two millennia ago, when the poet Lucretius found himself contemplating the doctrine of atomism, and with it, the possibility that humans were simply bits of matter to be scattered in eternity, he turned to song, writing a consolation that gave shape to the life lived without an immortal soul.[15] More recently, when Alan Shepard was asked why he wanted to be an astronaut, he replied: "Buck Rogers." While earlier generations had shuddered when the Copernican revolution bumped the earth from the center of the universe into a sprawling chaos of innumerable worlds, he found direction in a literary tradition that began when Jules Verne and H. G. Wells transformed the collapse of the old astronomy into the inspiration for a fresh heroism. Although recent scholars have looked at science to address the questions raised by literature, long use thus shows that this relationship can work the other way. Works like *Hamlet* can be more than problems. They can be problem solvers.

Introduction

The Descent of Ethics

I am aware that some persons maintain that actions performed impulsively...cannot be called moral. They confine this term to actions done deliberately...But it appears scarcely possible to draw any clear line of distinction of this kind.
—Charles Darwin, *The Descent of Man*

When Darwin sat down to write *The Descent of Man*, his aim was to show creationists that natural selection could explain the "noblest" of human faculties, not simply language and intelligence, but sociability, sympathy, and the other hallmarks of "the moral sense."[1] And yet in tracing moral behavior back to material biology, he found that he had severely constrained the future course of ethics. If our social behavior was to be improved—and certainly, there were indications that it was lacking—then it would seem necessary to change our underlying biology. Social reform must become identical with eugenics.[2] This did not sit well with Darwin, who thought it "evil" for societies to select who should live and who should die.[3] In addition, he felt it naive to suppose that even enlightened societies were capable of infallibly identifying the good. After all, different tendencies were useful in different ways, allowing "some advantage" to behaviors that were not traditionally perceived as moral.[4] Unwilling to sanction an active manipulation of human biology, Darwin therefore chose to strip ethics of its progressive function. Assuming that the existence of humans was evolutionary justification for their current sense of morality, he made it the business of ethics to reinforce the social instincts that people already possessed. Good laws, good teachers, good customs would not carry us away from our nature, but would reflect the way we naturally were.[5]

In its own time, Darwin's cautious naturalism failed to convince many of his followers, but in ours, it has become the accepted norm of the biological sciences. In no small part, this trend has been encouraged by the search for the neural basis of our social instincts, a search that has not only upheld Darwin's hypothesis that our "moral sense" is innate to our biology, but rooted this sense in the more ancient parts of our brains. Physiologists have linked our judgments about the goodness of others to the ventral pallidum and other subcortical structures that are themselves heavily linked to emotion.[6] Behavioral economists have pointed out that people are so passionate about fairness that they will pursue it at the expense of their own rational self-interest.[7] Physical anthropologists have discovered that our commitments to justice, loyalty, and other noble behaviors are shared not just by other primates, but by rodents such as the prairie vole.[8] Neurologists have observed that patients with a diminished capacity for emotion also show a diminished ability to act morally.[9] Although moral philosophers have often assumed that there are two competing volitional centers of the human brain—the calculations of reason and the impulses of emotion—the successors of Darwin have thus shown that the latter are overwhelmingly dominant and possibly exclusive.[10] While the newer and more flexible structures of our cortex have the capacity to invent original moral theories, such theories are only translated into actual behavior if we *feel* that they are right.[11] As Darwin suspected, morality seems less a function of deliberation than of impulse.

At the same time as our moral decisions have become associated with the less plastic regions of our psyches, there has also been a growing recognition of another constraint imposed upon ethics by natural selection. While Darwin was wary of eugenics, he did allow room for progress, supposing that more intelligent people would generally have higher survival rates.[12] Modern evolutionary biologists, however, have questioned whether this confidence in the goodness of the intellect is compatible with natural selection. Given that the engine of life is a "blind, unforesightful, nonteleological, ultimately mechanical process,"[13] the ultimate source of survival cannot be intelligence, or indeed, any other single trait. Rather, the source of survival is quite simply a variation of function, for it is this variation that provides the raw material upon which selection operates. To the extent that intelligence allows for behavioral plasticity,[14] it is thus certainly an aid, but highly intelligent individuals are often inflexible in their behaviors, while dimly intelligent creatures (e.g., the cockroach) can be extremely adaptive. Meanwhile, the tradeoffs for intelligence are high. Humans have longer breeding cycles and less flexible genomes than simpler organisms, putting our adaptive brains in conflict with another source of functional variety: genetic diversity. So it is that life has hedged its bets, not progressing toward more and more intelligent forms, but diversifying, treating intelligent life as one possibility among many. From the perspective of natural selection, a more reasoned and mindful way of life is thus not necessarily a better way of life, throwing up a second obstacle to the practice of intentional ethics. While humans have tended to see their own distinctive intelligence as distinctively good, there is nothing in our minds to guide us infallibly through the challenges of life, no innate quality of our mental logic that we can rely on absolutely. Although our minds open up the prospect of intentional decision-making, they are as provisional as everything else in nature. And so even if we could consciously revise our moral attitudes, there seems no way of knowing how we should.

Despite the apparently fatalist consequences of Darwin's theory, however, this book will endeavor to show that natural selection can be developed into an active ethics. This ethics, moreover, does not lead us back toward the absolutism that Darwin found so repulsively fatuous about eugenics, social Darwinism, and other like-minded efforts to translate his theory into deliberate practice. Instead, it is characterized by skepticism, pluralism, and many other qualities typically associated with a progressive politics. As will become clear over the remainder of this chapter, I am not the first person to propose this evolutionary ethics. It has existed from the earliest days of cognitive science, tracing its origins all the way back to William James' suggestion that Darwin's biological approach to the human mind could ground an ethical practice known as "pragmatism." In spite of its distinguished origins, though, this evolutionary ethics has all but disappeared from circulation. The reasons for its vanishing act are complex: in part it has to do with the increasing specialization of academic disciplines, a specialization that has made it much harder than it was in James' day to link together fields like cognitive science and ethics; in part, it has to do with the usurpation of pragmatism by "neo-pragmatism," a school of ethics that includes various speculative theories that are incompatible with experimental science; and in part it has to do with a broad mischaracterization of pragmatism as a circular (even cynical) method of justifying the way things already are. But as I will suggest over the remainder of this chapter, the primary reason for the disappearance of pragmatism's evolutionary ethics is that its early advocates failed to substantiate the most original and counterintuitive part of their theory: the claim that natural selection could best be translated into an active ethics by turning to poems, paintings, plays, and all the other human creations that fall under the heading of "art." Pragmatism, in short, tried not only to stitch together biology and ethics, but to use another distinct set of practices as the thread, and while this feat of connection would seem to require the most firm and patient hands, it was instead accomplished by quick (and often disordered) strokes that quickly burst apart. Over the following pages, I will therefore try to remedy this fault by providing pragmatic aesthetics with the binding that its original authors neglected, illustrating the practical possibilities of art with a string of examples drawn from an immensely influential performance tradition: *Hamlet* and the other English tragedies of the seventeenth century. In the process, I will provide evidence that a pragmatic aesthetics not only can work, but *has* worked, suggesting that art may after all provide the missing link in an evolutionary ethics.

The origins of pragmatism's evolutionary ethics were laid by William James' *The Principles of Psychology* (1890). In this sprawling work, James extends Darwin's conclusions in *The Descent of Man* by further reducing the mind to a series of biological processes,[15] establishing the foundation for what would become modern cognitive science.[16] Soon after James published his theory of the mind, it was then developed by another self-described pragmatist, John Dewey, into a practice-based ethics. Starting from the premise that the foundation of life in a Darwinist universe is functional variety, Dewey urged the development of plural societies that maximized the behavioral possibilities for human life.[17] This pragmatic investment in pluralism led Dewey to champion the merits of scientific communities, of student-centered pedagogies, and of democracies. Yet Dewey reserved his highest enthusiasm for an apparently unrelated practice: art. Describing the conscious production of art as "the greatest intellectual achievement in the history of humanity,"[18] he claimed it as the original and most effective means of negotiating our biological drives into ethical practice.

To understand why Dewey places so much confidence in art, it is first necessary to understand the view of human psychology that he derives from pragmatism. While many evolutionary thinkers (including Darwin) have interpreted the relative newness of intelligent life as a sign that the mind represents a higher stage of development,

Dewey supposes the opposite, taking it as evidence of the subordination of the mind to more material processes. For if natural history proves anything to Dewey, it is that bodies can exist without minds, but that minds never exist without bodies. Following James, who dismisses abstract speculation into topics like free will as fruitless, Dewey therefore distances himself from philosophers who treat the distinctive functions of the mind as the highest end of life. Instead, he sees these functions as a means of supporting the more essential processes of the body. By gathering and organizing the experiences of the body, the mind puts itself in a position to help when the body encounters physical difficulties, using its cache of stored experiences to propose solutions that the body then tests through practice. Against moral philosophers who urge their students to use their minds to discipline their bodies, Dewey thus suggests that the way to end experiences such as pain and hunger and fear is not by trying to suppress them with cognitive willpower, but by helping the body find physical solutions to its wants. Like the present-day heirs of Darwin, he views the mind less as the master of our impulses than as a tool for serving them.

Unlike more recent Darwinists, however, Dewey does not take this view of the mind as an obstacle to developing a progressive ethics. Instead, he takes it as an opportunity to reform society by actively arranging minds after the model established by the human body. The body, as Dewey notes, is composed of a variety of specialized organs such as the heart and the lungs and the gut. If any of these organs are removed from the whole, they perish, for they have sacrificed their self-sufficiency for specialization. And yet by becoming mutually interdependent, they have formed an organism that has a greater total diversity of function, making it more resilient to the unpredictable winnowing of natural selection. By becoming less flexible, in effect, the individual parts of the body have made the whole more so. In this method of organization, Dewey sees a model for human society. Pointing out that even the most basic societies naturally adopt some division of labor that in turn leads to an interreliance of function, he defines progressive societies as those that actively improve upon this process of organic association. Continuing the example of the human body, such societies hedge against natural selection by encouraging their individual members to participate in a network of specialized functions.

Given the enormous intricacy of the human body, the task of using it as a social blueprint might seem formidably complex. But rather than copying the current structure of the body, Dewey instead recommends that we imitate the core process that has brought this structure into being: "problem-solving."[19] The body, after all, did not intentionally set out to become such a complex network of functions. Rather, this network developed gradually over millions of years in response to the physical problems of existence, and Dewey suggests that an emphasis on problem-solving can do the same for progressive societies. Since a problem reveals the limits of our current way of living, it demands that we reach beyond our present habits and search out different ones, rummaging through our past experiences, borrowing behaviors from others, and experimenting with newly invented practices. The result of problem-solving is thus a push toward functional variety, and when this labor is undertaken in groups, it becomes a natural source of specialization. Since there is no practical purpose in repeating a problem-solving approach undertaken by another individual, the pressure is to develop a different one, yielding a community that is linked together by different strategies of responding to the same concerns. As evidence for this process, Dewey points to the example of modern experimental science, which has emerged out of the drive to address basic physical questions, but has developed into an immensely rich web of cooperative specialties. Simply by imitating the body's attention to physical problems, science has mirrored its organic pluralism, and Dewey suggests that the same can be true for society as a whole. Rather than attempting the daunting (and distinctly conservative) task of imposing a particular social structure through endless legislation, enforcement, and education, progressive societies can develop pluralism organically from within, making problem-solving the source of broad and mutually sustaining divisions of labor. In short, just as science expands the natural practice of the body, so should progressive society enlarge the practice of science, using problems to encourage cooperative specialization.

By rooting this process of specialization in the insentient operations of the body, Dewey would seem to commit himself to a version of the acquiescent naturalism that Darwin adopts in *The Descent of Man*. However, while Dewey sees problem-solving as a natural process, the course of human history suggests to him that it is not an inevitable one. The mind may have evolved as an aid to the body, but it often gets airs, becoming intoxicated with its own creations. Rather than recognizing its ideas as tools for solving specific physical problems, it mistakes them as a window into a higher and more permanent realm of being, carrying us out of practice and into the cloud castles of faith and philosophy. When the mind decouples ideas from physical application in this manner, moreover, it actively compromises collaborative pluralism. Without the common standard of physical utility to adjudicate differences of opinion, the mind has only speculative standards such as the true, the virtuous, the rational, the sacred. And beside the fact that such mental-stuffs are necessarily subjective, there is the added difficulty that they are often generated by entirely different systems of speculative logic that cannot be put into conversation with one another. Let alone agreeing over the nature of truth, how can a Kantian and a Calvinist, a Leninist and a libertarian, even agree upon a shared language of ideas that would permit them to disagree? As efforts at consensus—and communication—break down, idealists thus retire further into their own limited worldviews, portraying their opponents as irrational, uneducated, unenlightened, ego-driven, dissembling, morally bankrupt, evil. In short, although organic pluralism is a natural process, there is an element in human nature that presses against it. Left to their own devices, our minds often retreat into intolerance, withdrawing from the practical diversity that sustains human life.

In Dewey's day, the most obvious examples of this trending into ideological extremism were communism and fascism, but as Dewey was careful to note, idealism was also endemic to democratic societies. Democracies frequently championed immaterial things such as liberty or justice or equality as good in and of themselves, and while this activity was presented as a means to promote tolerance and diversity, its actual result was a romanticization of one's own policies, a vilifying of political opponents, and a slumping into partisanship. The threat to democracy was thus not just external, but internal, driven by the idealism that lurked within all of our minds, and to guard against self-destruction, Dewey urged democratic societies to remember their pragmatic origins:

> When democracy openly recognizes the existence of *problems* and of the need for approaching them *as* problems as its glory, it will relegate political groups that pride themselves on refusing to admit incompatible opinions to the obscurity which is already the fate of similar groups in science...[for] it is of the nature of science not so much to tolerate as to welcome diversity of opinion.[20]

Like modern science, democracy has emerged and flourished not because it is more right or more rational or more fair, but because "diversity of opinion" is a useful instrument for helping human life adapt to the physical turnings of the world. Against those "political groups" that would twist democracy into its own form of ideology, progressive societies would therefore do well to remind their citizens that freedom and justice are not high and holy works that authorize us to sacrifice each other on their altar. Instead they are humble things, tools for solving hunger, sickness, and other earthbound cares. Progressive societies, in short, must be actively pragmatic, using a rigorous focus on material concerns to check our natural impulse toward idealism.

Against this vision of active democracy, it might be supposed that there is little need to humble our minds when nature itself is only too happy to do so. Our individual lives are a constant succession of physical difficulties that frustrate the abstract simplicities of our mental models, and on a social level, physical problems are no less intrusive: what government does not wrestle with war and poverty, budget shortfalls, and discontented citizens? In such moments, when our gods forsake us and our ideologies lose their magic touch, our only recourse is to turn to each other, taking advantage of our differences to generate new species of practice. One way or another, life makes pragmatists of us all. Still, there is a major practical problem with relying upon nature to turn our minds to problem-solving: it places a potentially lethal stress upon our bodies. To wait until problems blossom into full-blown crises is like delaying until a cancer has metastasized—we have long passed the point at which the difficulty can readily be treated. Moreover, if we have not already laid the groundwork for cooperative problem-solving, our last desperate efforts at shedding our prejudices and working together are unlikely to succeed. We may need to be pragmatic, but we do not have the practical experience. For after all, organic pluralism is not an idea. It is a physical practice, and like other practices, it cannot be thought into being. When our minds are faced with the terrifying prospect of extinction, they may suddenly wish to be open-minded and cooperative, but such techniques can only be instilled by repeated use. And so it is that we would do well not to rely upon nature to remind us about problems. Better that we find an artificial reminder, one that helps us practice problem-solving before it becomes a matter of life-and-death, one that lays and maintains the infrastructure for cooperation by encouraging diverse habits of thought and fostering open relations between them.

It is in the service of this proactive ethics, Dewey suggests, that art becomes useful. In order for physical problems to become cooperative concerns, they must be communicated, and of all the possible forms of communication, Dewey claims art as the "most effective" because of its power to convey the fullness of lived experience.[21] Art, that is, does not dwell in immaterial abstraction, but taps into the more physical parts of our minds: our narrative logic, our emotions, our sense of color and sound. Indeed, this capacity is precisely why so many moral philosophers have distrusted art—from the days of Plato, they have wondered whether it is simply a pleasure technology, a poetic opiate designed to stimulate the bliss-centers of the brain. Or worse, perhaps it is a tool for unreason, a means to manipulate the naive by playing upon their fears and hatreds. And certainly, the art of the past century provides much to validate such concerns. There are the swelling volumes of pulp fiction and blockbuster movies and other self-gratifying fables. And there are D. W. Griffith's *The Birth of a Nation*, and Leni Riefenstahl's *Triumph of the Will*, and innumerable other examples of artful propaganda. Nevertheless, pleasing and preaching are not the only possible ends of art, for far from offering instant satisfaction or easy answers, a great deal of art involves its audience in a struggle, a conflict, a crisis. *Hamlet*, for example, deals with the difficulty of losing a father, and although there is much in Shakespeare's play that is innovative, its exploration of crisis is a practice inherited from the ancients. Two thousand years earlier, Sophocles had dramatized Antigone's own efforts to cope with bereavement, and hundreds of years before that, Homer had opened the *Iliad* by announcing the rage of Achilles. Put in the language of Dewey's ethics, these works begin with problems, and no less significantly, when these works are finished, problems remain. The *Iliad* ends with an armed funeral procession in which the Trojans bury one of Achilles' victims while gripping their weapons close—lest the Greek's anger reassert itself. *Antigone* closes with an orgy of violence that, as the Chorus grimly observes, leaves the future as uncertain as ever. And of course the part of *Hamlet* that has engraved itself into the popular imagination is not an answer but a tortured question. Whatever other functions art might have, history thus shows that it has long been used to communicate problems, embroidering them vividly in our imaginations and urging us to keep them as part of our society.

From the standpoint of Dewey's ethics, moreover, the problems communicated by works like *Hamlet* are of special importance. Although these problems originate in what seem like purely personal concerns, their quick result is to place the individual in conflict with the greater community: Hamlet's grief destabilizes the normal operations of the Danish court; Antigone's insistence on burying her brother reopens the fresh-healed wounds of civil war; Achilles' irascible retirement threatens the morale of the Greek army. These problems, in effect, are what Darwin's heirs in the biological sciences now refer to as ethical problems: practical instances of the tension that inheres between our awareness of our own individual circumstance and our wider investment in the society that sustains us. These problems invite us to connect our individual survival to the collective good, asking us to consider not just what is in our own immediate interest, but what kinds of social concessions might improve our long-term odds. By doing so, they present an opportunity not afforded by other categories of problems. Because the effectiveness of any particular social practice must be measured in its impact on individual experience, ethical problems cannot be resolved without the participation of all the individual members of a society. These individuals are the final authorities on their own personal experience, and so if there is to be a mutual solution, they must be mutually engaged. Unlike the problems of science, which limit open-minded cooperation to a narrow population of specialized researchers, ethical problems thus allow us all to practice experimental inquiry together. Put simply, they enlarge the problem-solving subculture of science into the basis of culture itself.

Viewed in this light, works like *Hamlet* have an immense potential significance to ethics. For if the most progressive response to natural selection is the practice of ethical problems, and if art has historically served to make such problems vivid and immanent, then problem-based art would seem to offer a time-tested method for translating Darwin's discouraging theory into working practice. With art, we can live intentionally in a nonintentional world. As intriguing as this possibility is, however, it has had no impact on the development of an evolutionary ethics. In part, the reason for this can be traced to Dewey himself. Dewey is so invested in establishing the communicative function of art that he focuses overwhelmingly upon its capacity to generate a sense of "unity."[22] In *Art as Experience*, such unity comes to seem the ultimate purpose of aesthetic experience, so that instead of serving as a means to disseminate problems that then serve as the basis for a social ethics, communication becomes an end in itself.[23] This antipragmatic bent is further reinforced by Dewey's method, which eschews detailed, empirical studies of particular artworks in favor of broad-stroke panegyrics about the power of art in general. The overall impression is that Dewey's enthusiasm for art has cost him his sense of its physical aspect, and while this is a clear departure from the method of pragmatism, it is a trend that has been reinforced by subsequent work in pragmatist aesthetics. Instead of making natural selection the justification for aesthetics, recent pragmatists have made aesthetics the justification for natural selection, treating Darwin as a "poet." The result, as Richard Rorty explains, is an approach to ethics that continues the original pragmatic emphasis on functional variety, but revalues this variety from the source of biological survival into a source of aesthetic pleasure:

> To say that moral progress occurs is to say that the later societies are more complex, more developed, more articulate, and above all, more flexible than their predecessors. It is to say that later societies have more varied and interesting needs than earlier ones, just as squirrels have more varied and interesting needs than amoebae.[24]

Here, Rorty precisely reverses Dewey's account of the relationship between problems and social diversity. It is not that social diversity helps us solve problems, but that social diversity helps us *produce* problems—specifically, "interesting" problems that make human life more varied and so more enjoyable. Like a good poem, progressive societies proliferate interpretive cruxes, shifting problem-solving from a physical necessity into a form of speculative play. Rorty's poetic pragmatism has been much attacked, but other recent pragmatists—including Cornel West, Richard Bernstein, Richard Shusterman, and even Giles Gunn—have reinforced his decision to treat the aesthetic as an activity that lies apart from the brutal necessities of natural selection.[25] Outside of pragmatism, meanwhile, Dewey's vision of an evolutionary ethics has not been seriously explored, largely because pragmatism was misunderstood for much of the twentieth century as a rival to later branches of cognitive science.[26] While Dewey's ideas on pedagogy, politics, and science have gathered receptive audiences,[27] his sense of the potential value of art in a universe of natural selection has thus found itself orphaned.

Over the following chapters, I hope to remedy this neglect by providing evidence for Dewey's instincts about the ethical value of art. In particular, I will offer support for the three major claims that Dewey's ethics implies but does not substantiate. First, that art offers an effective means of communicating the experience of ethical problems; second, that this communication can encourage communities to practice pluralism; and third, that this plural practice has a progressive purpose in an everchanging physical world. To offer evidence for these claims, it will be necessary to abandon the feature of Dewey's aesthetics that has most obviously restricted its place in current discussions of the biological function of art: its idealist method. Instead, I will return to the core method of *The Principles of Psychology*—natural history—for this is the method that pragmatism inherits from *The Descent of Man* and that it continues to share with contemporary work in the biological sciences. Given the vast history of art (which in Dewey's view, embraces every object intentionally crafted to communicate a physical experience), there are many possible sources of evidence for this natural history, but by focusing on *Hamlet* and the other tragedies of seventeenth-century England, the following chapters will content themselves with one of the more obviously promising. Written in the wake of both the Reformation and the collapse of Aristotelian-Scholastic philosophy, these plays emerged at a moment in which the driving force behind ethical inquiry was not a unified (and generally accepted) method, but rather the need to engage with a host of new problems. These problems ranged from Luther's doubts about the afterlife to Copernicus' questions about the celestial spheres beyond, from Descartes' paranoia about a deceiving spirit to Hobbes' anxieties about deceiving men,[28] and as they ranged, so did the proposed methods for resolving them. In Dewey's terse summation: "moral theory developed and altered as now this, now that, problem was uppermost."[29]

Dramatic tragedy, moreover, enjoyed a special relationship to these problems. Philip Sidney noted at the end of the sixteenth century that the long purpose of tragedy was to communicate moral doubt,[30] and three features of seventeenth-century tragedy allowed it to leverage this traditional function into the basis of a problem-based ethics. First, tragedy was free to treat problems as problems. Unlike moral philosophy, which was expected to answer the problems it posed,[31] tragedy was not burdened with the task of supplying plausible solutions, but could push problems to the point at which minds and bodies raged against each other, destroying life. Second, because tragedy was a fictional form, it was not tied to an absolute standard of presentation. It could adapt itself to different audiences and different times, using its formal flexibility to maximize the possibilities for communication, and seventeenth-century tragedy is rich with innovative aesthetic techniques that did just this. And third, tragedy was a public activity, a place where bodies physically met, making it a ready source of the communal pluralism that is the end of problem-solving. Because of both its particular historical situation and its particular historical form, seventeenth-century tragedy was thus well-placed to establish itself as the foundation of a problem-based ethics, and to trace its achievement is to see how it converted this potential into practice.

It is not just the achievement of seventeenth-century tragedy, moreover, that makes it a useful source for Dewey's evolutionary ethics. It is also the decline. The method of ethics developed by plays like *Hamlet* did not endure indefinitely, but was replaced by one that violates the Darwinist framework of pragmatism. This newer ethics was initiated at the end of the seventeenth century by John Locke, who was alarmed at the creeping transformation of ethics into a patchwork of ad hoc responses to local problems. In Locke's view, this situation was an invitation to anarchy and violence, and to eliminate it, he rolled all possible questions (not just those that had actually been posed by past thinkers, but all those that could potentially be posed by future ones) into an originary mental blankness he termed the "tabula rasa." This innate state of mind provided a private starting point for inquiry, allowing individuals to root ethics in a personal accounting of their own cognitive processes. Locke thus transformed the origin of ethics from a public engagement with problems into an introspective study of one's own free thought, and although Locke's blank slate violates the theory of mind set forth by pragmatism and reinforced by recent cognitive scientists,[32] his reform proved historically decisive. Following Locke's death, it became the cornerstone of classical liberalism and then went on to inspire successive waves of liberal and radical thought: J. S. Mill used the concept of the blank slate to ground the leveling policies of social liberalism, and after being fashioned by Hume and Kant into the idea of "the skeptic," Locke's notion of total doubt was appropriated by Nietzsche and made the

basis for radical antimorality. Indeed, these new forms of philosophy so thoroughly displaced tragedy that successive waves of literary thinkers—from Adam Smith to Nietzsche, from New Critics
to New Historicists—began to interpret plays like *Hamlet* through
their lens. The plays that had once guided human life were absorbed
by their opposite, an ethics rooted not in the public practice of physical problems, but in the private speculation of autonomous minds.

This profound historical shift demonstrates that to defend the
practical worth of seventeenth-century tragedy is not to describe the
inevitable. It is to prescribe the possible, to urge the reversal of the
tabula rasa and the other liberal and radical innovations that have
subordinated the public problems of seventeenth-century tragedy
to the private introspections of philosophy. It is, in short, to eschew
Darwin's acquiescent naturalism for the foundational practice of
Dewey's evolutionary ethics: a promotion of problem-based art. In
the chapters that follow, I will therefore sketch a natural history
of *Hamlet* and a dozen other plays written in the rough century
between the emergence of the London playhouses at the end of the
sixteenth century and Locke's proposal of the blank slate at the end
of the seventeenth. Like the natural histories that form the basis for
the theory of evolution, this history will study the interrelationship
and development of function in a particular ecosystem.[33] And like
these natural histories, it will necessarily be more observational than
experimental. Unlike Darwin's records of the Galapagos finches,
however, it will not deploy the tools of anatomy, morphology, or
the other biological sciences. Rather, it will rely on the tools devised
by literary critics and cultural historians to uncover the origin
and function of theatrical productions. The result will be a series
of in-depth readings that touch on historical particulars ranging
from Luther's take on riddles to Cicero's views on mourning, from
Descartes' theory of optics to Hobbes' analysis of social conflict.
At times, these matters will seem digressions from the broader concerns of the book, and yet like the sketches of beaks and wingspans
gathered on the voyage of *The Beagle*, they are the details on which
the whole rests. Revealing the practical function of problem-based
art, they show that Darwin's discovery need not reduce ethics to a
mixture of impulse, luck, and acquiescence. Instead, it can be a way
to find progress in a world of blind descent.

Chapter 1

Faustus, Macbeth, and the Riddle of Tomorrow

Incarnate man, fast bound as earth and sea,
Spake, when his pride would fain set Faustus free.
　　　　　—A. C. Swinburne, Prologue to Doctor Faustus (1896)

When Swinburne introduced *Doctor Faustus* to late Victorian audiences, he faced the formidable task of explaining why a play that had been all but forgotten for two hundred years had suddenly regained its relevance.[1] Undaunted, he insisted that what seemed a moldy fable of demon-summoning was in fact an exploration of the human drive to transcend "incarnate" nature, an exploration that had only become more urgent in the wake of the many new medicines and machines that H.G. Wells had darkly referred to a year earlier as "the growing pile of civilization…a foolish heaping that must inevitably fall back upon and destroy its makers in the end."[2] Swinburne's instincts proved good. While the initial revival of *Faustus* was brief, it laid the groundwork for a more ambitious performance schedule,[3] and the play has since become part of the standard repertoire of Elizabethan theater. In focusing attention on the vexed issue of our "fast bound" state, moreover, Swinburne helped set in motion a lively and ongoing discussion about the source of Faustus' doom.[4] Some interpreters have approached the play from a theological perspective, debating whether it illustrates the Catholic view that we are free to sin or paints Calvin's grim vision of the reprobate. Others have preferred the vantage of contemporary philosophy, debating whether the play is evidence that our choices are conditioned by larger cultural and ideological forces or is a sign of the possibility of "affirmation" and other radical forms of self-determination. And still others have taken a literary tack, debating whether Faustus shares Oedipus' tragic fate or his self-inflicted arrogance. Once forgotten, *Faustus* has thus made good on Swinburne's claims, establishing itself as the center of a deep and engaging conversation about whether we are destined or born free.

This revival of *Faustus* would seem a tidy illustration of the potential of seventeenth-century tragedy to serve as the source of a problem-based ethics. Gathering Catholics and Protestants, historians and philosophers, and moralists and radicals around the question of human agency, Marlowe's play appears a useful instrument of pluralism. In fact, however, the diversity of opinion that has come to surround *Faustus* is very different from the one urged by pragmatists like Dewey. To begin with, the issue of free will is what pragmatists refer to as a "false problem."[5] Unlike hunger, sickness, and other problems that draw attention to the needs of the body, free will is not a physical concern. It is a *meta*physical concern, and like other metaphysical things, it lies above the grasp of physical creatures such as ourselves. From the perspective of physical life, debate over such problems can therefore offer no practical gain, and indeed, pragmatism suggests that it can cost us something dear. By expending effort on the purely theoretical question of free will, interpreters of *Faustus* have tacitly implied that problem-solving is not an *instrumental* good, that is, a tool for keeping us alive. Instead, they have established it as an *intrinsic* good, something that is its own reward. This is a fundamentally nonpragmatic understanding of the purpose of problem-solving, and with it comes a nonpragmatic view of pluralism. Most of the interpretive theories that have been applied to *Faustus*—beginning in the 1930s and 1940s with liberal works such as J. C. Ransom's *The New Criticism* and continuing through more radical approaches such as postmodernism, deconstruction, and cultural materialism—have treated pluralism as the ideal end of human life.[6] This end has been framed in different ways: while liberal critics take democracy as the most socially just form of politics, radicals tend to frame indeterminacy as the most self-actualized mode of being. But what binds all these approaches together is that they treat pluralism as an innate good. It is not that pluralism is a useful tool for enduring the particular challenges of our world; it is desirable in itself.[7]

As Dewey notes, this idealist view of pluralism leads to a practical problem: instead of fostering organic interdependences, it encourages "atomistic" collectives of individuals who perceive their own survival as fundamentally autonomous from that of the group.[8] In response to crisis, the members of such a community will thus not take advantage of their colleagues, but will instead withdraw more tightly into their own personal perspectives, fracturing the group rather than strengthening it. And indeed, such has been the general dynamic surrounding recent interpretation of Marlowe's play. Scholarship on *Faustus* has fallen increasingly into the domain of English departments, which have themselves splintered over the past half-century into a series of competing methodologies that— far from being interdependent in the sense of biology, chemistry, physics, and other scientific disciplines—are often fiercely exclusionary, treating each other as hostile entities. Radical critics of *Faustus* often accuse liberal interpreters of naiveté and even oppression, while liberal critics treat radical interpretations as a pernicious assault on the possibility of meaning. This "theoretical turn" has been taken by biologists as evidence that literary criticism is a distraction from more useful pursuits,[9] and such needling aside, it is certainly true that speculation about the agency of Marlowe's doctor has not functioned as a source of organic community, or functional pluralism, or any of the other practical benefits that Dewey associates with modern science's culture of problem-solving. Instead, like the scholastic metaphysics that Faustus himself abuses, it has served as a sink of irresolvable disputes. What Swinburne proposed as a forward-looking play thus seems in retrospect to have fostered a highly regressive style of inquiry.

As I will suggest over this chapter, however, the disappointing results of Swinburne's approach should not lead us to relegate *Faustus* once again to our ethical past. For rather than treating the crisis of the play as a metaphysical concern, it is possible to take this crisis as the sort of physical problem that Dewey credits with fostering progressive society. When Faustus announces his discontent with heaven, hell, and the rest of the Catholic Church's grand eschatology, he divorces himself from the system of punishment and reward that past generations had used to gauge the virtue of present actions, plunging himself into a state of confusion: with no firm sense of the ends of life, he struggles to decide which way to step. This problem anticipates the focal concern of Darwinism—the place of intentional action in a world of uncertain consequences—and as I will show over the following pages, Marlowe's play inspired other playwrights (most notably Shakespeare in *Macbeth*) to make

Faustus' concern into the beginnings of a practice-based ethics.
By tracing these beginnings, this chapter will lay the foundation
for the rest of the book in two complementary ways. First, it will
offer a practical illustration of what I mean by "natural history." In
Darwin's usage, natural history is the study of the way that popula-
tions acquire new functions in response to environmental concerns,
and to adapt this model to seventeenth-century tragedy, I will rely
on both the findings of cultural historians and the techniques of
formal literary criticism—the former to illuminate the particular
ethical problems of the English seventeenth century, and the latter
to identify new tragic structures developed in response to them. Put
in biological terms, cultural history will be my ecology and formal
criticism my morphology, and while this may seem a curious strategy for studying plays, its practical result will be a set of readings
that are organic in their origins and fresh in their conclusions—
readings, in short, that meet the usual standard of dramatic criticism. Second, this chapter will provide a rationale for pushing on to
further case-studies of seventeenth-century tragedy. For if *Faustus*
and its heirs managed to orient communities around the experience of a problem, then perhaps they were not alone. Perhaps in
other seventeenth-century tragedies we can find evidence of other
practices and other problems—evidence, that is, of the functional
pluralism that Dewey predicts as the benefit of problem-based art.
Though Dewey's evolutionary ethics has long been without either
a method or a motive, the following pages will thus take the first
steps toward securing both, using *Faustus* simultaneously as a model
case-study and a justification for more.

   Faustus opens with a problem. After a few lively, even ebul-
lient, moments in which the doctor disowns logic, medicine, and
law as useless exercises, the mood abruptly shifts when he settles
on what he takes to be the central teaching of theology: "we must
die an everlasting death" (A. 1.1.48; B. 1.1.46).[10] Confronted with
the brute fact of his own mortality, the doctor crumbles into blunt
dismay: "that's hard." This emphasis on death was by no means
original to Marlowe's play. A decade earlier, Death himself had
appeared on the London stage to crow, "What are tragedies, but
acts of Death?" and whether served with piles of corpses, acts of
cannibal revenge, or defiant suicide, a bloody end was a certainty
in tragedy.[11] Traditionally, however, tragedy had worked to make
death less terrible.[12] Many tragedies were explicitly moral, providing their own tidy perspectives on the afterlife, and even those that

offered themselves as sheer spectacle tended through their excess to make death more familiar. Against this trend, Faustus finds the thought of his coming end endlessly strange. It costs him his faith in mortal authors—what, after all, can the living know about death?—and drives him to seek out a devil for insight. And yet even with a member of the damned to answer his questions, Faustus remains dissatisfied, repeatedly interrupting his spell-casting to badger Mephistopheles further about hell. For the doctor, death is thus such a pressing problem that it does not just disturb his thoughts; it physically disturbs the business of living.

On the surface of it, Faustus' problem may seem little different from the "problem" of free will. After all, there is no way to solve the problem of death, no way for the doctor to see past his own mortality and penetrate the dark mystery of tomorrow. And indeed, one of the characteristics of ethical problems is that they do not admit of absolute answers. These problems carry us to the limits of our own awareness, to the moment at which our individual experience intersects with the experience of others, confronting us with a social consciousness that is vast, unstable, and elusive. This sense of incomplete connection to a greater without is why death has traditionally been a major—perhaps the major—concern of ethics. On the one hand, our anxieties about death are social: if we did not connect our fate to the fate of others, then their demise would not seem to portend anything for our own particular case. But on the other hand, our anxieties about death also reveal the limits of our social understanding: if we could get could get into the heads of others, then death would not be a problem, for the first time we saw another person die, we would grasp exactly what it meant. Death is thus a puzzle as compelling and confounding as any metaphysical mystery—and yet even so, it is different in one important respect from the "problem" of free will: instead of being a byproduct of speculation, it is a product of experience. The death of others causes us physical suffering, triggering shock, confusion, and grief, and so unlike the problem of free will, the problem of death cannot be banished by not thinking about it. It is a recurring part of our bodily experience of life, and so it is, from a biological perspective, that this problem has a practical value. Death teaches us that our own existence is limited—to survive we must invest in our kin and our community. Unlike the problem of free will, the problem of death thus offers itself as an instrumental good. Instead of catching us in a roundabout of our own making, it opens a path to society.

Marlowe could not, of course, have seen this problem as a modern biologist sees it, but his own studies nevertheless introduced him to the possibility that death could form the foundation of a practice-based ethics. Marlowe spent three years pursuing a Master's in Divinity at Cambridge University,[13] where he encountered the writings of a social reformer who claimed the problem of death as a remedy to what he saw as the venal idealism of the Catholic Church. This reformer was Martin Luther, and in Luther's view, the church was guilty of a grand deception: although it had made itself rich by hawking visions of heaven and hell, it could not possibly know what lay in store for us in death. After all, death was literally the opposite of life, and so no living soul could honestly claim to grasp it.[14] To counteract the church's self-aggrandizing fabrications, Luther therefore reminded his readers obsessively of the problem of their mortality:

> I ask, what man does not shudder, does not despair, in the face of death? Who does not flee it? And yet because God wishes that we endure it, it is apparent that we by nature love our will more than the will of God. For if we should love the will of God more, we should submit to death with joy…Therefore we are discussing figments of our imagination. He loves God less than himself, even hates him, who hates or who does not love death.[15]

Here, Luther admits that death is so terrible that we naturally try to escape its consequences through gaudy theologies of heaven or secular imaginations of fame, but he insists that even though our nature pushes us to avoid the otherness of death, our relation to God requires that we fully embrace it. And yet no sooner has Luther insisted that we embrace death than he confesses that the task is impossible, for no living thing can have any idea of death beyond "figments of…imagination." Far from providing a coherent set of beliefs, Luther's assertions thus leave us with a problem. If we do not want to hate God, we must love death. But we cannot love death, for it is so alien to our experience that we cannot begin to know it.

The logical incoherence of Luther's counsel testifies to his deep distrust of speculative philosophy. In contrast to the traditional theology of his era, Luther had no confidence in the mind's power to untangle the deep mysteries of metaphysics, and his mature writings are so dismissive of human reason that they have often appeared incapable of supporting positive doctrines.[16] Despite his pessimism about speculative philosophy, however, Luther did not abandon hope of living ethically. For while he thought that the problem of death was intellectually irresolvable, he believed that it could encourage a style of practice that itself constituted the good life. As evidence for this, Luther offered the example of communion. This practice, he pointed out, was based on the baffling paradox that bread was also the body of Christ. Indeed, so baffling was this paradox that most theologians had felt forced to reduce it. Catholics sought refuge in the doctrine of transubstantiation, which claimed that while the eucharist seemed to be bread, it was actually Christ. Reform Protestants, meanwhile, took the opposite tack, suggesting that the wafer was purely a symbol of God's presence. Despite their obvious disagreement, both Catholics and Protestants thus agreed that the communion wafer was not both bread and Christ, but was really one or the other.

Against these rationalizations, Luther insisted upon fully preserving the paradox of communion, claiming of the eucharist: "It is…real bread and real wine, in which Christ's real flesh and real blood are present…Both natures [i.e., both God and bread] are simply there in their entirety…and though philosophy cannot grasp this, faith grasps it nonetheless."[17] As Luther concedes, his commitment to maintaining this paradox frustrates "philosophy," but as he sees it, this is no obstacle to ethical practice. For the function of communion is not to satisfy the mind, but to encourage a bodily experience:

> In the eucharist there are two things to be known and proclaimed. The first is the object of faith and the second is the faith itself…The first lies outside the heart and is presented to our eyes externally, namely, the sacrament itself, concerning which we believe that Christ's body and blood are truly present in the blood and wine. The second is internal, within the heart, and cannot be externalized. It consists in the attitude which the heart has towards the eternal sacrament.[18]

In taking communion, one part of our body (the heart) feels the presence of God, opening us to the prospect of bliss. And yet because another part of our body (the eyes) sees only bread, we are also reminded that we are not yet with God, but remain part of the gross, material world. The result is an intense cycling between hope and despair, as our heart strains toward a future bliss, while our eyes root us firmly in a degraded present.[19] Seen this way, communion is neither a puzzle to be solved nor the key that unlocks the mystery of our tomorrow. Instead, it is a physical reminder that we live on the edge of the here and the hereafter. "An incomplete act, always partly acquired and partly to be acquired,"[20] communion offers a means of practicing the problem of our mortality.[21]

Luther was so convinced of the efficacy of this practice that he called it "the whole Christian doctrine,"[22] and he dedicated his own written works not to clarifying the philosophical niceties of scripture, but to ceaselessly rehearsing the physical experience of mortality. As he writes in his commentary on Psalm 122, published in a popular English translation in 1577:

> Today alive and in good health, to morrow dead and gone. Yea how infinite are the troubles, calamities, tentations and daungers wherewith our life is tossed as a shippe on the sea, which so terrifie us that heaven and earth are to little for us, yea the whole creature is to us a very hell. This is the nature of flesh: which Satan moreover so inspireth and bewitcheth, that it seeth not God, but rather (as it judgeth) some great and horrible mischiefe: not life, but death and destruction. But this is no judgement, but rather a delusion of the flesh and of the devil: against the which we must fight, yea and beleve that even in our destruction (as to us it seemeth) God is present with us, and in our death Christ our King liveth: in whose sight our tribulations and afflictions, yea and death it self are altogither, (as you would say) but one nothing: and if we compare them unto God by the judgement of faith, we shall feele them so to be in deede. But who hath sufficiently learned thus to doe? Somewhat we may say, and teach other after a sort: but use and experience, with inward practise and feling is that which maketh a right divine and a true Christian indeede, so that he may be able boldely to affirme and say with David: He will not suffer thy foote to slyppe: that is to say, He will not suffer thee to be utterly overthrowne and perish. But the flesh saith the contrary, because it feeleth, not only thy foote to slyppe, but it selfe also to be troden under foote.[23]

This passage is marked throughout by sudden and complete reversals of perspective. Luther begins by discussing death, but then insists that what flesh sees as death is in fact life. This inspires a torrent of abuse toward flesh, leading Luther to urge his readers to fight flesh with faith. Abruptly, though, he hesitates at his own advice, wondering: "Who hath sufficiently learned thus to do?" This would seem a rhetorical question, and yet Luther hurries to answer it, noting that in fact some Christians have done so after all—as evidence, there is the example of David's defiant song. And yet rather than end on this positive note, Luther then plunges back into the perspective of flesh, commenting on the horror of being trampled under by death. Mimicking the cycling of hope and despair that attends the practice of communion, Luther's prose does not illuminate the theological meaning of the psalm. Instead, it offers the experience of struggling with a problem that cannot be resolved.

Luther's religious exhortations seem an unlikely source of an evolutionary ethics—what could be further from Darwin's godless vision of human life? Yet behind this theoretical tension lies a deeper practical consonance: an anti-teleological worldview, a rejection of speculative theology, and an investment in practice. Moreover, Luther's vivid communication of death as a problem—that is, not as an abstract philosophical question but as a grinding physical disarray—makes his writing a potentially useful starting-point for a problem-based ethics, and Marlowe and subsequent playwrights would make good on this opportunity, gradually peeling away the religious trappings of Luther's practice and translating it into a strictly secular context. English audiences displayed a broad enthusiasm for Luther's writing on death,[24] and it is perhaps this enthusiasm that encouraged Marlowe to think that a play centered on the problem of death would prove a success. Whatever Marlowe's ultimate motivations, however, he explicitly links his play to a Protestant ethos by making Faustus a doctor at the University of Wittenberg. This was famously the institution at which Luther and Calvin taught,[25] and although the doubts raised by *Faustus* push the play beyond the bounds of Calvin's metaphysics,[26] the doctor's struggle with death offers a dramatic enactment of Luther's physical practice. No sooner has the doctor signed the pact than he begins to press for answers about the afterlife, and though Mephistopheles willingly answers his questions, Faustus remains incredulous. He denies the devil's emphatic descriptions of the sufferings of hell and then attempts to distance himself from the consequences of his pact by asking edgily: "Why, think'st thou then that Faustus shall be damned?" (A&B 2.1.139). In effect, just as the eucharist introduces Luther to a future that is at once immanent and absent, so too does Mephistopheles stand as physical evidence of a tomorrow that Faustus can glimpse but not grasp from the today. And so just like Luther, Faustus finds himself pitched into a cycling of anticipation and dismay. He presses Mephistopheles with questions because in the devil's real presence, he senses that at last, satisfaction is near. But since Mephistopheles no more delivers Faustus into hell than the eucharist delivers Luther into heaven, no satisfaction is forthcoming. Hope breaks down, and

just as Luther experiences pangs of doubt after the joy of communion is past, so too does Faustus despair, denying that hell exists.
Yet he cannot rest in this state either, for as devils continue to parade
before his eyes, so tantalizingly close, the doctor again feels a sudden optimism that death is within his reach: "O might I see hell and
return again, how happy were I then!"

This endless rotation between rapturous expectation and gloomy
alienation yields the play's most curious element: the pact that
Faustus forms with Mephistopheles. The first curiosity about the
pact is that Faustus signs it at all. After the devil demands a blood
signature as security, the doctor hesitates for a moment, asking why
Lucifer wants his soul.

Mephistopheles:	*Solamen miseris socios habuisse doloris* [Misery loves company].
Faustus:	Have you any pain, that tortures others?
Mephistopheles:	As great as have the human souls of men.

(A&B 2.1.42–44)

That this conversation seals the deal, prompting Faustus to gladly sign
over his soul, seems at first incredible. Mephistopheles' admission that
"misery loves company" may be candid, but it hardly seems persua-
sive. Yet, as is revealed by Faustus' response—"Have you any pain, that
tortures others?"—the doctor's situation leads him to place emphasis
not on "misery" [*miseris*] but on "company" [*socios*]. For Faustus, misery is not a new state,[27] and it is therefore not something that draws
his attention. Company with the devil, however, is the very thing he
wants—after all, the doctor has summoned Mephistopheles to bridge
the distance between himself and death. To participate in the devil's
society of misery is to admit that the view from beyond is no different
than the doctor's own, and this joining of perspectives is in fact implied
by Mephistopheles' final line: "As great as have the human souls of
men." This line can be taken to mean that the devil's condition is fully
accessible to humans who are themselves in hell, or it can be taken to
mean that the devil's suffering is no different from that experienced
generally by humans, but either way, the end result would seem the
same: by confirming his place among the damned, Faustus can collapse
the gap between the here and the after. And so Faustus signs the pact,
believing that it will reveal to him what death is like.

In the end, though, the pact cannot deliver this satisfaction.
Faustus brushes away Mephistopheles' answers, labeling them fables
and "freshmen's suppositions," and he then rejects the spell-book

that the devil hands him, refusing to believe that Mephistopheles has actually anticipated his desires (A. 2.3.54–55; B. 2.3.53–54). Like the taking of the communion bread, which promises a future heaven that comes to seem more and more distant as we look about our current state, the devil's pledges about hell have a hollow ring. They are a sign of something Faustus cannot possess, and as the emptiness of his possession becomes apparent, the sign comes to seem empty as well. The devil that inspired such a sense of possibility when it first appeared now seems less substantial—false, perhaps even absurd. It is a deceiver, or no devil at all. To put faith in it is as ludicrous as putting faith in a piece of bread. What promised to bring Faustus closer to hell has thus simply made his distance more palpable, and so instead of finding peace, Faustus is twisted between a presumptuous certainty and a sudden despair, announcing that he is not in the least bit afraid of dying and then crying out in terrified anticipation of his fate. And herein lies the second curiosity of the pact: despite its failure to deliver any of the things that Faustus desires, the doctor passes up multiple opportunities to renege. As odd as this behavior seems, though, it is physically consistent with Faustus' root predicament. By virtue of his mortality, the doctor has already been born into an identical contract, one that also punishes him by raising high hopes and then violently frustrating them. All that Faustus' pact with Mephistopheles does is manifest this preexisting contract, and since he cannot rid himself of one, there is no practical advantage to getting rid of the other.

As Faustus loses hope in the pact, he resorts to distracting his mind from its revolutions by playing magical tricks upon the pope, a pompous knight, and finally a horse-courser. These pranks have often been regarded as filler, the hasty work of a collaborator who was hired to bulk up the play with some scenes of idle horseplay, and even if they are conceded to be Marlowe's, they have seemed to many critics to be inconsistent with a tragic tone.[28] Yet there is no contradiction between Faustus' comic antics and his painful uncertainty about death. Luther frequently counseled his friends to engage in gaming and even binge-drinking as a means to relieve their agonized speculation about their future state.[29] He feared that if they lacked this release, they risked slipping into a bottomless despair, and Faustus' pranks reflect a similar effort to ward off the grimness of his condition. As with all of his enthusiasms, though, this one can only last so long. After playing an absurd trick on the horse-courser, he ends up slumped in his chair, moaning: "What art thou, Faustus, but a man condemned to die?" (A. 4.1.139; B. 4.4.21). Like the taking of communion, pranks are not a permanent solution, but a practical therapy, and when the moment of euphoria passes, Faustus finds himself staring at the old problem of his mortal state.

Faustus' terrible failure made the play a great success. Where *Tamburlaine* made Marlowe's reputation by chronicling an incredible rise to glory, *Faustus* drew crowds to witness frustrated hope, and the similar popularity of Luther's grim consolations on death reveals that this was no aberration. The potential audience for such works is enormous, for all of us, by dint of our mortality, are vulnerable to the feeling of being born into a contract whose terms are hidden in an inscrutable future. Moreover, just as Luther fashioned a special prose style for guiding his readers through the cycle of hope and despair that he discovered in the problem of death, so too does *Faustus* develop an innovative formal style that immerses audiences in the doctor's predicament. The play combines two distinct methods of representation, intermingling psychological depictions of hell with physical materializations of devils. To many scholars, this mix of realism and allegory has suggested a play caught between a modern conception of tragedy and a cruder morality-play tradition,[30] yet the play itself resists this teleology by placing strong emphasis on the capacity of allegory to placate even the insatiable doctor. At the end of act 2, Lucifer attempts to quiet Faustus' yawning doubts by providing him with a pageant of the seven deadly sins. The strange procession of figures, which includes Pride cracking crude jokes and Gluttony ravenously inviting himself to dinner, is embraced wholesale by the doctor, who enthusiastically claims that it "feeds [his] soul" (A. 2.3.157; B. 2.3.154). Clearly, Faustus finds something deeply satisfying in this allegory of hell—something more satisfying, in fact, than the psychological description of hell he has previously been offered by Mephistopheles.

Like Faustus' other behaviors, this enthusiasm for allegory can be understood by turning to the practices that Luther developed out of his engagement with the problem of death.[31] For just as this problem led Luther to reformulate the taking of communion, so too did it lead him to a new style of interpretive practice. From the perspective of both the Catholic Church and Luther's Protestant successors, the purpose of hermeneutics was to establish the correct relationship between sign and signified. The question was not whether allegory itself was valid, but rather whether one particular allegory was better than another. In contrast, Luther's distrust of speculative efforts to clarify the paradoxes of mortal existence led him to reject allegory in favor of an insistence on the literal sense. Discussing the scriptural passage at the root of the eucharist—*Hoc est corpus meum* ("this is my body")—Luther lashed out against Catholics for "ignoring the grammatical sense" and turning the scripture into "allegories."[32] Catholics argued that Christ was not literally saying "this bread is my body," because it was inconceivable that bread and Christ could be the same thing. Therefore, "this" must refer to Christ's body, so that Christ was really saying: "My body is my body." This interpretation drew Luther's withering contempt—who were mortals to say what was conceivable for God? The grammar of the scriptures was not formed from human reason, and their meaning was clear: "the subject ['this'] obviously points to the bread and not to the body when he says: *Hoc est corpus meum* ['this is my body']."[33] Christ was not saying, "My body is my body," he was saying, "this bread is my body." At the same time, Luther was equally appalled by the Reform Protestants who insisted that the bread merely represented the body. After all, Christ had not said, "This represents my body," he had said, "this *is* my body." In response to the arguments of Catholics and Reform Protestants, Luther would therefore often just repeat, "This is my body...this is my body...this is my body," hoping to create the same wondrous confusion in his listeners that the eucharist had generated in him.

This denial of allegoresis is characteristic of Luther's whole theology. For Luther, there is never a real distinction between the word of God and its earthly sign; they are simply two different ways of looking at the same thing. Whether it appears to bodily eyes as a piece of bread, or a line of scripture, or anything else, the word of God is present as nothing other than itself. There can thus be no way of moving from sign to signified, in part because the two are identical, and in part because nothing in the way of flesh can lead to spirit. Because the sign is not something that points toward a greater reality, but is the way that flesh misreads that greater reality, the sign is at once the signified word of God and an indication of the observer's total alienation from that word. The dual function of the sign is therefore to bring the observer into the real presence of God while manifesting the infinite gulf of perception that exists between God and humankind. Reminding us of our mortal state, it leaves us not with satisfaction, but with a problem.

Given Faustus' frantic efforts to solve the problem that Luther describes as the lot of humanity, it is thus hardly surprising that he enjoys the allegorical pageant. To view hell as a collection of earthly forms is to follow Catholics and Calvinists in feeling the relief of knowing that the afterlife can be understood from this life, that there is after all a relationship between worldly sign and otherworldly signified. But of course, the central claim of Luther's theology is that such moments of forced resolution are not truly satisfying, and the hollowness of Faustus' contentment is immediately revealed when he cries: "O, might I see hell and return again, how happy were I then!" No longer satisfied with the pageant, Faustus now wants to see the thing itself, to be carried out of allegory and into immanence. Such moments reveal, in effect, that different styles of representation have different effects on Faustus, helping to drive his cycle between faith and disbelief. In the allegorical pageant, he finds a belief that edges quickly into doubt, and in Mephistopheles' grim confessions, a doubt that makes him hunger for new belief. And so too it is with Faustus' own audience. While the allegorical devils of Marlowe's play promise us a future clarity, the doctor's confessional soliloquies stir a present sorrow. By switching between these different methods of presentation, the play thus invites us to alternate between anticipation and despair. In other words, it invites us to undergo the same cycle as Faustus, to feel at moments that we can see into the doctor's soul—surely he is a free sinner, or an unlucky reprobate, or a glorious free thinker—and yet to feel at others that he is as inscrutable as death itself. So it is that when Faustus is dragged away in the final scene, the mood is terrible strange. As the doctor's hysterical screams drift out of a host of stage devils, we are uncertain where he has gone, whether he is waiting in the wings for another performance, or whether he really is in hell. We have seen death—but then again, we have just seen a sign, a show. Trapped in a doubled perspective that cannot be resolved, we experience the problem of mortality not as one to be answered, but as one that we will live until our life is used up.

By imparting this problem, *Faustus* leaves behind the medieval theory of tragedy recently set forth by Philip Sidney's *Apologie for Poesie* (c. 1580). In the *Apologie*, Sidney had summed up centuries of scholarship on the ethical function of tragedy by declaring: "Tragedie...teacheth the uncertainety of this world, and upon how weake foundations guilden roofes are builded."[34] Sidney, in effect, makes the problems raised by tragedy—the "uncertainety of this world"—into a vessel for a moral certainty: the better life beyond. In contrast, *Faustus* suggests that the ethical value of dramatic tragedy lies in the very feature that distinguishes it from this old doctrine. Unlike the moral philosophy of the church, tragedy can raise questions without answering them, shifting the origin of ethics from theological dogma onto problem-based practice. And while the practice of *Faustus* might itself seem a backward thing—after all, what purpose or foundation could it have outside of Luther's fervent Christianity?—the subsequent history of theater suggests the reverse. The logical endpoint of Luther's teaching was an end to organized religion. If there were no holy and unholy things, but only holy and unholy ways of practicing, then one place was as good as another for worship. Indeed, Luther himself admitted that the experience of the eucharist might just as easily be found in gazing on a mountain, a stream, or a tree, for Christ was everywhere. On this logic, not only was there no need for gaudy cathedrals, there was no need for any house of prayer; not only was there no need for the pope, there was no need for any clergy; not only was there no need for Catholicism, there was no need for any religion. All that was necessary for ethics was the experience of grasping the inscrutability of the time to come, and as Luther's writings revealed, this experience might be had simply by meditating on one's own impending end. For all of Luther's iconoclastic energy, however, his commitment to making the eucharist more available to the laity and to translating the Bible into the vernacular revealed that he never entirely abandoned the idea that some objects were more sacred than others. The idea that the playhouse was a suitable location for congregation, or that the scriptures could be replaced with theatrical scripts, would have struck him—as it struck many Puritan observers of the Elizabethan stage—as idolatry. In the end, this prejudice curbed the influence of Luther's problem-based ethics. For by keeping his ethics within the framework of Christian idealism, Luther prepared the way for subsequent idealists to appropriate his reforms. Calvin responded to Luther's destruction of Catholic eschatology by building his own complex *Institutes* upon the ruins, offering the theory of predestination as a calculus for determining the end of life, and setting the stage for later theologians to transform Luther's protest against dogma into the nest of doctrines known as Protestantism. Rather than accepting Luther's problem as the foundation of ethics, these theologians turned to speculative philosophy to find a new answer. Luther's practice had not so much ended the church as inspired another one.

In contrast, dramatic tragedy provided a space in which practice alone could form the foundation of ethics. For while Sidney's *Apologie* tried to retrofit tragedy with an idealistic purpose, its actual beginnings lay in its ability to engage audiences. In Athens, tragedy was staged as a popular competition, and in Marlowe's England, its survival depended upon its ability to draw paid spectators. Tragedy, in effect, was justified not by its origin in the divine, but by its physical function. Marlowe thus did not need Christian theologians to authorize his play, and though he took advantage of the morality play tradition that excites Sidney's idealism, he was free to add despairing confessions, comic jests, an inconclusive ending, and the other elements that focused on death as a practical problem. Moreover, while *Faustus* remained to some extent dependent on a preexisting metaphysics, relying on an audience that was willing to engage with Christian speculations about the afterlife, I will show over the remainder of this chapter that subsequent tragedy cut itself completely free. *Faustus* was enormously influential: no less a playwright than Shakespeare referenced it directly in *Richard III*,[35] *Troilus and Cressida*,[36] and finally *Macbeth*.[37] In the past, this line of influence has not been used to tie Shakespeare's Scottish play to a problem-based ethics—rather, *Macbeth* has usually been read either as a medieval moral on the dangers of temptation or as a postmodern exploration of the relativism of good and evil.[38] That is to say, *Macbeth* has usually been used to explore the sorts of speculative ethical concerns that Swinburne located in *Faustus*. As I will show over the remainder of this chapter, however, Shakespeare's play can instead be taken as an attempt to translate Faustus' physical predicament into a world devoid of Christian authority. Slipping the gods and altars that linger in Marlowe's play, *Macbeth* roots ethical congregation purely in the performance of our dark tomorrow. Practice replaces prophets, and the stage proves itself enough.

Like Faustus, Macbeth is introduced to the audience at a moment of earthly achievement: his glorious victory over the invading king of Norway. And like Faustus, Macbeth finds this satisfaction interrupted by an awareness of a coming time. On the way back from his triumph, Macbeth encounters the weird sisters, and their riddling prophecies trigger a sudden wonder at the gulf that yawns between his present and his future:

> This supernatural soliciting
> Cannot be ill; cannot be good...Present fears

Are less than horrible imaginings:
My thought, whose murther yet is but fantastical,
Shakes so my single state of man that function
Is smothered in surmise, and nothing is
But what is not.

(1.3.131–43)[39]

In this moment, Macbeth feels his "single state of man" split between two distinct perspectives—his awareness of the "present" and his "imaginings" of how things might be. Fantasizing about a future murder even as he is repulsed by his own horrible thoughts, Macbeth falls into the same practical difficulty that unsettles Marlowe's doctor. He has become oppressively conscious of his tomorrow, but knows that all he can see from his today is "surmise."

This problem continues to torment Macbeth in the following scene. Having agreed to ride ahead to Inverness, he abruptly declares: "Stars, hide your fires, / Let not light see my black and dark desires; / The eye wink at the hand; yet let that be / Which the eye fears, when it is done, to see" (1.4.51–54). The self-division in these lines is clear, and they are often cited as a demonstration of the struggle in Macbeth between his ambition to be great and his desire to be good. The immediate energy of this speech, however, derives from its temporal acrobatics, for Macbeth is talking to a midnight sky that does not yet exist. In this instant, what splits his single state is thus the very thing that divides Faustus when he sees the allegory of Hell: even as he feels the glimmering satisfaction of a coming time, he remains anchored in the now. And indeed, a few scenes later, Macbeth's worryings about the future blossom into a full-blown Faustian anxiety about the distance between this life and the next:

If it were done, when 'tis done, then 'twere well
It were done quickly. If th'assassination
Could trammel up the consequence, and catch
With his surcease, success; that but this blow
Might be the be-all and the end-all—here,
But here, upon this bank and shoal of time,
We'ld jump the life to come.

(1.7.1–7)

"Jump" is usually translated as "risk," but it also retains its literal meaning: "leap." For what Macbeth is imagining here is that action could become identical with consequence, that he could leap from the bank and shoal of time and reach the "end-all." With a single blow, the mind that spins so frantically, calculating possibilities, could rest in finished peace.

Yet as strongly as Macbeth feels this desire, he also recognizes it as a lunatic fantasy. There is no way to vault the individual steps that make up the long road to "success," no way to catch tomorrow's satisfaction without trudging through today. And so in the lines that follow, Macbeth attempts to gain satisfaction by another means. Fiercely suppressing his awareness of the "life to come," he briefly manages to convince himself that future justice inheres already in the working present:

> But in these cases,
> We still have judgment here, that we but teach
> Bloody instructions, which, being taught, return
> To plague th'inventor. This even-handed justice
> Commends th'ingredience of our poison'd chalice
> To our own lips.
>
> (1.7.7–12)

Instead of jumping to the day of last judgment, Macbeth now tries to find this justice in the "judgment here." Where he began by wishing that today could be tomorrow, he now wants to believe that the tomorrow inheres in the today. Yet clearly, his root impulse has not changed. Like Faustus, who cycles between rapturous anticipations of Hell and denials that there is any Hell at all, Macbeth now cycles to Armageddon and back because he craves a unifying of present action and future satisfaction. Desperately, hopefully, hopelessly, he tries to join his split state into one.

Like Faustus' interactions with the devils, Macbeth's encounter with the sisters thus awakens him to the problem of a coming time. Through their predictions, the weird trio make him aware of his tomorrow, filling him with an eagerness to know what this tomorrow holds. At the same time, though, the raw fact that Macbeth exists only in the present dooms his every effort to find future satisfaction. No sooner has he convinced himself that his future depends on his sword arm than he grows restless, seeking out the weird sisters for a second time. And even after hearing their prophecy that "none of woman born shall harm Macbeth," he resolves to make "double sure" of this by assassinating Macduff (4.1.94–97). Like Faustus, who wanders from his pact to his pranks and back, each fresh enthusiasm curdling quickly into discontent, Macbeth finds his hopes dwindling as soon as they are hatched. Far from discovering a resolution to his problem, he finds himself endlessly resolving it.

Macbeth's inability to find an answer to his difficulties has led a number of recent critics to suggest that the play offers a descent into pure subjectivity. Keying on the sisters' opening chant of "Fair is foul, and foul is fair" (1.1.11), Stephen Greenblatt, Stephen Booth, Alan Sinfield, and other radical scholars have argued that the same day can be simultaneously fair and foul only if these values depend entirely upon the observer.[40] Reversing the earlier consensus that the sisters' chant reveals their participation in an "evil" that is "not relative, but absolute,"[41] these later scholars have thus made *Macbeth* into a locus of relativism. However, while the sisters' chant does indeed suggest that they are not to be fixed on the pin of moral idealism, there is no need to follow these later scholars down the path to meta-ethics. For the sisters' initial riddle is not "Fair is foul, and foul is fair." It is: "When the hurly-burly's done, / When the battle's lost and won" (1.1.3–4). This observation that the same battle will be both "lost and won" emphasizes the subjective perspective of the different participants, but it does not imply a limitless proliferation of viewpoints. Instead, it suggests that there are precisely two ways of looking at the same thing. The same battle that will bring the victors joy will bring the losers anguish, so that one thing will be both fair and foul at once. The result, in effect, is not relativism, but the doubled sense of the future that Luther finds in the eucharist. On the one hand, the sisters remind us that certain aspects of the coming time are so certain as to seem immanent: there will be a battle, it will come to a conclusion, and there will be triumph and loss. And yet on the other hand, the sisters also remind us that the future is not so immanent after all, for we in the present cannot know for certain who will rise and who will fall. Only time will reveal the winner and the future king. Just like Faustus' pact, the sisters' riddles thus orient us to a problem that inheres in mortal existence: we know that the future will be fair for some and foul for others, that there will be a day of judgment that sorts out all our rewards. But we cannot grasp this judgment from the present, and so we cannot be certain how to act in the here and now.

As with Marlowe's use of allegory, Shakespeare's use of riddles has a precedent in Luther. Again and again, Luther compares the problem of mortality to the experience of being caught in a riddle: "The hiding place of God is darkness...because He dwells in the

riddle and darkness of faith...The shadow of peace is faith, the riddle of things to come."[42] For Luther, life is like a riddle because it
suspends us between two different perspectives, the present confusions of flesh and the future "peace" of spirit. As Luther illustrates
in his own attempt to solve "the riddle of Christ's humanity": "Not
that he is not God in us now, but He is in us wrapped in humanity.
But then He will be revealed as He is. Not that He will get rid of the
humanity, but that He will also show His divinity hidden there."[43]
In Luther's tortuous explanation, Christ's divinity is masked by
his humanity, and so he will in the future shed it and stand as he
is—but in doing so, he will retain his humanity. Understanding
is endlessly deferred to the future. In the present, we are trapped
uncomprehending in the riddle.

By likening ethical practice to an unsolved riddle, Luther established a highly unusual account of the physical connection between
rites and riddles. Anthropologists have found that riddles are frequently incorporated into marriages, funerals, and other similar
rites because they share a complementary aim.[44] The posing of a
riddle creates a disruptive sense of doubleness, forcing its audience
to imagine something with teeth that does not eat, or a door that
is not a door, or something that gets wetter the more that it dries.[45]
Just as a bride must reconcile her old sense of self with her new role
as a wife, or just as a mourner must reconcile life with death, the
audience of a riddle must grapple with two apparently incompatible
perspectives.[46] Once the solution to a riddle is offered, however,
this doubleness dissolves, bringing with it a sudden movement from
confusion to clarity. Riddles thus act as miniature instances of the
process of disruption and resolution that characterizes marriages
and funerals,[47] and this is why riddles are found in both the grave-
digging scene of *Hamlet* and the marriage caskets of *The Merchant
of Venice*.[48] Through their own metaphorical shifts, they help facili-
tate the transitions of perspective that underlie these rites.

Luther breaks completely with this view by suggesting that rites
are like riddles because both *refuse* transition. The perverseness of this
interpretation would seem to limit its appeal, and yet just as Luther's
writings on death enjoyed a popular following, so too did his conception of the eucharist as an unsolved riddle. No less a preacher than
John Donne explored the meaning of the eucharist by asking:

Do I see him at the window of bread and wine; Is he in that; or doe I
see him by the window of faith; and is he onely in that? still it is in a

riddle...I shall see Prophecies untyed, Riddles dissolved, but I shall never see that, till I come to this sight which follows in our text, *Videbo Deum*, I shall see God.[49]

Like Luther, Donne finds in the eucharist two perspectives: the "window of bread and wine" and the "window of faith." And like Luther, Donne describes not a sudden state of rapture, but rather a profound awareness of the distance that exists between the present and the future. Someday we will see God and riddles will be dissolved and prophecies untied. But for now we wander in the coils of reason, where the joy of God's revelation mingles with the confused turnings of our own thought.

Whether or not Shakespeare was aware of this Lutheran perspective, his own use of riddles tightly matches Luther's.[50] Luther sums up the riddle of human life as *simul justus et peccator*, "at once fair and fallen,"[51] and as Lady Macbeth notes early in the play, Macbeth embodies this contradiction: "Thou...wouldst not play false, / And yet wouldst wrongly win" (1.5.20–22). Macbeth is himself only too aware of this unresolved contradiction. From the moment he encounters the three sisters, he sees life as a riddle of fair and foul. The bright things he craves require atrocities. This riddle, Macbeth convinces himself, will dissolve at the moment of his coronation, but just as in Luther, the riddle stalls the rite. Although Macbeth is given the crown, he never feels that he is properly king. He has Duncan's sons to worry about, of course, but his real concern is the possibility that Banquo's line will one day assume the throne. As Macbeth sees it, he does not truly possess the crown if his blood does not rule Scotland in perpetuity, and so once again he finds himself in a state of suspended satisfaction. Before he kills Duncan, he is halfway to being king. And after he kills Duncan, he is halfway to being king. No matter how hard he labors in the present, he never secures the future.

In finding himself in this unending middle, moreover, Macbeth is not alone. For while he fusses over his coronation, the audience in the gallery are involved in their own ritual: playgoing. To attend a tragic play is to experience a sense of dramatic tension that was habitually justified in the early seventeenth century by claiming that it would lead to moral insight, or catharsis, or some other intellectual or emotional transition. Yet just as the sisters' riddles trap the would-be king in the midst of a ritual transformation, so too do they interrupt the ritual function of Shakespeare's play, ensnaring the audience in the same problem that troubles Macbeth. The grandest example of this experience is the sisters' final riddle, which unfolds entirely differently for Macbeth than it unfolds for his audience. This riddle is delivered to Macbeth following his coronation, when the sisters announce: "Macbeth shall never vanquish'd be until / Great Birnam wood to high Dunsinane hill / Shall come against him" (4.1.92–94). To Macbeth, this seems more a pronouncement than an interpretive puzzle. As he reasons: "Who can impress the forest, bid the tree / Unfix his earth-bound root?" (4.1.95–96). Macbeth's method of interpreting the riddle—and therefore his reason for achieving satisfaction—is revealing. Instead of taking the riddle literally as a true conditional, he applies his own earthly frame of reference, concluding that since it is inconceivable for trees to leave their moorings, he can himself never be vanquished. Keeping his own earth-bound root firmly fixed, he discovers the solace of allegory, accessing the hereafter through the logic of the here.

Just as in *Faustus*, however, this allegorical method is doomed to brutal failure. Macbeth is reveling in his invincibility when a messenger staggers up, stricken: "I look'd toward Birnam, and anon methought / The wood began to move" (5.5.32–33). Macbeth's reaction is immediate and violent:

> I pull in resolution, and begin
> To doubt th'equivocation of the fiend
> That lies like truth. "Fear not, till Birnam wood
> Do come to Dunsinane," and now a wood
> Comes toward Dunsinane. Arm, arm, and out!
> I gin to be a-weary of the sun,
> And wish th'estate o' th' world were now undone.
> (5.5.41–49)

Macbeth's agony in these lines stems not simply from the fact that the sisters' riddle is solved, but from the fact that its solution violates the logic of life as he knows it. For on the basis of the information he has been given by the messenger, he must accept that the wood is actually moving toward him. His allegorical reading of the weird sisters' riddle is torn apart and replaced with an event that violates all the laws of nature. The gulf of perspective that Macbeth has relentlessly tried to close is thus forced open once again, and he is confronted with the terrible realization that there is no analogy between the sisters' vantage and his own. No future logic can clarify the present. No present logic can contain the future.

What makes this scene remarkable, however, is that even as the riddle moves Macbeth to confusion, it stirs a very different experience in the audience. For we know that Birnam wood is not really moving toward Macbeth—in the previous scene we have seen that it is only a group of soldiers disguising themselves with branches. We thus perceive an allegorical relation between our earthly present and the future perspective of the prophecy, such that two things that seem in conflict are actually in harmony. We experience, in short, the typical experience of a riddle, in which an apparent opposition between two orders of meaning is neatly resolved by a metaphorical shift of reading frame. Where Macbeth despairs of understanding, we feel the satisfaction of grasping a larger logic, enjoying the same clarity that Faustus savors in the allegory of Hell. Together with Macbeth, we thus enact the two paired experiences of mortality— what for one is foul is for another fair. Far from resolving the puzzle of human life, the fulfillment of the sisters' prophecy has reintroduced the doubleness associated with their initial appearance. We have reached the solution of a riddle, but are in a riddle still.

The end of the play brings no release from this condition. In the closing moments, the future king Malcolm broods over the death of his soldiers, those who have been lost in the battle won. And when a bereaved father insists that his son could not have died "a fairer death...God's soldier be he!," Malcolm grimly replies, "He's worth more sorrow, / And that I'll spend for him" (5.9.13–17). Perhaps the soldier is in Elysium; perhaps not. Here on earth, we cannot see so far ahead. All we know is that even the fairest death is tinged with darker aspect. And so it is that the play ends without bringing us any closer to the ending. We have seen prophecies fulfilled and riddles untied. And so like Macbeth, we have grown hopeful, even expectant. We have felt that we understand the sisters, that we can grasp their logic from our present ken. But even as we have come to feel the future near, we can see no farther now than when we began. The ritual has brought us only halfway—our life beyond remains a riddle.

By offering this experience, *Macbeth* reveals the practical possibilities of the ethical project undertaken in *Faustus*. Like Marlowe's play, *Macbeth* presents the future not as a puzzle to be solved, but as an open question. Put in the language of Dewey's ethics, *Macbeth* treats the problem of our dark tomorrow "*as* a problem," inviting us to share Luther's experience of it as immanent and vivid and inescapable. Moreover, while *Faustus*, like Luther, relies on Christian eschatology to communicate this problem, *Macbeth* does not rely on any otherworldly ideal. Instead of God and Mephistopheles, it offers up a gang of creatures fashioned out of pagan lore, popular superstition, and poetic fancy. The weird sisters inhabit no known supernature, but are in the end simply theatrical devices. They exist nowhere—and so can exist anywhere, seeming as likely in any time and place. *Macbeth*, in short, exploits the fictional nature of theater to extend the experience offered in *Faustus*. Communicating Luther's concern to spectators whose only faith is in the stage, Shakespeare's play demonstrates that we do not need immaterial things to ground our ethical practice. Art alone can be enough.

While *Macbeth* may be enough to sustain Luther's ethical practice, however, it is not enough to substantiate Dewey's. It may show that seventeenth-century tragedy offered a means for gathering spectators around the experience of a particular problem, but it does not confirm pragmatism's more ambitious claims about problem-based art: first, that such art can encourage organic pluralism; and second, that this pluralism allows for a progressive response to natural selection. In the following chapter, I will therefore turn to exploring the first of these two claims, focusing in large part on the play that has given this book its title: *Hamlet*. As I will show, *Hamlet* formed part of a broader effort to explore the problem of our dark tomorrow from a very different direction than the one undertaken by *Macbeth*, a direction that channeled this problem not into a cycle of anticipation and despair, but into a therapeutic calm. When read alongside *Macbeth*, *Hamlet* thus supports Dewey's broader intuitions about the potential of problem-based art. For it shows that seventeenth-century tragedy did more than introduce audiences to the experience of a problem. It opened different ways of approaching the problem, encouraging the functional pluralism that sustains life.

Chapter 2

Partial Belief in *Julius Caesar* and *Hamlet*

Why farewell, Portia. We must die.
—Brutus, *Julius Caesar* (4.3.190–92)

With this blunt acceptance of human mortality, Brutus brushes aside the problem that torments Faustus and Macbeth. Though staggered by the news of his wife's death, he quickly recovers his composure, finding comfort in the thought that all that lives must die. For professing this sudden calm, he has been seen by some scholars as a true philosopher, by others as a fraud. To those in the first camp, Brutus reflects an evolution in Shakespearean tragedy that occurred after the death of the playwright's own son, Hamnet. Prior to this point, Shakespeare's characters seem either immune to suffering or overwhelmed by it,[1] but with Brutus, a more complex response to bereavement emerges. Guided by his Stoic philosophy, Brutus admits the horror of death without suffering permanently beneath it, accomplishing a remarkable transformation from anguish to tranquility. To those in the second camp, though, Brutus' transformation is *too* remarkable. Stoicism may view death as something to be philosophized away, but actual bereavement leaves a deep mark in flesh and blood. To this second group of critics, the Roman's recovery is therefore not to be trusted. Either he has not suffered as deeply as he appears, or his philosophy has not healed him as completely as he claims.

Although these camps offer very different theories about Brutus' behavior, I will suggest over the following pages that both are practically sound. As I will show, *Julius Caesar* promotes an

ancient approach to mourning that reframes death from a speculative problem into a physical one. Like hunger or any other bodily
pain, bereavement is thus made the target of a practical remedy,
dissolving the apparent tension between the claim that death cannot be philosophized away and the claim that its wounds can be
overcome. Brutus, in effect, is not a philosopher, but a pragmatist,
and although he has not earned a place in history as a model for
the bereaved, I will show over the second half of this chapter that
Shakespeare achieved a more memorable result in his next tragedy: *Hamlet.* Softening Brutus' blunt farewell into the prince's
long goodbye, *Hamlet* offers a more accessible introduction to the
Roman's experience of grief, communicating his practical remedy
to the great many of us who do not possess the steel of Roman
souls. *Hamlet* thus does for *Julius Caesar* what we saw *Macbeth*
do for *Faustus*, enlarging its problem-based practice into a wider
basis for society, and indeed, when viewed against the tragedies
discussed in the preceding chapter, *Hamlet* also enlarges the
practice of progressive ethics in another way. By using the same
concern that stirs Macbeth's restless ecstasy to encourage a very
different experience, *Hamlet* shows that the stage did not funnel
audiences toward a single response to the problem of human mortality. Instead, it was an engine of functional variety, allowing one
physical concern to be translated into multiple practices. *Hamlet*,
in short, confirms the second of Dewey's three hypotheses about
the progressive potential of art, and so though Shakespeare's play
has often been celebrated as the pinnacle of seventeenth-century
tragedy, the following pages will suggest that its ethical worth lies
in something quite different. Rather than being an ideal end, it is a
practical addition, an alternative that shows how tragedy can turn
problems into pluralism.

By all accounts, there is something odd about act 4, scene 3 of
Julius Caesar. A few moments after Brutus confesses to Cassius that
Portia has died, leaving him "sick of many griefs," Messala arrives
and asks whether Brutus has any recent news of his wife (4.3.144).
Brutus replies that he has not, and when Messala announces that
Portia is dead, Brutus responds, "Why farewell, Portia. We must
die, Messala. / With meditating that she must die once, / I have
the patience to endure it now" (4.3.190–92). For obvious reasons,
this sudden turnabout has puzzled audiences. Although Brutus
elsewhere seems scrupulous to a fault, here he not only lies directly
to Messala, but pretends to be a far better philosopher than he

actually is. Some critics have explained this as a textual error, arguing that Shakespeare wrote two different versions of this scene that subsequently got confused into a single account.[2] The problem with this approach, however, is that the surviving text of *Julius Caesar* is extremely clean and contains almost no errors, making a discrepancy of this magnitude improbable.[3] Moreover, this radical a solution is not actually necessary, for Brutus' previous insistence that the conspirators behave like "Roman actors" suggests that he is fully capable of espousing discrepant perspectives on the same situation. A number of critics have therefore argued that Brutus is being disingenuous when he professes a Stoic calm before Messala.[4] Hypocritically claiming a virtue he does not in fact possess, Brutus reveals the absurdity of Stoicism.

If this were the only possible reading of Brutus' remarkable calm, it would in the end hold a rather unremarkable place in ethics. After all, there is in the history of literature no shortage of reminders that virtue is easier to profess than possess. In fact, however, there is a more particular way to unpuzzle Brutus' behavior, one that links his abrupt reversal to a Stoic practice of mourning that had achieved a growing popularity in Shakespeare's day.[5] Prior to the Stoics, most philosophers had followed Plato and Aristotle in claiming that the soul housed two entirely different sets of faculties, the first containing emotions that stemmed from the body and the second containing rational thoughts that originated in the mind. The Stoics rejected this notion of two competing faculties, suggesting instead that passion and reason were two different ways of classifying the state of the soul. A soul that was in proper alignment with nature showed reason, while a soul that was disordered—placing excessive value on certain things and too little emphasis on others—was marked by passion. Passion and reason were thus descriptions—not causes—of cognitive states like grief and tranquility. The real source of these states, according to the Stoics, was belief, which ranged from certain knowledge to erroneous opinion. A mind filled with the true knowledge of virtue would be at all times coolly rational, while a mind stocked with disordered and conflicting beliefs would be prone to anger, misery, and other passionate states. This view of the origin of emotion led the Stoics to a new understanding of mourning. They claimed that we suffer when our loved ones die because we mistakenly believe that our loved ones are good—mistakenly, that is, because only virtue is good. And so it was that the Stoics counseled the study of philosophy as the best remedy to suffering, for by imbuing our minds with true knowledge, we immunized ourselves to pain.

In the end, this immunization proved too difficult for mere mortals, and the Stoic sage passed into the mists of legend, imagined but never seen. Nevertheless, one core feature of Stoic practice endured, passed down to Shakespeare's age in the form of a practical remedy described by Cicero, Plutarch, and Seneca. All three men had experienced the terrible pain of losing a loved one, a pain that had convinced them that no amount of Stoic meditation could inoculate the heart from loss. At the same time, however, these men felt that suffering could be managed and eventually eliminated because they accepted the plausibility of the Stoic view that emotion had its root in belief. As Cicero writes in *The Tusculan Disputations*, "The cause of sadness and of all the other passions is belief...and so he who grieves does so because he believes he ought to."[6] We suffer because we believe it is appropriate to suffer, a belief that often leads us to prolong our grief unnecessarily. As Seneca was fond of pointing out, while bereavement in animals is sharp but brief, humans typically extend their misery out of a sense of duty or guilt.[7]

Rather than following the original Stoics in trying to eliminate the problem of death entirely, these thinkers arrived at a revised position—which I will refer to as "neo-Stoicism"[8]—that simply sought to avoid unneeded suffering. Such was suffering that resulted not from the initial (and unavoidable) shock of loss, but from guilt, denial, and other emotions that flowed from the mistaken belief that the death of the loved one was abnormal. To combat this belief, moreover, the neo-Stoics did not prescribe philosophical speculations on virtue. Instead, they counseled a physical practice, urging the bereaved to study examples of the commonness of death. Such examples dissolved the sense of extraordinary circumstance precipitated by loss, for he "who demonstrates that the calamity is one which is common to many, and less than the calamities which have befallen others, changes the belief [*dócan*] of the one in grief and gives him a similar conviction."[9] Though it relies on the original Stoic view that emotional states are dependent upon belief, this practice thus does not seek to transform the bereaved into granite sages. Instead, it softens grief by providing models of patient endurance that lead the suffering out of their extraordinary sense of bereavement and into the conviction that loss is common and physically endurable.[10]

As the neo-Stoics were quick to point out, this reliance on examples was not their invention. It had been tested by the experience of others, most notably the Cyrenaics, who claimed that "premeditation on future ills lessens their actual arrival, for they have long been anticipated."[11] To bring this strategy of premeditation in line with their own experience, however, the neo-Stoics found it necessary to modify it. Because they felt that the shock of physical loss was unavoidable, they suggested that it was frequently necessary to premeditate *after* the calamity occurred. As Cicero writes, "I believe that the effect of prior meditation [*ante meditantur*] upon the wise parallels the effect of the passing of time upon others, except that it is a process of reasoning that heals [*sanat*] the former, while nature itself heals the latter."[12] By using the term *sanat*, which describes the restoration (not the preservation) of health, Cicero introduces a strange temporal inversion into his account of premeditation. Somehow *pre*meditation occurs *after* the wound, so that a preventative functions as a therapeutic response. As peculiar as this formulation seems, however, Cicero is simply suggesting that our response to grief take the form of a belated premeditation. Because true wisdom is an impossible ideal, because loss is by its very nature shocking, no amount of forethought can stave off the experience of tragedy. And so premeditation must often be undertaken afterward, allowing us to re-experience the tragedy with the insight gained by our subsequent use of examples. Though metaphysically impossible, neo-Stoic premeditation thus offers a practically useful bending of time, taking advantage of hindsight to show us "that what seemed great is in fact not."[13]

The works of the neo-Stoics were largely disregarded in medieval Europe in favor of the strict *contemptus mundi* of the Latin fathers, but in the mid-fourteenth century, Petrarch's *De Remediis* reintroduced neo-Stoic views on psychotherapy to a wide audience, and by the sixteenth century, the original works of Cicero, Plutarch, and Seneca were broadly available in vernacular translation.[14] Neo-Stoic practice was not simply known, moreover; it was embraced. Despite the wide variety of situations in which Shakespeare's characters comfort each other for loss, there is not a single mention of the Christian consolations that dominated medieval literature.[15] Instead, there is universal reliance—even by clearly Catholic figures like the Friar in *Romeo and Juliet*—upon classical authors, the vast majority of them neo-Stoics. By virtue of its own classical context, *Julius Caesar* provides a natural setting for this ancient tradition. Like Cicero, the historical Brutus was an Academic Skeptic with Stoic leanings, and Shakespeare's portrayal of Brutus' grief is an exacting depiction of the neo-Stoic account of mourning. Initially admitting the enormous pain that Portia's death has caused him, but then claiming that premeditation of this same event has given him the patience to endure her passing without sorrow, Brutus follows the path described in neo-Stoic consolations. Indeed, his precise language—"With meditating that she must die once, / I have the patience to endure it now"—echoes Cicero's own use of the term *meditatio* to imply an act that is imaginatively shifted from the present to the past.

This scene then further reinforces neo-Stoic practice by emphasizing both the uncommonness of Brutus' suffering and the method by which he recovers from his shock. Portia's death is by all accounts extraordinary. Brutus reveals to Cassius that Portia died when she "swallow'd fire," a form of suicide that Messala explicitly calls a "strange manner" of death (4.3.156; 4.3.189). No surprise, then, that Brutus is unprepared at first to deal with it. However, by subsequently denying to Messala that he has news of Portia, Brutus gives himself the opportunity to undergo the process of bereavement again. This time, the emphasis falls not on the distinctiveness of Brutus' situation, but upon its commonness: "Why farewell, Portia. We must die, Messala." By approaching Portia's suicide from the plural first-person "We," Brutus generalizes the terms of his loss and eases himself out of shock. He is not the only one to suffer bereavement, for as he reminds himself, death is our common lot.

Brutus' example is inspiring—he recovers rapidly from a terrible shock and never again dwells on the matter of his wife's death. And yet it is also intimidating—surely, the rest of us could not recover so fast. Brutus may not be a Stoic sage, but he is so far beyond the realm of the ordinary that for all practical purposes, he may as well be the stuff of myth. Nevertheless, as subsequent scenes make clear, Brutus is not the only one capable of this neo-Stoic practice. There is also the more humble example of Cassius. After witnessing Brutus' response to Portia's death, Cassius renounces his own Epicureanism, confessing to Messala that he is worried that the carrion circling overhead are a "canopy most fatal, under which / Our army lies, ready to give up the ghost" (5.1.87–88). Alarmed by this revelation, Messala counsels against a belief in omens. Cassius responds, "I but believe it partly, / For I am fresh of spirit and resolv'd / To meet all perils very constantly" (5.1.89–91). Like Brutus, Cassius thus reacts to a disruptive sense of the extraordinary by reordering his belief—"I but believe it partly"—and the result is a new emotional resolve. Brutus may be unusual in his practice, but he is not entirely alone.

Yet even as the example of Cassius seems to confirm the wider possibilities of Brutus' neo-Stoicism, it also prompts a fresh concern. Cassius follows his friend's practice so exactly that scholars who doubt the genuineness of Brutus' response have often found something suspicious in Cassius' use of the word "partly." This qualification has been taken to indicate a gap between what Cassius believes and how he is determined to act, such that his resolution is a public persona he has adopted to mask his inner doubts. Strengthening this interpretation is the fact that Cassius' profession of a fresh spirit and constant resolve recycles the language of Brutus' earlier exhortation to the conspirators to bear themselves as "Roman actors do, [w]ith untired spirits and formal constancy" (2.1.227–28). From this vantage, Cassius and Brutus seem superficial characters who—as one critic has written—"see themselves as actors, [and] conceive of virtue as the consistent playing of a part...Lacking self-knowledge, they try instead to act artificial parts imposed on them by their society, the expectations of others, and their own moral aspirations."[16] In short, perhaps Cassius' practice does not elevate him to the level of Brutus; perhaps it diminishes Brutus to the level of Cassius, revealing them both to be as devoid of moral substance as theatrical actors.

This negative view of theatricality, however, is predicated on the very view of psychology that Brutus' neo-Stoicism rejects. Rather than drawing a firm line between outward performances and inner states, the practice-based psychology of neo-Stoicism led to the view that all human behavior was essentially role-playing. As Cicero explains in *Tusculans* and *De Officiis*,[17] we develop our belief system in the same manner that an actor discovers his performance.[18] To test the worth of his dramatic choices, an actor must commit himself fully, performing them with total confidence. If these choices fail to convince his audience, he will become aware of a conflict between his expectations and his actual effect, and like a wise man struggling with unexpected calamity, he will falter in his performance. And just like this wise man, the actor must find his way ahead by revising his past choices and recommitting himself to new ones, boldly climbing back onto the stage to try again. This analogy between acting off-stage and on establishes an equivalence between beliefs and dramatic choices. In order to function, our beliefs demand from us the same level of conviction that we invest in a dramatic choice, so that we commit ourselves to our beliefs as though they reflected the deep order of our minds. If I believe that I need great wealth in order to be a valued member of society, then I will do my best to acquire money. However, because beliefs—like dramatic choices—are provisional, they can be revised in retrospect if we become aware of some unexpected consequence of our behavior. If my ruthless pursuit of wealth costs me my friends, I may revise my view that avarice is the best path to good standing. In short, our performances reveal whether our beliefs are in alignment (in neo-Stoic terminology, "rational") or whether they produce a conflict of expectations ("passionate"). The shock of feeling grief or anger or shame makes us conscious of a conflict between what we expected and what actually has occurred, allowing us to rethink the beliefs at the root of our public acts.

To clarify this account of learning, Cicero turns to a comparison of the soul with the eye. In Dolman's 1561 translation of *Tusculans*, the passage reads: "The soule is not able in this bodye to see him selfe. No more is the eye whyche although he seeth all other thinges, yet (that whiche is one of the leaste) can not discerne his owne shape. But admit that the soule can not consider him selfe: howebeit perhaps he may. His operacions... it doth well ynoughe perceyue."[19] Like the eye, the soul cannot look directly at itself, but just as the eye can see its reflection in other things, so too can the soul come to understand itself by studying the effects of its actions upon others. The emphasis here is on function, as opposed to being, for self-knowledge is revealed through performance. Like an actor, the eye discovers itself by doing. Cicero's *Tusculans* is dedicated to Marcus Junius Brutus, and this very figure introduces the philosopher's simile of the eye into Shakespeare's *Julius Caesar*. In the opening act, after revealing to Cassius that he is caught in the midst of an unsuccessful struggle to order the contents of his mind, Brutus admits that "the eye sees not itself / But by reflection, by some other things" (1.2.52–53). The common Shakespearean pun on "eye" captures both terms of Cicero's original simile, and by resorting to this analogy at a time when his own private introspections have proved fruitless, Brutus acknowledges the neo-Stoic claim that we can best know ourselves by studying the effects of our public acts.[20] Just like the eye, we see ourselves not through mental reflection, but by witnessing our actions reflected in others.

Read in this light, Brutus' insistence that the conspirators bear themselves as "Roman actors do" does not implicate him in a misguided attempt to suppress his human nature. Instead, it reveals him pursuing the same therapeutic practice that allows him to find peace after Portia's death. This same practice, moreover, informs Cassius' claim that his conversion has led him to believe "partly." While scholars have taken this as a sign that Cassius is trying to cloak his private reservations with a public face, this interpretation jars with the understanding of belief held by Shakespeare and his contemporaries. At the time that *Julius Caesar* was written, "belief" implied total assent.[21] Not until later in the seventeenth century did belief come to assume its modern valence of degrees of conviction.[22] Prior to *Julius Caesar*, moreover, Shakespeare scrupulously follows traditional usage. Cassius' remark is the first indication in any of the dramatist's works that belief can be anything but total.[23] A shift in meaning has clearly occurred, but it is not necessary to follow recent critics in supposing that Shakespeare has anticipated subsequent generations and abruptly shifted to a modern equation of "belief" with "opinion." Instead, Cassius' usage holds onto the traditional idea that the effect of belief is total, but adds the neo-Stoic view that the foundation of belief is contingent. Seen this way, Cassius' response to Messala is evidence not of hypocrisy, but of dynamic learning. In the moment that he is challenged by Messala, Cassius realizes that he feels uncomfortable with the way he is acting, and he makes a sudden decision to alter his behavior. This involves an examination of the beliefs that drove his previous actions, prompting him to recognize that his earlier belief in supernatural portents was provisional, something he believed only "partly." And so like a Roman actor who leaves behind one set of dramatic choices for another, he decides to set aside this belief in favor of a different one. Once this revision is complete, moreover, Cassius commits himself fully to his new set of beliefs—the word "partly" is associated only with his old belief in portents, while his revised beliefs are never characterized as anything but total. And as is the case with a new dramatic choice, the result is a shift in Cassius' performance. Not only does he announce that he is fully resolved to meet all perils constantly, but he leaves behind the petty selfishness of his early actions. Mirroring the determination of Brutus, he does not crack under the world's weight, but adapts to the vast extraordinary without.

The therapeutic benefits of this neo-Stoic practice are confirmed in the play's closing moments by the contrast that Brutus' death provides with Caesar's. Caesar spends his final breaths making grand assertions about his inflexibility: "I could well be mov'd, if I were as you; / If I could pray to move, prayers would move me. / But

I am constant as the northern star" (3.1.58–60). Here, Caesar
expresses the heroic constancy typically associated with Stoicism in
the Renaissance. This emphasis on constancy was traceable less to
any Stoic treatise than to Senecan tragedy, which dramatized the
Stoic belief that the individual could remain firm in the face of great
stress simply through an act of will.[24] In displaying such will, the
heroes of Senecan tragedy frequently imagined the universe as their
own personal mirror,[25] a technique that underscored not only their
importance but also their constancy. Instead of being crushed by
adversity, they were upheld by the order of nature itself.[26] Caesar's
comparison of himself to the northern star has the same effect. Like
a Senecan hero, Caesar projects himself onto the world outside,
satisfying his self-importance by finding his image reflected in the
way of things. In doing so, Caesar briskly distinguishes his personal
brand of Stoic idealism from Brutus' neo-Stoic practice. In place of
the reflexive, evolving universe described by Brutus' comparison of
himself to an eye, Caesar imagines a universe in which the virtuous man is unaffected by anything else, persisting eternal. Almost
as soon as it is expressed, however, Caesar's view of constancy is
proven false by his brutal murder, which makes it clear that he is
subject to the same larger forces as everybody else. In a cosmos in
which movement is the way that things come to know themselves
and grow together, there is no room for an individual who would
be the northern star. Though Caesar is the title character, he is gone
before the fourth act.

Set against Caesar's collapse, Brutus' death establishes a different
standard for ethics. Like many of Brutus' actions, his decision to kill
himself is preceded by an upheaval of belief. After Cassius asks him
what he will do if they lose the upcoming battle, Brutus frames his
response as a condemnation of Cato's suicide:

> Even by the rule of that philosophy
> By which I did blame Cato for the death
> Which he did give himself—I know not how,
> But I do find it cowardly and vile,
> For fear of what might fall, so to prevent
> The time of life.
>
> (5.1.100–105)

Here, Brutus describes his philosophy as a collection of rules, condemning Cato for violating its precepts. Brutus' intense attachment

to these precepts is then underlined a few moments later by his association of the rules of philosophy with "the providence of some high
powers / That govern us below" (5.1.106–7). Brutus' aversion to
suicide, it would seem, is tantamount to religious faith.

Given this fervency, it comes as something of a surprise when
Brutus utterly reverses his belief a few moments later. Abandoning
his commitment to "the rule of that philosophy," he announces that
he would rather kill himself than be led defeated through Rome.
This reversal has long created problems for critics, who have in general felt that it must reflect either a textual error or a flaw in Brutus'
moral character.[27] There is, however, no need to see any inconsis-
tency in this scene. By seeing rules as absolute prescriptions that can
nevertheless be revised in retrospect, Brutus is holding fast to his
neo-Stoic philosophy, which gives ethical rules the same status as
beliefs.[28] Just as beliefs are both prescriptive and provisional, so too
are rules an absolute guide that may be modified to cope with unan-
ticipated circumstances. And indeed, despite Brutus' stated certainty
on the matter of suicide, there is an interesting hiccup in his speech.
Wedged between his declaration of his own future actions and his
condemnation of Cato is the frank admission: "I know not how."
The placement of this phrase suggests that Brutus is simultaneously
unsure about both his own future actions and his precise reason for
condemning Cato. Even as he holds fast to a system of rules, Brutus
thus admits that he is uncertain how to extend it.

This conflict—between the fierce adoption of a fixed system of
behavior and the awareness that this system cannot account for the
unexpected—is the very conflict contained in the practice of partial
belief, where belief is at once the determiner of definite action and
the provisional basis for an evolving system of knowledge. And in
fact, the figure that lurks at the center of Brutus' conflicted relationship to philosophical rules is the same figure that the historical
Cicero invokes to explain how rules can be violated without being
invalidated: Cato. According to Cicero, although suicide is in general a crime, it was proper for Cato to kill himself, for nature had
given him an extraordinary [*incredibilem*] austerity.[29] Cicero then
goes on to argue, however, that the appropriateness of Cato's act
does not invalidate the rule. The other conspirators were not as
exceptional as their leader, and so it was appropriate that they did
not take their own lives. Here is the flexibility created by Cicero's
view that rules are descriptive not prescriptive, and it is this flexibility that lies at the root of Brutus' hesitation. Although rules give

solid guidelines for general behavior, the exceptional is by its very nature beyond their grasp.

Nevertheless, as Brutus' subsequent actions demonstrate, there is a way to bring the exceptional into the domain of practice. To begin with, even though Brutus is uncertain about the future course appropriate for him, he makes a definitive declaration about what he will do in the event of a defeat, insisting that he will not kill himself. As we have seen, such firm decisions provide neo-Stoics with the impetus for a performance that can then be altered if it is disrupted by a sudden emotion, or an unexpected peer response, or some other similar shock to the system. In Brutus' case, this disruption comes from Cassius, who fills in the fate of those republicans who did not kill themselves with Cato: "Then, if we lose this battle, / You are contented to be led in triumph / Thorough the streets of Rome?" (5.1.107–9). Here, Cassius challenges Brutus' sense of certainty by drawing on a past example. By doing so, he functions as a mirror, allowing Brutus to glimpse the physical effects of his decision. The effect on Brutus is immediate: "No, Cassius, no. Think not, thou noble Roman, / That ever Brutus will go bound to Rome" (5.1.110–11). In this moment, Brutus thus decides to make a different dramatic choice. The extraordinary act of Cato's suicide becomes the example that he now patterns his life after, bringing with it the belated composure typical of neo-Stoicism.

Brutus' final words to Cassius preserve this neo-Stoic dynamic, expressing a conviction that is nevertheless implicitly incomplete: "this same day / Must end that work the ides of March begun. / And whether we shall meet again I know not" (5.1.112–14). The conjunction "and" is crucial here. It yokes together sureness and doubt, joining a calm resolve to an acceptance of the limits of human knowledge, and moments later, Brutus offers a final proof that these apparently irreconcilable states of mind can be brought into alignment:

> O that a man might know
> The end of this day's business ere it come!
> But it sufficeth that the day will end,
> And then the end is known.
> (5.1.122–25)

Here, Brutus runs up against the very same problem that confronts Macbeth, the recognition that the future is inherently unknowable.

But unlike Macbeth, Brutus reminds himself that he has lived many days and each has ended. And so too, he tells himself, must this one. This conclusion is not, of course, an answer to the problem of the future. It does not bring the end of the day closer, nor does it stop the march of future days. Yet though Brutus is no better able to solve the problem of the future than Macbeth, he shows that it is possible to practice it differently. Where Macbeth turns to his sword arm, Brutus turns to the example of past experience. One problem has generated two distinct styles of ethical practice.

For all its potential, however, Brutus' example is by itself a fragile one. Brutus is an austere figure and his perspective frequently seems remote. He recovers from his wife's suicide with astounding alacrity and embraces the necessity of his own death with remarkable calm. The play itself, moreover, does little to make his perspective more accessible. Brutus is constantly idealized by the other characters, even in death: "This was a man!" (5.5.75). In short, far from suggesting that Brutus is a model for us all to follow, the play implies that he is extraordinary. Like Cato, he is more to be admired than emulated. Cassius, meanwhile, may take the edge off Brutus' singularity, but he is hardly the focus of the action, nor is he an emotional tether for most audience members. He may offer the hope that Brutus' example can be broadly accessible, but he does not deliver on this promise himself. And so it is that *Julius Caesar* fails to live up to the standard of *Macbeth*, which as we saw in the last chapter, takes advantage of theater's dramatic dimension to involve its audience in the experience of wrestling with a problem. Instead, *Julius Caesar* is more expositional than engaging, more a treatise than a tragedy. As I will suggest over the following pages, however, this lack was remedied in Shakespeare's next tragedy: *Hamlet*. Brutus has long been seen as a model for Hamlet, and as I will show, *Hamlet* elaborates the therapeutic ethics depicted in *Julius Caesar* by joining it to the prince's deep and painful experience of bereavement. Where *Julius Caesar* allows the audience to remain observers of suffering, *Hamlet* invites them to experience the problem of loss themselves, encouraging them to test the efficacy of Brutus' practice firsthand. Like my previous readings, this reading of *Hamlet* will depart from previous scholarly accounts of the play's ethical worth, and once again, my justification for this departure will not be that the evidence I present is somehow more correct than the evidence that other scholars have laid out—after all, how could one human brain possibly absorb and evaluate the vast mountains of philosophical, historical, and literary evidence that have been piled around this endlessly interesting play? Rather, my justification for this departure will be simply that it is useful. For not only does it allow us to experience Shakespeare's play as a remedy to our own difficult bereavements, but it opens the possibility that this remedy can be part of a greater one: a practical pluralism that addresses the problem of human life in our inhuman world.

Hamlet begins by portraying a character with clear connections to some form of Stoic perspective: Horatio. Horatio declares in the play's final scene, "I am more an antique Roman than a Dane" (5.2.341), and he is described by Hamlet in the terms typically associated with the austere Stoicism of sixteenth-century tragedy: "A man that Fortune's buffets and rewards / Has't ta'en with equal thanks...that man / That is not passion's slave" (3.2.67–72). Despite the positive implications of this description, a number of critics have suggested that Horatio's connection with Stoicism does not in fact lend dignity to his behavior.[30] Rather, it makes him seem vaguely absurd. His rigid outlook leaves him unprepared to deal with the universe he inhabits, and Hamlet himself chastises his friend: "There are more things in heaven and earth, Horatio, / Than are dreamt of in your philosophy" (1.5.166–67). As the play's opening scene reveals, however, the prince errs in associating his friend's philosophy with the rigidity that leads to Caesar's inglorious fall. For far from being vainly inflexible, Horatio is in touch with the adaptive practice elaborated by Cassius and Brutus. After encountering the ghost, Horatio and the night watchmen get into a discussion about portents. Like the riddles of the weird sisters, such portents are embodiments of the extraordinary. They remind their witnesses of the uncertainty of the future, inviting the unquenchable curiosity that unsettles Macbeth. But rather than follow the footsteps of the doomed Scotsman, Horatio remarks, "So I have heard and do in part believe" (1.1.165). Like Cassius, Horatio responds to a supernatural portent by invoking partial belief, becoming the second of Shakespeare's characters to reference this core principle of neo-Stoic psychology.[31]

The context for this remark, moreover, reveals that Horatio's view of belief is not just a gesture toward neo-Stoic psychology, but an integral part of his ethics. After seeing the ghost, Horatio is struck immediately with a sense of "wonder," and he insists that the ghost is "strange," incompatible with any of his "particular thought[s]" (1.1.44; 64; 66). Horatio is thus powerfully aware of the weirdness of the ghost, a realization that seems to place him—despite all of his school-learning—in precisely the same situation as the night watchmen. Without warning, however, Horatio suddenly reverses his view of the ghost's visitation, declaring it a "mote...to trouble the mind's eye" (1.1.112). The extraordinarily strange has now become insignificant, almost commonplace. Horatio's abrupt shift comes as a surprise, and yet the strategy of thought that produces this shift should not, for it is the same strategy that Brutus and Cassius employ in *Julius Caesar*. As Horatio explains, even worse events—from walking dead to astral anomalies—preceded the death of Julius Caesar. He then goes on to point out that similar signs are even now being presented by heaven and earth to the Danish people. Horatio, in effect, relieves his sense of shock by returning to a prior framework that restores his sense of normalcy. Like Brutus and Cassius, Horatio recovers a state of calm not by suppressing emotion with reason, but by reconfiguring his beliefs with past examples.[32] There are stranger things than dreamt of in his philosophy, but his philosophy can unstrange them.

If Hamlet's critique of Horatio's philosophy does not point to a problem with neo-Stoicism, however, it does point to a problem with the prince's own practice. For what Hamlet sees as his friend's tendency to resist the extraordinary is in fact an indication of his own propensity to exaggerate it. Hamlet's belief in the uniqueness of his situation emerges in his initial exchange with his mother. Here, he makes the very mistake that Seneca and the other neo-Stoics warn against, insisting that his experience of loss is distinct from any other:

> *Gertrude*: Thou know'st 'tis common, all that lives must die,
>   Passing through nature to eternity.
> *Hamlet*:   Ay, madam, it is common.
> *Gertrude*:   If it be,
>   Why seems it so particular with thee?
> *Hamlet*:   Seems, madam? Nay, it is, I know not "seems."
>
> (1.2.72–76)

At first, there appears to be a total disconnect between the first four lines of this conversation and Hamlet's final response. Gertrude, after all, is discussing the nature of death when Hamlet seizes suddenly upon the word "seems" to switch the discussion to one about the authenticity of his grief. Because of this apparent disjunction, scholars have generally ignored Gertrude's remarks on death when

attending the prince's claim that he has "that within which pas-
seth show." In the process, they have tacitly divorced Hamlet's distinction between seeming and being from his mother's opposition
between the commonness of death and the strangeness of her son's
mourning.[33] Indeed, the desire to separate these two contrasts is so
strong that it has been suggested by one critic that the change of
topic is actually initiated by Gertrude.[34] On this view, the queen's
"it" should be taken to refer not to "all that lives must die" but
to Hamlet's behavioral response to his father's death. For otherwise, the "it" in Hamlet's "Nay it is" must also be taken to refer to
"all that lives must die," a reading that implies that the prince thinks
that "his father's death *is* exceptional rather than *seems* exceptional"
(404). Such a belief—this critic suggests—would be incredible, for
who would actually think that death is exceptional?

But while many of Hamlet's critics, including Claudius and
Gertrude, are baffled by the idea that the prince could actually
believe that his father's death is exceptional, the preceding pages of
this book have shown that many individuals of his era did experience death as extraordinary, even when they intellectually realized it
was not. Hamlet would thus hardly be out of place if he felt that his
father's passing was remarkable, and there is every indication that
he does. In his subsequent soliloquy, the prince repeatedly insists
upon the lofty nature of his father, comparing him first to Hyperion
and then to Hercules even as he reduces the rest of the world to
satyrs and unreasoning beasts. Even before Hamlet suspects foul
play, he is therefore clearly predisposed to view his father's death
as unusual—the death of an extraordinary man is an extraordinary
event. And so where Hamlet's admission of the commonness of
death strikes his mother as evidence that he should cease his wild
grief, Hamlet believes precisely the reverse. For him, the commonness of death is the backdrop against which the uniqueness of his
own case emerges. If death were in itself an extraordinary event,
then the death of the older Hamlet would not stand out. It would
be just one more extraordinary event among many. Once the commonness of death is conceded, however, the exceptional nature of
the old king's passing can be established. Moreover, as the only person at court who recognizes the strangeness of this event, Hamlet
establishes himself as exceptional as well. Where others play at grief,
he is genuinely aware of the tragedy that has transpired. Where others are all outward show, he has a private space of suffering. When
the prince transitions without warning from Gertrude's comment

on the uncommonness of his mourning to his distinction between being and seeming, he is thus exploiting the force of his mother's contrast to emphasize the uniqueness of his own interiority. He is saying, in effect, "As particular as my suffering appears, that is how particular my private perspective *is*."

In this moment, Hamlet reveals that his sense of his own place in the world depends upon a logic of the strange. Unlike his mother, he does not see extraordinary events as aberrations to be brought back into the domain of the ordinary. Instead, he wants to preserve the extraordinary, for it is by admitting the possibility of one exception that others become possible. In making sense of the prince's response to his mother, however, this logic exposes a potential problem with his assertion about his inner self. While this assertion has historically been taken as a mark of the prince's unusual intellectual maturity, it in fact rests on a fragile foundation: the unusualness of his father's death. For if it turns out that this death is after all no more exceptional than any other, then Hamlet's claim to possess a unique interiority crumbles. He becomes as ordinary and as external as all the suits of grieving that he scorns. Hamlet's whole sense of identity, in effect, depends upon him establishing the uncommonness of a common occurrence, and it is this need to believe in the exceptional that leads Hamlet a few moments later into his conflict with Horatio over the ghost. Where Horatio reacts to the ghost by searching his memory for past precedents, the prince responds by swearing to empty his head of all its previous contents: "From the table of my memory / I'll wipe away all trivial fond records, / All saws of books, all forms, all pressures past" (1.5.98–100). Although it is normal for exceptional circumstances to briefly separate individuals from their prior beliefs, Hamlet attempts to jettison these beliefs permanently. To confirm the importance of the ghost's visit, he makes it an originary moment that abnegates everything prior to it, a literal blank slate. The wailing of ghosts and the poisoning of kings might be a commonplace when considered from the vast library of examples that Horatio and Hamlet have acquired through their bookish studies.[35] But rather than compromise the foundation of his own interiority by acknowledging such, Hamlet chooses to ridicule his friend, admonishing him: "As a stranger give it [the ghost] welcome" (1.5.165). Where Horatio resists the exceptional, Hamlet exists upon it.

The contrast between these two friends is elaborated further in Hamlet's famous "To be" soliloquy. It has long been recognized that there are a host of verbal parallels between this soliloquy and a portion of John Dolman's 1561 translation of Cicero's *Tusculans*.[36] Previous scholars, though, have paid so much attention to stylistic similarities that they have failed to see that the prince completely reverses the neo-Stoic logic of his source. From the perspective of Hamlet's essentialist view of the self, his opening formulation—"To be or not to be?"—is the most profound question he can pose, for being and not-being are the fundamental categories of his universe. From the perspective of Cicero's theatrical ethics, however, the opposition between being and not-being is a blind alley. According to Cicero, any attempt to discuss the fate of the self after death runs into the logical impossibility that something which is dead—and therefore not-being—is approached in terms of being: "Whom you saye not to be he you say afterwardes is: where is your wit?"[37] Cicero therefore moves to curb this speculation, which fails to yield a use-able result, and instead focuses attention on practical action. He does so by drawing on his view of partial belief, exhorting individuals to still their contemplation of the future by willing themselves to believe that a good fate awaits them after death: "Let us thinke that day which is so terrible to other[s], to be a blessed and a happye daye to us...Whiche hope taken away, who is there so mad, that would continually live in laboure and daunger?"[38] As is typical of Cicero's neo-Stoic practice, this passage of *Tusculans* directs attention from what cannot be known to what must be done, using the ethical crisis created by death to generate the impetus for an election of belief.

This is the very perspective modeled in Brutus' final moments, where he turns from the uncertainty of death and instead focuses upon a belief that allows him to act confidently. But where Brutus is able to take comfort in partial belief, Hamlet is led by his obsession with the singularity of his circumstance to reverse Cicero's logic. Instead of turning his gaze onto physical examples, Hamlet tries to probe the mysteries of death, and the result is a wandering and inconclusive speculation. After entertaining the thought that death might just be an endless sleep, he then wonders about the exis-tence of hell and finally admits that the "something after death, / The undiscover'd country, from whose bourn / No traveler returns, / puzzles the will" (3.1.77–79). In effect, by focusing on the catego-ries of being and not-being, and then attempting to penetrate the impossible relation between the two, Hamlet traps himself in an endless maze of thought. Where Cicero's text moves from specula-tion into choice, the prince begins by framing a choice—"to be or

not to be"—that evaporates into speculation, and so where Brutus
and Horatio are able to regain a practical basis for action by relating
apparently extraordinary events to other occurrences, the prince's
philosophical essentialism leaves him as unable as Caesar to move.
Perceiving himself as a being surrounded by such instances of not-
being as the outward shows of the court, Hamlet loses his capacity
to relate to others and lapses into solipsistic inactivity.

The opening scenes of *Hamlet* thus offer two contrasting views on
the neo-Stoic practice modeled in *Julius Caesar*. Horatio embraces
it, using it to regain a relaxed sense of the commonness of his situation. Hamlet resists it, and the result is an exaggerated sense of
the singularity and isolation that normally follows in the wake of
disaster. Like the guilty mourners that Seneca describes, he has not
healed himself, but made himself sicker. The remainder of the play,
however, resolves this difference between Hamlet and Horatio by
revealing the prince's gradual incorporation into the neo-Stoic practice he initially opposes. This process begins during Hamlet's plan
to catch the conscience of the king. Although this scheme would
seem to require conscious forethought, the prince in fact stumbles
upon it accidentally.[39] After instructing the players to perform a
revised version of *The Murder of Gonzago* before Claudius, Hamlet
delivers a soliloquy that begins with him berating himself for being
unable to take action, but ends with a sudden epiphany:

> About my brains! Hum—I have heard
> That guilty creatures sitting at a play
> Have by the very cunning of the scene
> Been strook so to the soul, that presently
> They have proclaim'd their malefactions.
>   (2.2.588–92)

This passage is often read not as a moment of discovery, but as
Hamlet's explanation for his earlier instructions to the players. There
is, however, a problem with this usual interpretation: if Hamlet has
previously hit upon the idea of using the play as an instrument of
justice, then why is he now raging against himself for his failure to
act? Instead, the passage makes more sense as a genuinely new idea
that has just occurred to Hamlet as a way out of his crisis of inac-
tion, and indeed, there is every indication that the prince is having
a revelation. Not only does the passage begin with Hamlet exhorting himself to think—"About my brains"—but it then shows him

frozen in a moment of thought: "Hum." Far from unspooling a prelaid plot, the prince is engaged in a moment of discovery: the realization that his earlier instructions to the actors have unintentionally laid the groundwork for his current plan. Like Horatio, he has found the power of acting then reacting.

It is not until Hamlet confronts Laertes at Ophelia's funeral, however, that the prince becomes fully aware of the potential of this neo-Stoic practice. Witnessing Laertes' powerful grief at his sister's death, Hamlet boorishly interrupts, insisting that his own suffering is worse. At root, Hamlet's behavior is driven by the attempt to usurp Laertes, to play the part of the bereaved better than Laertes himself. As Hamlet announces when he emerges from his hiding place to disrupt the proceedings:

> What is he whose grief
> Bears such an emphasis, whose praise of sorrow
> Conjures the wand'ring stars and makes them stand
> Like wonder-wounded hearers? This is I,
> Hamlet the Dane!
>
> (5.1.254–58)

At first, Hamlet appears to be making a genuine inquiry about the identity of the mourner before him, demanding to know whose grief bears such emphasis. However, his subsequent announcement— "This is I, Hamlet the Dane!"—seems as much an answer to this question as it does an introduction, and the effect is to translate the qualities initially associated with Laertes onto Hamlet himself. He too has a sorrow that stops the stars.

Hamlet's subsequent behavior toward Laertes continues this course, culminating with the tirade:

> 'Swounds, show me what thou't do.
> Woo't weep, woo't fight, woo't fast, woo't tear thyself?
> Woo't drink up eisel, eat a crocodile?
> I'll do't. Dost thou come here to whine,
> To outface me with leaping in her grave?
> Be buried quick with her, and so will I.
> And if thou prate of mountains, let them throw
> Millions of acres on us, till our ground,
> Singeing his pate against the burning zone,
> Make Ossa like a wart! Nay, and thou'lt mouth
> I'll rant as well as thou.
>
> (5.1.274–84)

The most notable feature of this passage is its emphasis on acting. Distancing himself from his earlier claim that outward shows of mourning are not reflective of inward suffering, Hamlet is instead concerned to argue that the magnitude of his grief can be discerned in what he does. By weeping, fasting, fighting, ranting, by *doing* all these things, Hamlet is demonstrating the greater suffering. His "that within" can after all be shown.

This emphasis on acting seems sudden, but it is prepared by the peculiar exchange between the gravediggers that begins the funeral scene. The pair are discussing the legality of Ophelia's burial when the first gravedigger makes an attempt to clarify the law surrounding suicides:

> It must be *se offendeno*, it cannot be else. For here lies the point: if I drown myself wittingly, it argues an act, and an act hath three branches—it is to act, to do, to perform; argal, she drown'd herself wittingly. (5.1.9–13)

The digger's wandering remark is a specific reference to *Hales vs. Petit*, the odd case of James Hales, a judge who drowned himself in 1554. Because suicide was considered a crime, the crown confiscated Hales' lands. Hales' wife, however, refused to leave and sued to keep her husband's property. Noting that her husband's land passed to her at the instant of his death while her husband's decision to kill himself became apparent only *after* he had died, she argued that her claim to the land was technically prior to that of the crown. Despite this intriguing argument, she was defeated by the defense, who though they admitted that James Hales' intention only became clear after his body was discovered, asserted that his intention must nevertheless have preceded his death. And since the crown's claim rested on this intention, while the claim of Hales' wife rested on the resulting act, the seizure was justified.

The gravedigger's garbled reference to this case seems comically random, and yet its legal framework is directly relevant to the prince's struggles. In upholding the crown's seizure, the defense took the stance that an act consisted of three parts, imagination, resolution, and execution, suggesting that Hales conceived of the idea of drowning himself, consciously decided to do so, and then put his plan into action. In the digger's version, however, forethought and intention are effaced to produce a view of human behavior in which action is predicated on nothing other than itself: "an act has three branches:

to act, to do, to perform."[40] With this division, the digger eliminates the sense that behavior is the result of imagination, resolution, or any conscious intention. Instead, he suggests that the fundamental source of action is itself. At the same time, the conclusion drawn from this division—"argal [ergo], she drowned herself wittingly"—upholds the view that Ophelia's behavior possess intentionality. For although action does not spring from intention, intention is the consequence— the "argal"—of action. This account spectacularly reverses the traditional relationship between thought and deed, and yet it is consistent with Horatio's belief that purpose always lags behind action. To see itself, the eye first must look; to discover the appropriate performance, we first must act. In short, like the ethics he espouses, the digger may not intend to be wise, but he is accidentally so nevertheless.

Following on the heels of the digger, Hamlet spends the remainder of this scene stumbling toward neo-Stoic practice. After the prince promises to prove his own suffering by outdoing Laertes, he quits the stage with the remark: "Let Hercules himself do what he may, / The cat will mew and dog will have its day" (5.1.291–92). Earlier, Hamlet had used Hercules' example to prove the exceptional virtue of his father, insisting "My father's brother, but no more like my father / Than I to Hercules" (1.2.152–53). Now, however, Hercules is used to stress not singular achievement, but the inevitability of the everyday. Instead of being the final term of a rhetorical climax, responsible for providing the whole meaning of Hamlet's comparison, the demigod is introduced to be forgotten amid the actions of the most insignificant of creatures. This diminished sense of the extraordinary reveals the effect of the prince's newly theatrical practice of grief, and a few moments later Hamlet abandons his sense of his own exceptionalism entirely, claiming that his suffering and the grief of Laertes mirror each other: "For by the image of my cause I see / The portraiture of his" (5.2.77–78). Looking at himself, Hamlet discovers not a unique interior, but the external shape of another.

This new approach to life shapes Hamlet's behavior throughout the final act. After the funeral, the prince describes to Horatio how he seized upon Claudius' fatal writ while on the boat to England. As he explains, his discovery was not the product of any conscious intention, but rather an act that came to make sense after it was impulsively accomplished:

> Rashly—
> And prais'd be rashness for it—let us know

Our indiscretion sometimes serves us well
When our deep plots do pall, and that should learn us
There's a divinity that shapes our ends,
Rough hew them how we will—

(5.2.6–11)

This short passage has created a great deal of disagreement among scholars, for it seems to suggest that Hamlet has undergone a very rapid change, abandoning his firm commitment to an autonomous selfhood and instead embracing determinism. Scholars who are invested in preserving Hamlet's selfhood therefore tend to argue that this is not a real conversion at all, but another of the antic masks that the prince uses to preserve the mystery of his being. Against this reading, scholars who want to read Hamlet as a cultural artifact tend to point to this scene as evidence that even the prince eventually realizes that he is the product of larger social forces.

Like the rest of the play, however, this scene can be read as something other than a drift into the speculative matter of free will. Hamlet's explicit claim in the above passage is that action precedes understanding. This is the same claim upon which Horatio bases his ethics, and indeed, Horatio greets Hamlet's assertion with the enthusiastic: "This is most certain" (5.2.12). After winning Horatio's approval, Hamlet then further aligns himself with neo-Stoic practice by remarking: "We defy augury. There is special providence in the fall of a sparrow. If it be now, 'tis not to come; if it be not to come, it will be now; if it be not now, yet it will come—the readiness is all" (5.2.219–24). Hamlet's rejection of augury is thus based upon the view that even the most common events are unusual. Like Cassius and Horatio when they are confronted by the idea of portents, Hamlet admits the omnipresence of the exceptional in order to make it ordinary, and this pattern of response continues through his following string of conditionals: "If it be now, 'tis not to come; if it be not to come, it will be now; if it be not now, yet it will come." This line expresses a well-known Stoic axiom[41] and is probably derived from a very similar passage in the 1567 translation of Epictetus' *Enchiridion*: "I must die: if instantly, I will die instantly; if in a short time, then I will dine first; and when the hour comes, then I will die."[42] But just as the neo-Stoics reworked Stoicism, so too does Hamlet rework this axiom to fit his new ethical practice. In the Stoic original, there is no progression of thought, but simply a relentless certainty. Humans die. Whether it comes now or later, the end is unavoidable. Hamlet's neo-Stoic adaptation, in contrast, begins with a true conditional—I may die now—and then builds a series of more definite pronouncements. An opening formulation so obvious as to be devoid of meaning—if I die now then I cannot die later—is reworked into a genuinely nonintuitive statement—if I am not slated to die at any future moment, then I must die now—and finally into the conclusion that death is inevitable. Moving from a true conditional to a firm belief, Hamlet discovers Cicero's adaptive ethics: "the readiness is all."

In gaining the practice of neo-Stoicism, however, Hamlet also loses something: his availability to the many members of his audience who do not already grasp this practice. Horatio may react with immediate enthusiasm to the prince's new ethics, but no less than Brutus' emotional reformation, Hamlet's conversion is a difficult one for spectators to follow. For hours, we have experienced Hamlet's intense grief, and whatever we may feel about it, we cannot be expected to shed this feeling with the rapidity that Hamlet sheds his. Hamlet, after all, has had days and months to reflect on things; we are still caught up in the first few hours of shock. Despite its increased attention to the process of mourning, *Hamlet* thus seems in the end to go the way of *Julius Caesar*: the play may convey suffering more effectively, but it is no less abrupt in communicating the neo-Stoic remedy. In fact, however, *Hamlet* does not abandon us to wonder whether neo-Stoicism physically works or whether we have just witnessed a stage trick. Instead, it invites us to test Hamlet's practice firsthand, for over the remainder of this scene, it puts us in the prince's shoes, bereaving us. After battling Claudius, Hamlet lies dying, and the shock of his situation unsettles him. He turns to Horatio and pleads: "What a wounded name, / Things standing thus unknown, shall I leave behind me…If thou didst ever hold me in thy heart…tell my story" (5.2.344–49). Overwhelmed by the extraordinary nature of his circumstance, the prince reverts to his belief that he is an exceptional being whose motives lie hidden from public view. In effect, just as neo-Stoicism predicts, no sense of progress is permanent. Each moment of life brings with it the possibility of unforeseen shock, requiring that purpose be recovered again. The new shock for Hamlet is the realization that his death-blow differs significantly from the previous traumas he has endured. No longer will he be around to determine the significance of his suffering. Instead, he must rely on others to look back and narrate what it portends.

From the perspective of Hamlet's recently discovered neo-Stoicism, Horatio is the perfect person to undertake this labor. He too sees life as a series of performances lent coherence in the retelling, and in response to Hamlet's request, Horatio promises an account of "carnal, bloody, and unnatural acts" (5.2.381). Scrupulously attending to the *events* of Hamlet's life, he omits any mention of his friend's private uncertainty and grief. In effect, just as Horatio retells his own encounter with the ghost by focusing upon the outward actions that occurred, so too does he describe the prince's recent life as a string of happenings. Like Brutus' belated premeditation of Portia's death, this strategy eliminates the initial sense of confusion that accompanies crisis, preparing for an imaginative recovery of the narrative that preceded it. Though Hamlet's sense of purpose can no longer be reclaimed by the prince himself, Horatio's retelling restores it for him. In the process, Horatio makes explicit one of the most remarkable aspects of neo-Stoic ethics. Because of its theatrical approach to life, this ethics does not insist upon the continuities required by an essentialist approach to psychology. We have already seen Brutus efface the consciousness that suffers at the news of Portia's death, denying it as part of his actual experience, and Horatio's retelling of the prince's life literalizes this split. It is not as if Hamlet's peace of mind is recovered by some else. It *is* recovered by someone else.

This passing of responsibility for Hamlet's narrative onto another teller allows Shakespeare's play to communicate the experience left unconveyed by *Julius Caesar*. For Horatio does not actually give his account of Hamlet's life. Instead, he simply leaves the stage promising to do so. The play thus ends by insisting upon the importance of a retelling that it does not itself provide, inviting the audience members to assume this responsibility themselves. If they choose to do so, they will have two distinct models as their guide. The first is Horatio's neo-Stoicism, which encourages them to reconstruct Hamlet's life as a series of events, recovering a sense of tranquil order. The second is found in Hamlet's initial promise to remember the ghost, a promise that brings with it the burden of preserving the deceased as extraordinary, particular, unlike any of the saws and records of common memory. From this perspective, Horatio's method seems cold and impersonal, a confusion of his friend with the very revenge-tragedy clichés the prince labors to escape. And so against Horatio, this latter approach seeks Hamlet in his dreams, his wordplay, his declarations, and above all, his soliloquies. These are the windows into Hamlet's distinctive mind. They must be preserved and celebrated if Hamlet's example is to mean anything. Where the first model of retelling is associated with a process of recovery, the second thus prolongs the initial shock of bereavement, placing an emphasis upon the extraordinary that makes the present seem meaningless and the future seem overwhelming. In having to decide between these two models, audiences are thus invited into Hamlet's own struggle, so that the public form of tragedy provides a forum to extend the prince's ethical quandary into the world beyond the stage. Taking advantage of the physical gathering of theater, *Hamlet* makes the prince's problem the center of a communal practice.

Experienced this way, *Hamlet* supports Dewey's ambitious claim that problem-based art can encourage pluralism. It is not simply that the formal flexibility of seventeenth-century tragedy allowed the playwrights of this era to develop the riddles of the weird sisters, or the painted devils of Faustus, or the promised narrative of Horatio, or other innovative techniques for communicating the experience of a problem. It is that this formal flexibility allowed these playwrights to develop techniques for exploring *different* experiences of a problem. As we have seen over the preceding pages, the neo-Stoic practice of Brutus and Horatio (and ultimately Hamlet) offers a very different approach to the problem of our dark tomorrow than the one explored by Macbeth and Faustus. Instead of agonizing over their distance from death, these neo-Stoics react to the present and then build a narrative out of what has passed. Play-acting and then plotting, they improvise their way ahead. And though this neo-Stoic ethic may seem in certain ways more practical than Luther's restless ecstasy, the performance tradition of these plays suggests otherwise. Shakespeare did not follow *Macbeth* with *Hamlet*, but the other way around, and over the remainder of the century, both plays existed alongside each other in the repertoire of London theater. Where Luther and Cicero each had to throw in their lot with a particular approach to life, the audiences of seventeenth-century tragedy were able to participate in both at once. In the process, they experienced the potential of a problem-based ethics to not simply encourage practice, but discourage idealism. For as seventeenth-century tragedy demonstrates, the result of pluralism is the end of the ideologues Luther railed against. By revealing that there is practical value to different styles of ethical practice, tragedy forestalls the possibility of one absolutely right way of living, and with it, the ideological basis for those jealous deities who promise ever-after in exchange for martyrdom and conquest. Instead of urging us to spill human blood for neverland, tragedy uses death to find a more social life.

The formal innovations described over the past two chapters do not, of course, exhaust the ingenuity of early seventeenth-century tragedy. *Faustus, Macbeth, Julius Caesar,* and *Hamlet* are all exceptional, but it was a time for exceptional works, and there are surely many other tragedies from this period that found compelling ways to practice the problem of our dark tomorrow. Since the four plays already discussed are enough to support Dewey's claim for the organic diversity of problem-based art, however, the following chapters will take us away from the early seventeenth century in order to pursue the third unproven claim of Dewey's ethics: that the organic diversity of problem-based art can also be adaptive. That is, we will shift from looking at the way that art can offer multiple approaches to a single problem and instead examine the way that art can adapt itself to new problems. By themselves, the plays we have just discussed are not sufficient to demonstrate this function. Although the problem they explored was in some sense new—collapsing confidence in the moral authority of the Catholic Church had done wonders to remind people of their mortality—the problem of death was itself an ancient one, so much so that Shakespeare could find consolation in a therapy that was nearly two millennia old. On the evidence presented, then, tragedy too might simply be an ancient form, one that was roused out of its own quiescence in the late sixteenth century when people remembered that there were ethical traditions that predated the church. Far from being an adaptive instrument, it was simply a forgotten one.

To eliminate this possibility, the following chapters will explore the further adventures of English tragedy over the seventeenth century. As they will show, tragedy was pressed during this period by a painful new ethical problem described by Descartes, Hobbes, and other mid-century thinkers. Unlike the problem of death, this problem was genuinely new—it is not described in ancient sources, nor had it been explored by previous playwrights. To address it, tragedy therefore had to adapt, and as I will show over the following three chapters, adapt it did, developing a style of theater as revolutionary as the problem itself. Over these chapters, moreover, I will show that tragedy did not simply adjust itself to this new problem; just as it had done in the early years of the seventeenth century, it used the problem of the times to encourage different styles of ethical practice. The new problem, that is, became the source of a new pluralism. In keeping with the practice of the previous pages, I will uncover this pluralism through a series of case studies, but first, I will attend to the emergence of the problem itself, tracing its impact on a popular and much-imitated seventeenth-century tragedy: *Othello*. As I will show, *Othello* was adapted dramatically over the seventeenth century to fit it for a function that Shakespeare never imagined, an adaptation that revealed not only the new ethical concerns of the age, but the need for an entirely new form of tragedy.

Chapter 3

Othello and the Subject of
Ocular Proof

In William Congreve's *Double-Dealer* (1694), Maskwell tricks Lord Touchwood into suspecting that his wife has been unfaithful, prompting a fit of swaggering outrage in which the lord exclaims, "Give me but proof of it, ocular proof!"[1] Echoing Othello's demand that Iago give him "ocular proof" of Desdemona's infidelity, Lord Touchwood imagines himself vaulting to the heights of tragic pathos. Instead, however, he catches himself in the low coils of dramatic irony.[2] Othello was famous not as a betrayed husband, but as a dupe. Hoodwinked into a ridiculous jealousy that strips him of his nobility, he is more like Touchwood than the lord himself recognizes. Still, if the joke is on Touchwood, he was hardly the only one in the Restoration to rush into identifying with the Moor's demand for ocular proof. As the number of similar parodies attests,[3] *Othello* was one of the most popular plays of the later seventeenth century. When public tragedy returned in 1660 after two decades of civil war, *Othello* was the first of Shakespeare's plays to be revived.[4] And while Shakespeare's other tragedies only pleased Restoration audiences after enduring heavy revision, *Othello* was left relatively unchanged. *Macbeth* was transformed into a musical and *King Lear* into a comedy, but *Othello* merely had its running-time trimmed.[5]

This restraint has resulted in a rare moment of agreement between the Restoration and our own time. In general, the scholars of the past hundred years have been baffled by the tragic sensibility of the Restoration: enamored with spectacle and happy endings, Restoration playwrights not only mauled Shakespeare, but produced the strange mix of exoticism and imperialism known as the heroic play.[6] Despite this indifference for the Restoration, how-ever, recent scholars have shared its particular interest in *Othello*. In the mid-twentieth century, *Othello* was celebrated by New Critics as a particularly "modern" play because of its awareness that "we all have a touch of paranoia in us,"[7] and of late, it has been seen as more prescient still.[8] To the scholars of the past thirty years, the play has seemed to anticipate not only the modern drive for visual certainty, but also the post-modern critique, offering a cautionary tale on empirical science, the male gaze, and "modern philosophical thought."[9] In effect, just as Congreve ridiculed Touchwood for his naiveté, so have many recent critics seen Othello's paranoid demand for ocular proof not just as a sign of the times, but as a satire on them. Following down the path blazed by the Restoration, we have taken Shakespeare's play as an augur of the problems of today.

The irony of this shared enthusiasm for *Othello* is that it almost certainly misconstrues Shakespeare's original intent. When the play was written in 1603, the senses were seen as highly unreliable sources of knowledge; it was not until the emergence of Cartesian philosophy in the mid-seventeenth century that visual evidence was given the status of a "proof" that could legitimately substantiate violent paranoia. In effect, since the problem that subsequent audi-ences have discovered in *Othello* was not in fact a problem until sev-eral decades after the play was first performed, we are left with two possibilities: either Shakespeare somehow managed to anticipate the course of history, or Restoration and modern audiences are guilty not of a mutual appreciation but of a mutual misreading. Out of veneration for Shakespeare, we might prefer the former, supposing that modern paranoia did not emerge at a single stroke, but was the culmination of a long-gathering trend that an intelligent play-wright could have foreseen.[10] Over the following pages, however, I will suggest the opposite. Tracing the reception history of *Othello* over the seventeenth century, I will show how midcentury writers adapted Othello from a victim of self-doubt into an icon of para-noia, transforming Shakespeare's original into the play we know today. With this reading, I will necessarily divest Shakespeare of any prophetic powers. In recompense, though, I will invest seventeenth-century tragedy with the progressive function that Dewey claims as the third characteristic of a progressive ethics. Playwrights may not have been able to predict the future, but they were able to react to it once it arrived, changing the form of tragedy to keep pace with the problems of the times.

The horror of *Othello* is the speed with which doubt ruins. In a few hours, Othello undoes a lifetime of military service, suffocating his wife and then killing himself. The crucial scene for this disaster is 3.3, where Iago plants the suspicions that pervert his commander's mind. At first, Iago offers only misdirections. He asks whether Cassio and Desdemona have long been familiar, confesses that he is himself overly suspicious by nature, warns that it is impossible to recover lost honor, and then suddenly bursts out: "O, beware, my lord, of jealousy!" (3.3.165). Othello initially seems more baffled than upset by this sequence:

> Why? why is this?
> Think'st thou I'ld make a life of jealousy?
> To follow still the changes of the moon
> With fresh suspicions? No! to be once in doubt
> Is once to be resolv'd. Exchange me for a groat,
> When I shall turn the business of my soul
> To such exsufflicate and blown surmises,
> Matching thy inference. 'Tis not to make me jealous
> To say my wife is fair, feeds well, loves company,
> Is free of speech, sings, plays, and dances well;
> Where virtue is, these are more virtuous.
>   (3.3.176–86)

While a beautiful, companionable wife might cause some husbands worry, Othello insists that Desdemona's social graces make her honesty all the more admirable. If Desdemona had no opportunity for infidelity, her virtue would simply be another name for necessity.

Just when it seems as if Othello has escaped Iago's insinuations unscathed, however, his admiration for his wife's qualities stirs an anxiety about his own:

> Nor from mine own weak merits will I draw
> The smallest fear or doubt of her revolt;
> For she had eyes, and chose me. No, Iago,
> I'll see before I doubt; when I doubt, prove.
>   (3.3.187–90)

Noting his "own weak merits," Othello abruptly transforms the proceedings from an examination of Desdemona into an examination of himself. Initially, he brushes aside any consideration of his own deficiencies—"[f]or she had eyes, and chose me"—but no sooner has he brought up the matter of his wife's sight than than he asserts: "No Iago, / I'll see before I doubt." In effect, once he raises the matter of his own merit, Othello finds his sense of certainty rapidly erode. Not only does he abandon his earlier position that "to be one in doubt / Is once to be resolved," but he raises the possibility that his own virtues might suffer from close inspection. He has stopped looking at his wife's social graces and started looking through her eyes at his own flaws. And having seen, he begins to doubt.

Iago seizes on this opportunity. He begins by noting that Venetian women are well known for their deceptions. And when Othello hesitates, Iago offers the following example:

> She did deceive her father, marrying you,
> And when she seem'd to shake and fear your looks,
> She lov'd them most.
>
> (3.3.206–8)

Here, Iago latches onto Othello's attempt to see himself from his wife's perspective, offering a portrait of a young woman who loved the Moor's looks while appearing to fear them. This is visual evidence alright, but it is evidence of Othello and not of Desdemona, and its purchase is not in Desdemona's character, but in her husband's sense of self-worth. Reminding Othello that his appearance was enough to make Desdemona tremble in fear, Iago prods him to question what she sees in him.

At this point, Iago drops his insinuations. Fervently repeating his love for Othello, he cautions him not to make too much of idle doubts. Othello, meanwhile, broods: "I do not think but Desdemona's honest…yet how nature erring from itself—" (3.3.225–27). Before Othello can finish his thought, Iago pounces and drives the knife home:

> Ay, there's the point; as (to be bold with you)
> Not to affect many proposed matches of
> Of her own clime, complexion, and degree,
> Whereto we see in all things nature tends—
> Foh, one may smell in such, a will most rank,
> Foul disproportion, thoughts unnatural.
>
> (3.3.228–33)

If these lines are about Desdemona, their real object is Othello. His complexion and degree make him unsuitable. He is strange and out-of-place. A woman like Desdemona could love him only if she were foul and depraved. Iago gives Othello a vision of himself through Desdemona's eyes, showing him a monster that only a monster could love.

Othello is broken by this moment: "Why did I marry?" (3.3.242). His agonized question is then followed by a harsh self-portrait:

> Haply, for I am black,
> And have not those soft parts of conversation
> That chamberers have, or am declin'd
> Into the vale of years (yet that's not much)
> She's gone. I am abus'd; and my relief
> Must be to loathe her.
>
> (3.3.263–68)

In these lines, Othello returns to the anxieties that prepared the way for Iago's scheme, blaming his own weak merits for his misery. Nevertheless, the true source of Othello's agony lies deeper than his anxieties about his blackness or his age. These are just the symptoms of a more profound sense of alienation. He has been made to feel an outsider, an usurper, and finding himself incapable of self-love, he cannot accept that anyone worthy would love him either. Although he will turn his agonies outward, castigating and eventually killing Desdemona, it is not others he suspects, but himself.

When Shakespeare's play was revived in the Restoration, this scene was radically altered.[11] The cuts are not extensive, but they eliminate Othello's growing self-doubt and instead play up the mood of paranoia. While Iago's rants against jealousy are preserved, Othello's first pangs of introspection—"Nor from mine own weak merits will I draw / The smallest fear or doubt of her revolt; / For she had eyes and chose me"—are excised. Without this passage, the audience is given no indication that Othello's desire for ocular proof springs from his study of his own flaws. Instead, the Restoration adaptation suggests that the Moor is moved purely by a suspicion of his wife. The next cut is brief, but it is also significant. In the original version of the play, Iago punctuates his discussion of Desdemona's deception with a remark about her father: "He thought 'twas witchcraft" (3.3.211). Iago thus turns Othello's memory to the opening act of the play, when Desdemona's father was so distraught at his daughter's behavior that he was convinced it must have been wrought by spells. At the time, Othello diffused this accusation by relating that he had charmed Desdemona with tales of his exotic adventures in other lands:

> She thank'd me,
> And bade me, if I had a friend that lov'd her,

I should but tell him how to tell my story,
And that would woo her. Upon this hint I spake:
She lov'd me for the dangers I had pass'd,
And I lov'd her that she did pity them.
This only is the witchcraft I have us'd.

(1.3.163–69)

Even as he brushes off the notion of witchcraft, Othello admits that Desdemona may have fallen more for his beguilements than his substance. She loved him for his "story," for "the dangers" he passed, and Othello's account suggests that any "friend" who recounted these events would similarly have won her love. By reviving this memory in the third act of Shakespeare's original, Iago thus further destabilizes Othello's self-confidence, raising the concern that Desdemona loves him not for who he is, but because he is strange and exotic. And so when the Restoration *Othello* purges this concern, it also strips away another moment of self-doubt. Shakespeare's careful depiction of Othello's insecurities is again ignored.

The Restoration revision of Shakespeare then culminates in the elimination of Iago's entire speech about Desdemona's "unnatural" preference for Othello over suitors of "her own clime, complexion, and degree." This is a spectacular deletion, one that disposes of the climax of Shakespeare's original scene. Without the rising drama of Othello's self-doubt, however, Iago's speech has become superfluous. In the Restoration *Othello*, there is no need for an extended look at Othello's blackness, for what is at issue is not his opinion of his own worth, but his jealousy of Desdemona. So it is that Othello's angry abuse of women is left intact, but his references to his own advancing age are purged. Where the original Iago forces Othello to scrutinize himself, his Restoration counterpart drops the mirror and points directly at Desdemona.

In the past, scholars have treated these deletions as an effort to satisfy Restoration expectations of heroic behavior.[12] As far as it goes, this interpretation is not wrong. By ridding Othello of his creeping inadequacy and investing him with a prideful anger toward his wife, the Restoration adaptation does make him more closely resemble Montezuma, Almanzor, and the other heroes of the post-war stage. To account for the changes in *Othello* by aligning them with a broader dramatic trend, however, is not to explain why it would have been seen as more becoming of a hero to jealously suspect his innocent wife than to examine his own failings. Instead, it substitutes a description of historical events for an explanation of their origins. This cursory account, moreover, contributes to the impression that Restoration theater was itself a largely cursory affair. Rather than bothering to conceive of heroism in any great detail, Restoration dramatists just pruned their heroes of self-doubt and any other potentially awkward complexities. If such pruning did not produce a wholly logical account of virtue, this was of little concern. The audiences of the period went to the theater to reinforce their assumptions about social decorum, not to think deeply about ethics. Previous criticism on the Restoration *Othello*, in effect, participates in an endlessly self-reinforcing assumption about the English drama of the 1660s. The more it is presumed that the Restoration was an uncritical age, the less that modern critics attempt to plumb the logic behind its dramatic choices. And the less that modern critics look beneath the surface, the more superficial the drama of the period appears.

There is, however, a great deal beneath the surface of the Restoration *Othello*, for far from being the product of an uncritical age, its portrait of heroic paranoia reflects a hugely ambitious effort to reshape the foundations of ethics. By the mid-seventeenth century, Aristotelian-Scholastic philosophy was crumbling under the skeptical critiques of Luther, Montaigne, Bacon, and many other aggressive new thinkers.[13] And yet far from achieving a new consensus over metaphysics, these thinkers had fallen into thickets of disagreement. Indeed, the situation had become so dire that it was prompting doubts about whether consensus would ever be forthcoming. Perhaps, as many of Montaigne's seventeenth-century followers argued, the lesson of skepticism was not the need to do away with the bankrupt speculations of the schools. Perhaps it was the need to do away with the idea of universal philosophy altogether. In the late 1630s, Descartes stepped forward with a different proposal.[14] As he saw it, the philosophical disagreements of the times stemmed from a proliferation of idiosyncratic methods for gathering knowledge, and to winnow this glut, he outlined a method that could fashion a unified science from undisputed rational principles. Despite the considerable disagreement at the time over what actually constituted reason, Descartes suggested that certain absolute principles—that is, certain "innate ideas"—were implanted in each mind at the moment of its inception. The task of philosophy was thus not to weigh and balance all existing doctrines to see which were most rational. Rather, all that philosophers needed to do was attempt to rid themselves of all of their ideas—the ones that survived this purge were innate, the principles of a universal method. Seen this way, skepticism was a source not of fracture, but of unity. By washing away the gaudy constructions of contemporary metaphysics, skepticism did not destroy the possibility of a universal science. Instead, it laid bare an ancient and immutable foundation, providing every philosopher with a common foothold in reason. The doubts that Montaigne had seen as the end of philosophy became for Descartes a more solid beginning.

This account of the private origins of science reinforced the ancient ideal of philosophy as a heroic pursuit. Although Descartes was careful to insist in his published works that philosophers should not do anything that might upset civic authorities, his insistence that his readers free themselves from popular opinion and wrest truth from their own minds fostered an ideal of total self-sufficiency. Indeed, Descartes put so much emphasis upon self-sufficiency that his method spawned a distinctly solipsistic ethos. By refusing to accept the veracity of anything other than his own innate ideas, he verged upon denying the existence of everything beyond his mind.[15] As one of his critics demanded: "Suppose that whenever you have thought you were thinking while awake, you were not really thinking while awake, but merely dreaming that you were thinking while awake?"[16] In a world constituted entirely of private thoughts, what hope was there for public distinctions such as the difference between waking and dream?

Despite Descartes' grand ambitions, the objections of his critics thus revealed that he had not been successful at ending doubt. Indeed, it soon became clear that his method was connected to a terrible new ethical concern. Where Luther, Montaigne, and other previous thinkers had seen the mind as an errant, unstable entity prone to making poor judgments and contradicting itself, Descartes was sure that his mind was not only invested with absolute reason, but completely transparent to itself. When doubts persisted, Descartes therefore could not blame his mind; the source of uncertainty must originate without. Descartes' heroic quest for certainty thus became inextricably paired with a paranoid suspicion of the world beyond, and although Descartes was quick to insist that he believed in God, he floated the idea in his *Meditations* that all of his impressions could be traced to the deceptions of a malicious demon. Many of Descartes' readers were struck by this strange new paranoia, and rather than curbing it, his English followers expounded on its social consequences. Descartes' works began circulating in

England in the 1640s, the same time at which the country became embroiled in civil war. Religious enthusiasm and political extremism gathered into an atmosphere of distrust, and in 1651, Thomas Hobbes drew upon Cartesian rationalism to develop the grim solution of *Leviathan*.[17] In Hobbes' view, the dominant emotion in a state of nature was fear. Isolated and alone, each of us had to constantly look out for our own protection, for no sooner had we accumulated a few good prospects than our fellow man was attempting to murder us for them. Eventually, though, we realized that there was a more rational alternative: banding together into civic polities that looked out for our mutual safety. Not that we ever liked each other, of course—we simply realized that the logic of self-interest dictated civility. Hobbesian society was thus the political endpoint of Descartes' meditation: a multitude of rationalist paranoiacs who combined confidence in their own powers of mind with distrust for everyone else.

This new attitude of paranoia permeates the Restoration *Othello*, and evidence that it was the driving force behind the revisions can be gathered from other post-civil war interpretations of Shakespeare's original. Thomas Rymer—who composed the preface to Hobbes' *Historia Ecclesiastica*—argued in his notorious assessment of the play that the apparently crucial events of 3.3 were utterly pointless.[18] After remarking on how inappropriate it was for Desdemona to plead aggressively with Othello for the reinstatement of his young lieutenant, Rymer continues sarcastically:

> And then comes the wonderful Scene where *Iago* by shrugs, half words, and ambiguous reflections, works *Othello* up to be Jealous. One might think, after what we have seen, that there needs no great cunning, no great poetry and address to make the *Moor* jealous. Such impatience, such a rout for a handsome young fellow, the very morning after her Marriage must make him either to be jealous, or to take her for a *Changeling*, below his Jealousie. After this *Scene*, it might strain the Poets skill to reconcile the couple, and allay the Jealousie. *Iago* now can only *actum agere*, and vex the audience with a nauseous repetition. (118)

In Rymer's view, the sheer fact that Desdemona has developed an attachment for a young man other than her husband is grounds for violent suspicion. The entire scene with Iago is irritatingly unnecessary. Like the adapter who produced the Restoration version of *Othello*, Rymer thus displays no interest whatsoever in the Moor's painful self-scrutiny. Instead, he takes it as a given that Othello's doubts are directed entirely toward his wife. Indeed, he is so attuned to this ethos of paranoid distrust that he is able to discover grounds for it in the mere fact that Desdemona takes up Cassio's case, an event that by itself has little significance in Shakespeare's pre-Cartesian play.

Because of his general contempt for *Othello*, Rymer balked at according its title character the heroic mantle worn by the Cartesian philosopher. Rymer's reluctance was not universal, however, and it is possible to trace the emergence of an infallible, paranoid heroism in the transition from pre- to post-civil war retellings of *Othello*. The most popular retelling from before the civil wars was Francis Beaumont and John Fletcher's *Philaster, or Love Lies a Bleeding*.[19] First produced around 1610, *Philaster* has a fantastical plot that has often seemed an anticipation of the heroic drama of the 1660s and 1670s.[20] Its title-character, the usurped heir to the throne of Sicily, is in love with Arethusa, the daughter of the usurper, and hopes to marry her. His happy prospects are suddenly cast in doubt, however, when his friend Dion hears a rumor that Arethusa has been unfaithful with a boy, Bellario. This cannot be true, for Bellario is in fact a woman in disguise, but Dion is unaware of this detail, and he passes the rumor onto Philaster, encouraging him to put aside his feelings for Arethusa and claim his rightful heritage. Philaster is instead hurled into a jealous despair, and before he is finally subdued, manages to stab both Arethusa and Bellario. All seems lost—but before things collapse utterly, Bellario is revealed as a woman. Order is restored, and Philaster gets both his lady and his crown.

Philaster thus strips *Othello* of two of its most powerful elements: the malicious deceiver and the ruined protagonist. Instead, it opts for the stock characters, sharp plot-twists, and triumphant ending that would become characteristic of the heroic tragedy of the later seventeenth century. And yet despite its apparently forward-looking form, *Philaster* remains firmly rooted in the ethical concerns of its own historical moment, preserving Shakespeare's vision of a man torn by self-doubt. In the third act, when Philaster confronts Bellario and demands that he confess his crime, Bellario so fervently defends himself that Philaster wonders:

> Why, who can but beleeve him? He does sweare
> So earnestly, that if it were not true,
> The gods would not endure him. Rise *Bellario*,
> Thy protestations are so deepe; and thou

Doest look so truely, when thou utterst them,
That though I know 'em false, as were my hopes,
I cannot urge thee further.

(3.1; 39)[21]

In this moment, Philaster crashes into the limits of his perception, crumbling into self-division: "though I know 'em false, as were my hopes, / I cannot urge thee further." Not only is he unable to reconcile the contradictory testimonies of Dion and Bellario, he is hoping against reason that Arethusa is faithful, and so far from feeling certain about anything, Philaster is a tangle of inner conflict. In the fourth act of the play, Philaster then snaps and attacks Arethusa, wounding her with his sword, but still, he gains no sense of certainty: "I have done ill, my conscience calls me false...She may be abusde, / And I a loathed villaine" (4.1; 56). Pulled out of his angry fervor, Philaster seems on the verge believing that Arethusa is innocent—and yet he hesitates again, concluding only that he "may" have been mistaken. In the final act, this self-questioning gives way to open despair. Philaster berates himself as "a wretch" that "shall dye loath'd," and he is only saved from ruin by a providential turn and a royal pardon (5.1; 61). Even in this moment of success, moreover, Philaster is not allowed to forget his failings. Instead, the king joins him to his bride with the declaration: "Let Princes learne / By this to rule the passions of their blood / For what Heaven wils, can never be withstood" (5.1; 78). With this closing reminder of Philaster's deficiencies, the play arrives at a typically pre-Cartesian view of our doubts about others. As Montaigne explains in his *Essais*, such doubt "presents man naked and empty, acknowledging his natural weakness, fit to receive from above some outside power" (375). Our suspicion, in short, is not an indictment of the honesty of others; it is a revelation of the frailty of our own powers of knowing.

   In stark contrast to *Philaster*, there is the most popular retelling of *Othello* from after the civil wars: Thomas Porter's *The Villain* (1662).[22] The enthusiastic reception of *The Villain* in the Restoration has often been attributed to its revival of the blank-verse and bloody violence of early seventeenth-century tragedy,[23] and on surface inspection, its plot seems almost a direct rip of Shakespeare's original: after the soldier Beaupres falls for the lady Bellemont and secretly marries her, the machinations of the wicked Maligni drive Beaupres to end his marriage in murder. Despite this apparent throwback to an earlier time, though, the plot of *The Villain* hinges on the ethical problem of its own time: the paranoia described in

the Restoration *Othello*. Things begin during the couple's prenup-
tials, when Bellemont tells her lover: "Know, all that pleases you,
brings such content / Unto my mind, that I shall study still, /
Out of self interest, how to please you most" (2.1; 21). Bellemont's
mention of her own "self interest" is accomplished with charm,
but this term nevertheless aligns her with a recent strain of English
political philosophy that took a highly cynical view of interpersonal
relationships. Prior to the 1640s, social networks had been justified
on the basis of love, justice, divine right, and other similarly idealized concepts, but the general chaos of the civil wars had provided
an impetus for a different kind of political thinking. People clearly
could not be expected to respect the king, the church, or each other
because of a shared belief in the sacred. Moreover, while traditional
political philosophy had made allowances for antisocial behavior by
ascribing it to evil, passion, or other forms of irrational behavior,
this explanation was of little practical use. To admit that there was
some facet of human life that eluded reason was to admit a permanently unpredictable force into social relations. If civic order was to
be maintained, the motiveless malignancy of irrationality thus had
to be replaced by a more useful understanding of human drives,
and to do so, political thinkers turned increasingly to the concept
of self-interest. Hobbes' *Leviathan* is the most notorious example
of a political philosophy rooted in the belief that people would
always act in their own best interest, but a similar conviction influenced a wide range of midcentury thinkers, from royalists to radical republicans.[24] As Marchamont Nedham bluntly put it: "If you
can apprehend where a man's interest to any Game on foot doth
consist, you may surely know, if the man be prudent, whereabout
to have him, that is, how to judge of his designe."[25]

Bellemont's use of the term "self interest" is the first in English
tragedy, and it reflects this new concern over the grounds of trust.
Bellemont is assuring Beaupres that he can trust her because her
love for him is in her own interest, and his response betrays a similar
mingling of charm and suspicion. Producing a friar and insisting
that they wed at once, Beaupres declares:

> And I most blest in this delivery:
> But I will now be base as Tradsmen are,
> Not trust, without the bond be sign'd, and seal'd;
> 'Tis all my wealth, of which I'm Covetous.
>
> (2.1; 21)

No less than his lover, Beaupres is open about his self-interest. Framing marriage as a form of economic possession, he bluntly admits that he is covetous of his anticipated wealth. In his rush to formalize his relationship with Bellemont, however, Beaupres draws notice to a worrisome aspect of their arrangement. To Hobbes and other like-minded theorists, a contract could not bind people to act permanently against their own self-interest. Rather, a contract simply identified a state of affairs that benefited its signers. If their interests changed, or if they had been tricked into agreeing to unfair conditions, the contract was void. People who enforced a contract that threatened irreparable damage to its other signers were guilty of acting against the ends of nature: instead of recognizing the general pull of self-interest, they were ruthlessly pursuing their own. There is thus, as Beaupres himself admits, something "base" in pouncing on Bellemont and insisting that her bond be "sign'd, and seal'd" at once. Greedily eager to conclude a transaction that is in his own self interest, he pays no mind to Bellemont's long-term happiness. Instead, like the avaricious tyrants that Hobbes condemns, he seems willing to enforce his contract at her expense.

At this moment in the play, it is easy to overlook this scene as banter. Nevertheless, the fragility of interpersonal connections in a world of self-interest is exposed in the closing act by the sudden violence with which Beaupres' suspicions emerge. Beaupres is highly gullible, requiring no proof of his wife's infidelity beyond a badly forged letter. In direct contrast to Iago, who carefully stokes Othello's self-doubt, Maligni easily coaxes Beaupres into a misogynist distrust: "For I grow mad to see your excellent Nature / Thus Fever-shook by a fond Womans fault" (5.1; 89). The emphasis here is on a fault that lies without, and Beaupres is only too willing to believe that his own "excellent Nature" has been abused. A man who guards his own interest so closely that he can only trust a lover when her bond is signed, he slips easily into jealousy. Beaupres' overwhelming confidence in his own perspective then leads at the close of the play to its most disturbing moment. As Bellmont's waiting woman begins to provide evidence against Maligni—remembering one occasion on which he tried to rape Bellemont and others in which he tried to forge letters in her bed chamber—Beaupres interrupts the proceedings with proof of his own:

> I find my soul's a fleeting after her's
> And you'l have time enough t'examine this,
> See, Sir, the Sacrifice of Innocence,—
>   *Maligni discover'd peirc't with a stake.*

Now take my sword, 'tis not in Surgeon's Art
To cure the fractures of a Broken heart!
Besides that villain ha's been busie here;
Forgive me Dear Bellmont! Forgive a Crime
Caus'd by my too much Love.
    Dies.

(5.1; 94)

This violent end provides a stark contrast with Othello's final moments. Shakespeare's original offers a brutally exact portrait of his own failings, but Beaupres' inability to accept real blame is revealed in his treatment of Maligni. Where Othello turns his dagger against himself, Beaupres has Maligni impaled gruesomely upon a pike, a brutal act that stands as a reminder that Beaupres has after all been betrayed. The problem, in short, is not his paranoia—but rather that he trusted.

The unveiling of Maligni deepens this paranoid conclusion, moreover, by according a new meaning to ocular proof. When Beaupres impatiently preempts the careful sleuthing of Bellemont's waiting woman and urges the gathered audience to "See" what he has hidden behind the curtain, he establishes vision as the ultimate form of evidence. The *sight* of Maligni's wretched body is convincing in a way that a reconstruction of facts is not. This moment anticipates Touchwood's insistence in the *Double-Dealer* that the only proof he is interested in is "ocular proof," and it offers a new spin on the original events of *Othello*. Within the pre-Cartesian context of Shakespeare's original play, eyesight had been associated with the same gross defects that corrupted all human faculties. As Montaigne declared: "Man cannot escape the fact that the senses are the sovereign masters of his knowledge; but they are uncertain and deceivable in all circumstances."[26] This belief in the inadequacy of human faculties made visual evidence more a means to question oneself than a means to accuse others—as long as problems in perception could be traced to the observer, there were no grounds for suspecting that the outside world was intrinsically deceptive. So it is that the original *Othello* ends not with the guilty husband producing a grand visual testament to another man's traitorous duplicity, but with him blaming himself for placing too much weight in the impressions of his own sight.

Descartes had no such qualms about the reliability of the sight. Indeed, he believed that it could form the basis of public ethics. Because his skeptical method threatened to maroon him within his own innate ideas, Descartes was strongly interested in rehabilitating vision from the critiques leveled by thinkers such as Montaigne.[27] As he announces in the opening sentence of his *Optics*: "The conduct of life depends entirely upon our senses, and since sight is the noblest and most comprehensive of the senses, inventions which increase its power are among the most useful that can be." Shaped by rational reflection, but reaching beyond the mind's own private domain, the science of optics could be relied upon to guide "the conduct of life," countering the mind's isolation by connecting it to the world outside. Descartes' view of optics was noted approvingly by Hobbes,[28] and it is this willingness to make one's own eyes the basis of ethics that leads to the heroic investment in ocular proof caricatured in Congreve's play. Pompously secure in his own perspective, yet aware that he lacks certain knowledge of what goes on beyond, Touchwood demands visual proof of his wife's infidelity so that he might "justify" himself "to the World."[29] Touchwood's doubt thus leads him not to experience the general fallenness described by Montaigne, but rather to feel a defiant isolation. He is alone, but by confirming that his vision of things conforms to reality, he can make others see his point-of-view. In his loneliness, he sees a heroic opportunity to assert himself.

As *The Villain* reveals, though, there was an ominous aspect to this new science. If Hobbes and Descartes offered vision as a connection to the world without, they did so through unqualified confidence in powers of the individual mind. From this perspective, the shock of the unexpected was no longer a source of self-examination. Rather, it was a spur to suspicion and rage, granting the injured license to wreak absolute judgment upon their perceived tormentors. *The Villain* offers Maligni as a version of Descartes' deceiving genie, and far from dispelling this sense of paranoia, the unveiling of Maligni's mangled body intensifies it. There is no evidence in this corpse that the dead man is guilty of any particular crime. Rather, the horror of its sudden discovery is proof of something else: that the mind's inner peace might at any moment be interrupted by an unexpected violence beyond. As Beaupres announces, this is "the Sacrifice of Innocence," and the abrupt sight of the corpse ushers in such a terrible sense of fear and disillusionment that one of the witnesses dies from shock.

Although it is impossible to know with certainty what intentions lay behind the Restoration *Othello*, its revisions are thus consistent with the changing problems of the age. The central concern of ethics was no longer the fallibility of one's own mind; instead, it was the unknowability of others. Like the problem of death, moreover, this concern was one rooted in bodily experience. Although given popular shape in Descartes' skeptical meditations, the Cartesian *cogito* took hold of Hobbes and other English readers because it reflected a novel crisis in the practice of human relations, one that placed the structures of our mind under a new form of physical duress. When the social circuitry of our brain had evolved tens of thousands of years earlier, life had been a much simpler affair. Societies numbered in the dozens, not the millions, allowing us a clear sense of our social place.[30] With the rise of early civilizations, our social circuits were put under increased stress, but certain core practices helped to preserve our primitive experience of belonging. Families were held together by strong ties to their ancestors—Aeneas might have been forced to flee Troy, but he carried with him the ancient gods of his hearth, and right through the sixteenth century, it was common in Europe to be able to trace one's lineage back to a god, or a classical hero, or some other founder-figure. Big cities were divided into small boroughs, and even at the height of their empires, Athens and Rome retained a heavy focus on local politics—while a few campaigned to be consuls, many ran to be magistrates of the neighborhood *vici*. Further binding was provided by shared cultural experiences: from street festivals and civic architecture to live theater and public recitations. And finally, integrity was fostered by a pervasive cultural dualism: you were a Jew or a gentile, a Greek or a barbarian, a Roman citizen or a Roman vassal. Although our brains were in danger of being overtaxed by the bigness of our social environment, the workings of culture thus helped maintain a new equilibrium, and further helping matters in Europe at least was the collapse of the Roman Empire. Over the middle ages, human life fragmented back into smaller, more isolated communities, and the church wove a vast array of cultural practices—from pagan holidays to Aristotelian learning—into a shielding blanket. The stress on our biological hardware gradually lessened, and the problem posed by our physical expansion seemed to have passed.

From the fourteenth century on, however, the medieval sense of society began to unravel at an accelerating pace. Philologists such as Lorenzo Valla and Erasmus discovered that the ancient world was not as familiar as medieval scholars had claimed—it was filled with strange customs and beliefs, and perhaps more worryingly, it was not a stable point of origin, but a diverse entity that had changed over time. At the same time, Europe was colliding with new cultures—not just the sundry inhabitants of the new world, but the "skillful Turk" and the civilizations of Islam. Meanwhile, just as the outside world was coming to seem more various, people's sense of their own cultural unity was starting to fracture. The church disintegrated, ripped apart by the Reformation and a growing tide of literacy that allowed the faithful to interpret God's holy writ after their own personal inclinations. Copernicus kicked the earth from the center of the universe and his heirs promptly declared the universe infinite, making it without any center at all. Traditional dress became infused with foreign tailoring; traditional eating became infused with foreign spice. Towns swelled into cities and then into megalopoli—in spite of fire and plague, London's population quadrupled over the sixteenth century and more than doubled again over the seventeenth. No longer was there a stable cultural touchstone for the self; no longer was there a manageable number of others without. The ancient therapies, effective in their time, could not cope with the growing complexities of the modern landscape. Pushed to its limit, the mind's natural sense of social integrity began to fall apart.

This physical shift was building in England at the time of Shakespeare's original *Othello*, which itself makes reference to the new world Anthropophagi and the not "unskillful" Turk (1.3.144; 27). And yet, as the stage history of *Othello* suggests, the tipping point for England was the civil wars of the mid-seventeenth century. This was the moment when the old society shattered and individuals pulled into themselves, searching for innate ideas, or self-interest, or some other solid anchor amid the clatter and the noise. To say that the problem of the Restoration stage was new is thus not to say that it reflected some fundamental change in human biology or that it had never been felt in any form on earth before. Rather, it is to say that the English had no cultural precedent for understanding it. They could not, as Shakespeare had earlier done in *Hamlet*, turn back to the Romans or some other ancient model. Nor, as the example of *Othello* reveals, could they turn back to their own immediate history—for if even a play that explicitly centered on betrayal and cultural conflict did not address the problem of paranoia, but instead took the opposite tack of interrogating the self, then what relevant resources could the past possibly hold? The physical environment had shifted underfoot, opening a new ethical concern, demanding a new form of art. And so like the times themselves, *Othello* became paranoid.

By itself, of course, the example of *Othello* simply demonstrates that English tragedy was under pressure to adapt; it does not establish that tragedy actually did. For instead of fashioning a new form of tragedy, the editors of the Restoration *Othello* merely pruned away bits of the old. Or, to put it another way, the very quality that makes *Othello* a useful source of evidence for the changing ethical concerns of the times also makes it less helpful for illuminating the way that tragedy responded to them. Because *Othello* preexists the problem of radical paranoia, its performance history has been a good way to trace the emergence of this new problem. But at the same time, because *Othello* preexists this problem, it cannot contain a response to it. To find a response, we must hunt out newer tragedies, ones written after the problem emerged. As I will suggest over the following chapters, such tragedies are not hard to find. Indeed, they spilled off the pen of the most prominent playwright of the later seventeenth century: John Dryden. Dryden's tragedies have often been dismissed as either escapist nonsense or poor copies of Shakespeare, but as I will show, they are in fact both deeply serious and highly innovative. They pick up the problem described by Descartes and Hobbes, emphasizing its physical aspect by framing it in the context of the European encounter with the new world. As Shakespeare had done earlier, moreover, Dryden did not simply use his tragedies to provide a single approach to the problem of the times. Instead, he crafted different tragic forms that stimulated different styles of ethical practice. Read alongside the opening chapters of this book, the following pages thus demonstrate that tragedy was able to adapt its original function in its entirety. Just as it had done in the early years of the century, it used a variety of innovative formal techniques to take an ethical problem and make it the center of an organic pluralism. The only difference was that, this time, the problem was new.

Chapter 4

The Indian Emperour and the Reason of New World Conflict

In George Villiers' *The Rehearsal* (1672), love commands the gallant Volscius to doff his boots and bed his mistress. At the same time, honor commands him to set forth fully shod. Finding himself unable to reconcile this conflict of values, Volscius pulls off his boots, then puts them on, then pulls them off, then puts them on again. Finally, the befuddled knight hops off stage, wearing one boot and clasping the other. Volscius was a send-up of the heroes who had stormed the Restoration stage in plays such as *The Indian Emperour* (1664), and like any good parody, *The Rehearsal* is only barely an exaggeration. Throughout *The Indian Emperour*, the lofty ideals expressed by its characters seem less a window into an eternal realm of perfect virtue than an ironic comment on the fate of heroism in a world of material circumstance.[1] The Spanish commander Cortez has no sooner sworn his everlasting love to a woman than he admits to having previously made this same pledge to another, now dead. The Indian emperor Montezuma insists that he prefers death to ignominy, but then abandons his own daughter to the Spanish to thank them for calling off an ambush. The Indian prince Guyomar vows revenge on a Spaniard for killing his brother, only to experience a sudden remorse that inspires a futile attempt to resuscitate his mortally wounded foe. Fueled by this strange mix of fervor and forgetfulness, Dryden's heroes appear oddly adolescent. No less than the hapless Volscius, they are at once swashbuckling and scattered.

Dryden is himself lambasted in *The Rehearsal* for possessing similar qualities, but recent scholars have inclined to the view that he was aware of the contrast between his idealistic heroes and their inelegant heroics. In the preface to *The Indian Emperour*, he identifies himself as a "Sceptical" thinker,[2] suggesting that he possesses the critical self-awareness so distinctly lacking in the fanatics of his plays.[3] And yet far from improving the reputation of his tragedy, Dryden's admission of skepticism has further ruined it. To many critics, this admission has implied that the manic romanticism of his plays is a calculated pander: pitched to a generation exhausted by civil war, *The Indian Emperour* forsook the unflinching exploration of the human condition undertaken by earlier plays like *Hamlet* and *Macbeth* and instead offered the pleasant escapism of spectacle, bombast, and surprise.[4] Other critics, meanwhile, have taken Dryden's self-proclaimed skepticism as evidence that *The Indian Emperour* is a play of ideas, or a philosophical dialogue, or some other form of speculative enterprise.[5] And yet in trying to show that *The Indian Emperour* is more than candied peel, these critics have distanced the play even further from solid theatrical practice, associating it with a concern over the attainability of absolute knowledge, a willingness to sort through truth-claims in private, and other similarly theoretical topics. Villiers' parody, in short, seems largely on target. If it is too hasty in condemning *The Indian Emperour* for lacking intelligence, it seems right to sense a fundamental incongruity between the play's philosophical ideals and its dramatic action.

While this incongruity has struck critics from Villiers on, however, it did not bother Dryden's original audience. The play was a huge success, drawing enthusiastic crowds and making the playwright's reputation,[6] and as I hope to show in this chapter, a careful attention to Dryden's own statements on skepticism reveals why: far from treating doubt as a speculative exercise suited for the meditations of philosophy, he viewed it as a public practice rooted in the ethical problem discussed in the previous chapter. His play, in short, was not philosophically incongruous, for its aim was not philosophical at all. Rather, its intention was dramatic, and since the engine of the drama was the very concern that drove the Restoration adaptation of *Othello*, it is no surprise that the play appealed. Dryden, moreover, had an opportunity that the adaptors of *Othello* did not. Instead of having to gerrymander an old form, he was free to develop a new one. The result was a style of theater that offered audiences a tailored way of engaging with the problem of the times, providing them with the same sort of practical ethics that previous generations had been able to discover in plays like *Hamlet* and *Macbeth*.

When considered against the backdrop of the preceding chapters, *The Indian Emperour* thus confirms part of Dewey's third hypothesis about the progressive potential of art. Just as Dewey predicts, seventeenth-century tragedy was not limited to communicating traditional social practices. It could also develop new ones, offering itself as a source of ethical growth.

When Dryden identifies himself as "Sceptical" in the essay that introduces the 1668 edition of *The Indian Emperour*, he does so by identifying a specific limit to the power of reason:

> If Nature is to be imitated, then there is a Rule for imitating Nature rightly; otherwise, there may be an end, and no means conducing to it. Hither-to I have proceeded by demonstration; but as our Divines, when they have prov'd a Deity, because there is order, and have inferred that this Deity ought to be worshipped, differ afterwards in the manner of the Worship; so, having laid down, that Nature is to be imitated, and that Proposition proving the next, that then there are means which conduce to the imitating of Nature, I dare proceed no further positively. (*Works*, 9.14)

Here, Dryden proceeds by rational "demonstration" to prove that there are rules for producing art. Yet he is quick to admit that since reason does not reveal what these rules are, he dares "proceed no further positively." His basic point is that reason reveals the abstract truths of existence but says nothing about how these truths are to be put to actual use. To illustrate this point, he then draws upon a striking analogy with religion. Reason, he suggests, informs us that there is a God who must be worshipped, but it cannot tell us what form this worship should take—otherwise there would not be so many different religions. Where interpreters of Dryden's skepticism have debated whether the playwright saw reason as a scientific tool or a hopeless instrument, Dryden's account of religion suggests that this debate rests upon a false dichotomy. For Dryden, reason is both functional and futile: adequate for theorizing value, but insufficient for practicing it.

Dryden was unusual in taking this position, but he was not alone. For the very same account of religion had been set forth a decade earlier by one of the thinkers discussed in the previous chapter: Hobbes. As Hobbes explains in *Leviathan*:

> For the worship which naturally men exhibit to Powers invisible, it can be no other, but such expressions of their reverence, as they

would use towards men; Gifts, Petitions, Thanks, Submission of Body, Considerate Addresses, sober Behavior, premeditated Words, Swearing (that is, assuring on another of their promises,) by invoking them. Beyond that reason suggesteth nothing; but leaves them either to rest there; or for further ceremonies, to rely on those they believe to be wiser than themselves. (1.12)

Reason thus suggests that we should tender gifts to God, but does not tell us *what* gifts; it tells us that we should give thanks, but it does not tell us *how* to give thanks; and reason certainly does not provide for the elaborate ceremonies that organized religions take as their foundation. Instead, all this pomp and circumstance originates from men—men we "believe" to be wiser than ourselves. For this account of religion, Hobbes was quickly branded a cynic and an atheist.[7] He himself saw *Leviathan*, however, not as an attempt to spread unbelief but rather as a means to curb an antisocial skepticism. For well before *Leviathan*, there had been skeptics, most notoriously of late, Montaigne. Struck by the strangeness of both the ancient world recovered by philology and the new world reported by sailors, Montaigne had been moved to question his own religious practice. After all, if Egyptian pharaohs could marry their sisters and if Amerindians could eat human flesh, then perhaps the moral views of Western Europe were not as absolute as they seemed. Montaigne's revival of Pyrrhonist skepticism proved compelling to many readers, but many more—including Hobbes—were alarmed by its consequences. What hope could there be for social stability when even incest and cannibalism became debatable? In *Leviathan*, Hobbes therefore tried to reclaim a foundation for ethics by suggesting that behind the differences of behavior that held people apart, there was a fundamental rationalism that linked them all together: cultures might disagree about the appropriate form of religious observance, but they all believed in a divine power who should be worshipped.[8] Common reason thus connected even the most bewilderingly divergent ethical practices, providing a solid basis for society.

Hobbes' effort to restore social integrity earned him a small, but committed, group of enthusiasts. Of these, one of the most outspoken was Dryden. John Aubrey's account of Hobbes notes that "Mr John Dryden, Poet Laureat, is his [i.e., Hobbes'] great admirer, and oftentimes makes use of his doctrines in his plays."[9] To some scholars, this has suggested a dark aspect to Dryden's skepticism—brute cynicism[10]—but *The Indian Emperour* reveals that the playwright

did not succumb to the popular caricature of Hobbes as a godless misanthrope. Not only does Dryden's preface reproduce the
nuanced view of religion expressed in *Leviathan* 1.12, but the dramatic force of the play itself springs from a set of conflicts that illustrate Hobbes' account of the limits of reason. The play begins when
the Spanish discover Mexico, and no sooner have they touched the
beach than they find themselves at odds over the logic of their expe-
dition: while Cortez waxes lyric about the simple joys of a primitive existence, his lieutenants see a chance for personal enrichment.
This conflict of attitudes neatly captures the vigorous seventeenth-
century debate over whether New World peoples were noble savages or base creatures ripe for plunder,[11] a debate that Dryden's
close associate William Davenant had recently made the basis for
one of the earliest examples of English heroic tragedy: *The Cruelty
of the Spaniards in Peru*(1658).[12] Davenant's work initially questions imperial expansion by following Las Casas' *The Tears of the
Indians* in celebrating a lawless state of nature, but it abandons this
dim view of colonial rule in its final act when Cromwell's surprising
arrival in Peru prompts the Indians to burst into song about how
"th'*English* shall sit and rule as . . . guests."[13] The result is a work that
mirrors England's own anxieties about its imperial role, revealing a
deep uncertainty as to whether it is more noble to conquer others or
to let them live in peace.

    In offering its own mixed perspective on imperialism, the open-
ing scene of *The Indian Emperour* revisits this uncertainty. But
where *The Cruelty of the Spaniards* endlessly rehearses the conflict
between a desire to idealize the new world and an impulse to possess it, Dryden draws upon Hobbes to dismiss the cultural contrast
that grounds this Eurocentric debate. Instead of portraying the
Indians as either noble savages or unfeeling brutes, Dryden suggests that they are fundamentally similar to the Spanish, for linking
both cultures together is a shared rational dilemma. This similarity
emerges during the first interaction between the two groups, a discussion over religion. The conversation begins when Montezuma,
the Indian emperor, rushes up to Cortez and mistakes his unusual
appearance for an indication that he is a god. Before Cortez can
respond, Montezuma announces his pious willingness to honor
the heavens, but confesses that he has no idea whether it would be
more appropriate to offer as a gift "breath of incense" or "Human
sacrifice" and "hot reeking gore" (1.2.237–42).[14] The difference
between these two options is so great as to be almost absurd, and

yet Montezuma is entirely serious. Although he recognizes the rational necessity of honoring the gods, he also grasps that reason is not equipped to tell him how to worship. Like Hobbes, the Indian emperor thus finds himself certain in his piety but hesitant in his religious practice.

In the work of another dramatist, Montezuma's doubt might be part of a lesson on the need to supplement the vague dictates of reason with the divine light of Christianity. Dryden, however, has already revealed his own sympathy with Montezuma's position in the play's introduction, and subsequent events do nothing to shift the emperor's firm stance on the limits of human understanding. Although Montezuma listens intently to the Catholic priests, he remains unconvinced by their religious practices, and he declines to abandon his own. Now that he has ascertained that the Spanish are not gods, but humans who struggle with the same rational uncertainty as himself, he is not about to let them tell him what to do. The Catholic priests are less than pleased with Montezuma's stance, but Cortez is so moved by the emperor's piety that he demands, "Must I have War, yet have no Enemy?" (1.2.336). Equally impressed by the Spanish commander, the Indian emperor prays to the heavens: "Preserve this antient State and me, / But if your doom the fall of both decree, / Grant only he who has such Honour shown, / When I am dust, may fill my empty Throne" (1.2.339–42). Each man, in short, sees himself in the other. And indeed, they share the same predicament. Since reason has not only led them to the same standard of piety, but made them aware that there are no logical grounds for preferring one set of religious practices to another, neither man can yield his own religion without being irrational. Montezuma and Cortez recognize, in short, what the Catholic priests do not: the fatal problem is not that Montezuma is unenlightened. It is that he and the Spanish have equal reason.

Like Montezuma's bizarrely congenial declaration of hostilities, the ensuing conflict is thus marked by an atmosphere of tragic absurdity. Two cultures wipe each other out in a demonstration of mutual likeness, and even the conclusion of the war does nothing to resolve this disquieting situation. Following Montezuma's death, Cortez attempts to display magnanimity by offering the emperor's son Guyomar a role in his new government. The Indian prince, however, will have none of it—he leaves the stage vowing to start a new Aztec settlement, promising "No Spaniards will that Colony destroy" (5.2.373). Not to be outdone, Cortez concludes the play by paying "loud thanks...to the powers above," reminding his foe whose god has really triumphed (5.2.378). Such unresolved conflict was a self-conscious part of Dryden's skeptical method. As he writes in the preface to the 1668 edition of *The Indian Emperour*: "My whole Discourse [in *Essay of Dramatic Poesy*] was Sceptical...it is a Dialogue sustain'd by persons of several opinions, all of them left doubtful" (*Works*, 9.15). In a world in which reason leads us only to generalities, how can there ever be agreement over particulars? And yet even as Dryden allows his essay and his play to draw to an inconclusive close, he admits in his preface that life does not allow us to rest in a permanent state of doubt. In practice, we cannot be an artist unless we translate the rules of art into a specific tragic style; in practice, we cannot be pious unless we choose to worship a particular god in a particular way. Life, that is, forces us to do more than think. It forces us to act. There is thus the need for a means for translating the abstractions of theory into the particularities of practice, and so Dryden continues his preface by writing: "...all of them left doubtful, to be determined by the Readers in general; and more particularly defer'd to the accurate Judgment of my Lord Buckhurst." What reason has left theoretically open the "judgment" must practically decide.

In assigning this practical role to the judgment, Dryden followed the same thinker who had led him in the first place to his skeptical view of reason: Hobbes. Prior to Hobbes, the judgment had been a relatively minor component of faculty psychology. It had long been associated with what was reasonable, a nebulous domain that implied something that was logical yet lacked the full certainty of reason. As Hobbes saw it, this feature of judgment made it the perfect complement to reason—while reason could go no farther than the universal, the judgment could carry on into the particular, translating the rational abstract into physical practice. Even so, there was the clear problem that judgment varied from individual to individual. Although judgment resolved peoples' individual indecisions, it did so by steering everyone in a different direction. In the end, it reintroduced on a social level the very confusions it eliminated on an individual one. Hobbes was less interested in clarifying this murky epistemological situation than in finding a practical solution to the difficulties it precipitated. He therefore settled on the idea that one individual should be given authority over all others, so that one judgment would be used in all cases to determine what was reasonable:

> The only way to elect such a Common Power, as may be able to defend [one group of people] from the invasion of Forraigners, and the injuries of one another, and thereby to secure them in such a sort, as that by their owne industrie, and by the fruites of the Earth, they may nourish themselves and live contentedly; is, to confer all their power and strength upon one Man...and therein to submit their Wills, every one to his Will, and their Judgments, to his Judgment. (2.18)

Instead of allowing individual judgments to proliferate, Hobbes argued that everyone should submit to the judgment of a single ruler. The result of this arrangement would be an enforced uniformity of perspective that was also in full accord with reason. For in Hobbes' view, if there was a range of equally rational choices that could be made, then one was as good as any other. Indeed, one was better, for it did away with conflict altogether. In judgment was a path from universal reason to shared society.

By looking to "the Judgment of...Lord Buckhurst," the preface to *The Indian Emperour* thus aligns itself with Hobbes' socially-minded solution. And yet the action of the play itself derives from the fact that there is no Hobbesian monarch, no Lord Buckhurst, to past final judgment. Instead, there is a cohort of opposed heroes whose judgment carries equal weight, tipping life into endless struggle: Montezuma and Cortez battle over their different religious practices; Guyomar and Odmar come to blows over whether it is more noble to rescue one's parent or one's lover; and Cortez and Guyomar dissent over whether honor dictates an urge for conquest or a disinterest in acquisition. Although these heroes all agree on ideals such as piety, justice, and love, they all judge differently on how to translate their shared ideals into actual behavior. Lacking a Hobbesian autocrat, they exist in a Hobbesian state of nature. Just as Dryden's *Essay* demands that its readers use their own powers of judgment to produce resolution, so too does *The Indian Emperour* hand the matter over to its audience. Since there are many noble heroes and many virtuous choices, we must decide for ourselves which are best. In effect, like the heroes of the play themselves, we must use our own judgment to choose between a series of equally rational alternatives.

By encouraging us to judge in this way, *The Indian Emperour* offers an entirely different form of dramatic experience from previous tragedy. The broad inspiration for the form of Dryden's play comes from French heroic dramas like Corneille's *Le Cid*, but as one of the characters in Dryden's *Essay* notes, these earlier dramas "commonly make but one person considerable in a Play; they dwell on him, and his concernments, while the rest of the persons are only subservient to set him off" (*Works*, 17.38).[15] Modern scholars have been quick to contest this interpretation, pointing out that Corneille carefully crafted other perspectives to counterbalance the perspective of the hero,[16] and yet if anything, Corneille's careful balancing is precisely what makes his heroes so considerable. The most famous moment in Corneillian drama is the soliloquy in which the Cid weighs the competing demands of love and honor, balancing them carefully, deliberately...only to realize that a man cannot be worthy of love without his honor.[17] Honor is all, and "ashamed at having debated so," the Cid springs into action.[18] The Cid, in effect, sets up a balance of perspectives only to tip it decisively in favor of a single value, and the remainder of the play amplifies this dynamic. Though much of *Le Cid* is dedicated to emphasizing the "prudent" moderation of the king—a man so conscious of his place in a greater whole that he refers to himself merely as "a" king—equilibrium is no sooner established than it is violently upset by "the" Cid.[19] Far from counterbalancing the Cid's behavior, the play's judicious balancing thus has the practical effect of making his monomania all the more memorable, and indeed, this is precisely how Corneille's original audience experienced it. A contemporary noted of *Le Cid* that it inspired such "admiration" among the public that "they committed it wholly to memory in order to anticipate [*prévenir*] the actors who performed it."[20] The audience, in effect, modelled themselves directly after the Cid, finding purpose in single-mindedly disturbing the norm. As Dryden's *Essay* notes, they had found only one point-of-view considerable—the rest was simply there to set it off.

Against this clarity of purpose, Dryden's decision in *The Indian Emperour* to place "many shining characters in the play...that greatness may be opposed to greatness" forces audiences to decide which shining character they prefer (*Works*, 17.49). Before we can imitate, we first must judge, and the full consequences of this emphasis on judgment are revealed in the brilliant spectacle of the play's final scene. When Montezuma refuses to disclose the location of his gold, Pizarro and a Christian priest chain him to the rack and attempt to convert him. At first the Christians rely upon reason, but Montezuma easily rebuffs them with reason of his own, turning the exchange into a stalemate (5.2.39–82):

> *Christian Priest*:   Those Pains, O Prince, thou sufferest now are light
> Compar'd to those, which when thy Soul takes flight
> Immortal, endless, thou must then endure:
> Which Death begins, and Time can never cure.
> *Montezuma*:   Thou art deceiv'd; for whensoe're I Dye,
> The Sun my Father bears my Soul on high:
> He lets me down a Beam, and mounted there,
> He draws it back, and pulls me through the Air:
> I in the Eastern parts, and rising Sky,
> You in Heaven's downfal, and the West must lye.

Here, Montezuma responds to the Christian priest's version of heaven by offering his own, challenging the priest to provide a fuller justification of the Catholic faith. The priest, however, can only rail:

> *Christian Priest*:   Fond man, by Heathen Ignorance misled,
> Thy soul destroying when thy Body's Dead:
> Change yet thy Faith, and buy Eternal rest.
> *Indian Priest*:   Dye in your own: for our Belief is best.

This conversation too thus grinds quickly to a halt, as both priests stubbornly cling to their own personal views about the divine.

At this point, Montezuma intercedes, suggesting that the rational thing to do is to admit that since both faiths share a great deal of common ground, their similarity should take precedence over their differences:

> *Montezuma*:   Where both agree 'tis there most safe to stay:
> For what's more vain then Publick Light to shun,
> And set up Tapers while we see the Sun?

The Christian priest, however, rejects this as impiety:

> *Christian Priest*:   Though Nature teaches whom we should Adore,
> By Heavenly Beams we still discover more.

Montezuma:	Or this must be enough, or to Mankind
	One equal way to Bliss is not design'd.
	For though some more may know, and some know less,
	Yet all must know enough for happiness.
Christian Priest:	If in this middle way you still pretend
	To stay, your Journey never will have end.
Montezuma:	Howe're, 'tis better in the midst to stay,
	Then wander father in uncertain way.

The force of this exchange stems from the fact that Montezuma and the priest make equally practical points. Montezuma follows Hobbes in insisting that it is reason that leads us to the core truth that we should adore the heavens, and the priest concedes this point. However the priest makes an equally Hobbesian point when he notes that "if in this middle way you still pretend / To stay, your journey never will have end." The realization that God should be adored means nothing without a physical commitment to some particular form of worship, and Montezuma's own admission of this claim comes in the following couplet:

| *Christian Priest*: | But we by Martyrdom our Faith avow. |
| *Montezuma*: | You do no more then I for ours do now. |

Although the emperor recognizes his similarity to his Christian captors, he knows that this similarity can only emerge when they punish him for his difference. Abstract reflections about martyrdom are not enough; shared reason must be writ in blood.

The violence of this moment serves as blunt reminder that the ethical problem of the play is not a speculative matter to be batted round the chambers of the mind. It is a problem that leaves its mark in human flesh. And indeed, just as the rack confronts Montezuma with the bodily consequences of his heroic dilemma, so too does the remainder of this scene involve the audience, carrying us beyond a removed contemplation of the emperor's philosophical arguments and making his physical predicament immanent to our own experience. Having failed to convince Montezuma with argument, the Christian priest determines to produce closure by another means. He orders the ropes tightened: "I must by force, convert him on the Rack" (5.2.99). Where reason has failed, judgment must be employed. When he feels himself being further stretched, the Indian priest screams and asks his emperor for permission to reveal the secret of the gold. Montezuma's response is thunderously dismissive:

> Think'st thou I lye on Beds of Roses here,
> Or in a Wanton Bath stretch'd at my ease?
> Dye, Slave, and with thee, dye such thoughts as these.
>   (5.2.103–5)

As if on command, the Indian priest dies. This is the dramatic climax of the play, and it encourages a two-stage response. At first, Montezuma's rhetorical questions create the expectation that his state of mind is transparently obvious. Without ever directly expressing his experience of racking, the emperor draws his listeners into a feeling of intimacy with his perspective, for the very form of a rhetorical question implies that the answer is intuitively obvious. This sense of psychological closeness disappears almost immediately, however, when the Indian priest dies on the heels of Montezuma's command. Montezuma's judgment appears to have literally killed, making it seem as if he somehow has the power to alter reality through the action of his thought. The mind that moments earlier had seemed so familiar has now been invested with a strange and inscrutable power.

The effect of this dramatic reversal is intensified, moreover, by a clever theatrical device: the incomplete metaphors woven into the emperor's questions.[21] Although metaphors are a common part of the language of *The Indian Emperour*, the ones that Montezuma utters on the rack are unique.[22] The other metaphors in the play involve two terms, one of which is known through the other. But the metaphors that Montezuma uses in this scene have only one term. Take, for example, "Think'st thou I lye on Beds of Roses here?" The two terms established by this metaphor can be marked off as "Montezuma's experience on the rack" and "lying in a bed of roses," yet the incongruity of these terms causes the metaphor to immediately fall apart. Being racked is *not* like lying amid roses, and so to appreciate the absurdity of the emperor's comparison is to be left with only a single term: "Being racked is like ____." With this incomplete formulation, *The Indian Emperour* thus gives audiences the unusual opportunity to finish the metaphor themselves. The process of finishing metaphors was of great interest to Dryden, who remarked that "the first happiness of the Poet's imagination is properly Invention, or finding the thought; the second is Fancy, or the variation, driving, or moulding of the thought, as judgment represents it proper to the subject."[23] Metaphors, in effect, are generated by an act "judgment" that translates the abstract essence of a thought into a more particular form.[24] Finishing a metaphor thus involves precisely the same psychological faculty as a heroic choice, and so it is that Dryden's heroes are particularly good at making metaphor. No sooner has Montezuma escaped the rack than he launches into an extravagant six-line comparison of himself to a weary traveller, and when he dies a few moments later, it is with another likeness on his lips (5.2.200–205; 5.2.249).

By leaving his metaphors on the rack incomplete, Montezuma thus gives his audience a chance to participate in this heroic practice. Inheriting an unfinished thought, we may judge for ourselves what it means. This is not to say that we must actually settle upon a precise word or phrase that completes Montezuma's expression, for Dryden felt that the specifics of wording, or "elocution" as he put it, followed after the act of judgment.[25] It is to say, however, that we are invited more loosely to fill in the blanks of Montezuma's statement, achieving some personal impression about what he is feeling on the rack. We judge that he is experiencing terrible pain, or fierce determination, or something else that is not like lying in roses. Moreover, no sooner has the play prompted us to engage in this physical act of judging than it immerses us in the other bodily aspect of Montezuma's heroic dilemma: the experience of other people's judgment. For when the Indian priest abruptly dies on the heels of Montezuma's command "Dye!" we are bluntly confronted with the fact that the judgment does not just create new metaphors. It also strikes down alternatives. The same process that feels comfortably automatic from within feels shocking autocratic from without, so that in the transition between these experiences, we discover the ethical concern of Dryden's play firsthand.

By involving its audience in this killing decision, *The Indian Emperour* distances itself not just from the experience of French heroic tragedy, but from earlier English tragedy as well. The moment in Elizabethan tragedy that most anticipates the torture of Montezuma is the boiling of Barabas in Marlowe's *The Jew of Malta* (1590).[26] Like Montezuma, Barabas is hounded by a pack of Christians who urge him to convert. They are particularly stuck on the notion that their Christian charity makes them better than Jews like Barabas, and even Barabas' own daughter concludes that there is no "Pity in Jews" (3.4.48). Barabas seems

only too happy to live up to this unfortunate caricature, poisoning
nuns and hoarding gold, and in the play's climatic scene, he builds
an elaborate trap to pitch his Christian tormentors into a boiling
vat. Just when it looks like the ruthless Jew is about to succeed,
however, he runs afoul of his own contraption and plunges into
the fiery waters himself. A triumph of Providence, surely!—but at
the very moment that Barabas' Christian onlookers are reveling in
their salvation, the Jew screams out from the cauldron: "Help me,
Christians!...why stand you all so pitiless?" (5.5.69–70). With
this terrible shriek, the Jew lays bare the hypocrisy of a group
who espouse pity but who show none while a man boils before
them. What had been a moment of exhilaration twists into an
occasion for awkward introspection: the Christians are not so different from the Jew after all. This fusing of dramatic spectacle and
emotional reversal is preserved in Dryden's later play, but unlike
Barabas' death, Montezuma's torture alerts its audience not to the
fallibility, but to the *infallibility*, of their judgments. Since their
opinions are fully rational, just like everyone else's, the only way
to resolve difference is by force. So it is that Montezuma does
not follow Barabas in begging for mercy. Instead, he is himself
brutally imposing, condemning his own priest as a "Slave" and
crushing him for it. Where Marlowe's audience is made to regret
their judgments, Dryden's thus comes to feel that there is no other
alternative.

Although scholars have tended to read Dryden's skepticism as
a sign that tragedy had either passed its peak or veered into philosophical territory, *The Indian Emperour* thus moves in a very different direction. What sets it apart from earlier tragedy is not a
lack of seriousness—for the limit of human reason has fatal consequences. Nor is what sets it apart a philosophical method—for the
play is thick with drama. Rather, what makes Dryden's play innovative is that it adapts the form of tragedy to a new concern. The
spectacle of Montezuma's torture, the presence of multiple heroes,
the use of uncompleted metaphors—all of these are new formal
techniques developed to make the ethical problem of Dryden's
time as immediate as Hamlet's struggle with death and Macbeth's
anxiety about tomorrow. Where the Restoration *Othello* crudely
retrofits an old play to a new problem, hacking away the parts
that do not suit its purpose, *The Indian Emperour* grows with the
times, generating a new form for a new function. By adapting in
this way, moreover, *The Indian Emperour* opens up the possibility

of an even greater horizon. For if tragedy could engage with new problems, then perhaps it could also encourage different ways of experiencing them, continuing the example of ethical pluralism set forth by *Hamlet* and *Macbeth*. If so, seventeenth-century tragedy would fully confirm Dewey's claims for problem-based art, adapting itself to changing circumstance while maintaining a practical commitment to diversity. In my following and final case-study, I will explore this possibility. Shortly after completing *The Indian Emperour*, Dryden began working on an alternative response to the problem of his heroic plays, and as he developed it, he also developed a new form of tragedy to communicate it. As distinct in its experience as Horatio's unfinished narrative is from the riddle of Birnam Wood, this new form of tragedy suggests that new plays can do more than raise new problems. They can encourage new pluralities.

Chapter 5

Cartesian Generosity and the New Shakespeare

In *The Conquest of Granada* (1671), Dryden unleashed the greatness of Almanzor onto the Restoration stage. Soaring to grand new heights of self-importance, Almanzor is so confident in his own authority that he boldly scolds kings,[1] so lofty in his personal regard that he petitions his prospective father-in-law with the domineering: "Believe, old Man, that I her father knew: / What else should make *Almanzor* kneel to you?" (5.1.233–34). Even when the ghost of his own mother appears to warn him that his imperiousness is a quick road to moral disaster, Almanzor is implacable, wrapping himself in the paranoid individualism that Dryden had made a centerpiece of *The Indian Emperour*: "By Reason, Man a Godhead may discern: / But, how he would be worshipt, cannot learn" (II. 4.3.129–30). And when his mother's ghost rebukes him by insisting that his haughty behavior cannot be justified by any system of ethics, Almanzor continues to claim that egoism is the human lot: "Like a Captive in an Isle confin'd, / Man walks at large, a Pris'ner of the Mind" (II. 4.3.147–48).[2]

As Dryden's critical writings reveal, it was not just Almanzor who felt trapped by this problem; it was Dryden as well. By pursuing the problem of the times to its logical conclusion, the playwright had left behind the multiple heroes of *The Indian Emperour* and arrived at the outrageous singularity of one man's isolated judgment.[3] What had once been a wide road to dramatic conflict had tapered into a cul-de-sac of grating self-regard. It was enough to make Dryden despair, confessing in the preface to *Aureng-Zebe* (1675): "True greatness, if it be any where on Earth, is in a private Virtue; remov'd from the notion of Pomp and Vanity, confin'd to a contemplation of it self, and centring in it self."[4] With this claim, Dryden distances himself so completely from Almanzor that he seems to have turned his back not just on the heroic play, but on the theater itself. A private virtue, "confin'd to a contemplation of it self," might satisfy philosophy, but it hardly seems fare for the stage. Yet as I will show over the following pages, this new view of greatness would in time lead Dryden to an eminently dramatic model: Shakespearean tragedy. Or more precisely, it led to the eminently dramatic model that Dryden misimagined Shakespearean tragedy to be. During the late 1670s, Dryden came to believe that Shakespeare had found a way to use tragedy to translate the isolation of reason into a social generosity. As it happened, Dryden was wrong—this use for tragedy was first proposed by Descartes, decades after Shakespeare had died—but the error was nevertheless a fruitful one. When Dryden was unable to find more than scattered hints of generosity in Shakespeare's actual plays, he set out to complete what he believed the Bard had left unfinished, rewriting two of Shakespeare's tragedies to make them more generous. The result was not just a new Shakespeare, but a new response to the concerns of Dryden's heroic plays: where tragedy had once stimulated judgment, it would now move audiences to practice generosity instead. When placed alongside the previous chapters, moreover, this aesthetic shift has consequences beyond Dryden's own artistic development. It provides the final piece of Dewey's progressive ethics, demonstrating that art can translate emergent concerns into multiple styles of ethical practice. While chapters 1 and 2 have shown that tragedy can encourage different perspectives on the same problem, and while chapters 3 and 4 have shown that tragedy can shift attention to new problems, this chapter will thus show that both these forms of growth can occur together. In the rounding out of Dryden's personal development is the rounding out of an evolutionary ethics, evidence that art can take new problems and make them a source of new pluralities.

A few pages after musing in the preface to *Aureng-Zebe* that true greatness is best seen in the inward meditations of sages, Dryden turns to a more obviously dramatic model, confessing the "secret shame" that invades his "breast at *Shakespear's* sacred name" (*Works*, 12.159). As far back as *An Essay of Dramatic Poesy* (1668), Dryden had celebrated Shakespeare for having "the largest and most comprehensive soul," and although Dryden continued to feel that there was something rough and unfinished about Shakespeare's work, he became more and more convinced that Shakespeare's soul was greater than the "too narrow souls" of other writers: "The characters of Fletcher are poor & narrow, in comparison of Shakespears ... [for] Shakespear had a universal mind, which comprehended all Characters and Passions" (*Works*, 17.55; 13.13; 13.240; 13.247). As Dryden saw it, this greatness had a profound dramatic consequence: it allowed Shakespeare to produce characters that were "distinct" from himself, operating on their own unmistakable "inclinations."[5] Such characters instantly struck audiences as individual selves, that is, not as mouthpieces for the author but as distinct persons whose specific motives were worthy of attention.[6] Shakespeare's greatness, in short, generated dramatic interest—or in Dryden's term, "concernment." By remaining separate from his creations, the Bard had made it possible for audiences to connect with them.

In offering this reading of Shakespeare, Dryden seems to be anticipating certain later theories of the novel, which suggest that we connect with literary characters because we immerse ourselves in their motivations, identifying vicariously with them.[7] But in fact, Dryden thought exactly the opposite. He believed that to have concern for a character was to follow Shakespeare's example of greatness, remaining separate. Demonstrating this effect, Dryden quotes from Shakespeare's *Richard II*, challenging the reader, "refrain from pity if you can":

> As in a Theatre, the eyes of men
> After a well-graced Actor leaves the Stage,
> Are idly bent on him that enters next,
> Thinking his prattle to be tedious:
> Even so, or with much more contempt, mens eyes
> Did scowl on *Richard*: no man cry'd *God save him*:
> No joyful tongue gave him his welcom home,
> But dust was thrown upon his Sacred head,
> Which with such gentle sorrow he shook off,
> His face still combating with tears and smiles
> (The badges of his grief and patience)
> That had not God (for some strong purpose) steel'd
> The hearts of men, they must perforce have melted,
> And Barbarism it self have pity'd him.
> (*Works*, 13.246)

The most remarkable aspect of this passage is the distance that it creates from Richard's suffering. The audience is not given Richard's own description of his pain, but is instead told by York, a man who is balancing his regret at Richard's suffering with his belief that the king is nevertheless guilty of an abuse of power. Moreover, Richard's subjects do not actually feel pity, for their response is crushed by God. Instead this pity is felt by the audience members, who are safely isolated from the effects of Richard's behavior by their place in the gallery—and even they pity him not as Richard, but as a tedious actor. The effect is thus not sympathetic identification, but remove. Far from joining our perspective to Richard's, we inhabit the same attitude that allowed Shakespeare to write Richard in the first place. Like the playwright's great soul, we grasp Richard's condition while remaining apart.

With this reading, Dryden offers a rather singular account of Shakespearean tragedy. For far from being typical of Shakespeare, the sense of distance generated by the suffering of Richard II is unusual—so unusual in fact that Dryden would soon find himself rewriting Shakespeare to generate further examples. And indeed, to credit Shakespeare for inspiring Dryden's new view of greatness would be a mistake. For while Dryden found Shakespeare a useful prop, his real inspiration was more contemporary. A few years earlier, Walter Charleton—the subject of one of Dryden's odes, and also the man who nominated the playwright for the Royal Society—had explained in his *Natural History of the Passions* (1674) that there were two forms of pity.[8] The pity experienced by most people is driven by an ignoble fear for their own safety, but it is not merely the weak who feel pity:

> It hath ever been observed, that men of the most generous and Heroick spirits, such who having by brave resolutions, and habitual magnanimity, elevated their souls above the power of fortune, and so could fear no evil that she could bring upon them; have nevertheless been prone to Commiseration, when they beheld the infirmity of others, and heard their complaints; because it is a part of true Generosity, to will well to everyone. But the Grief of this Heroick Commiseration is not (as the other) bitter, but like that which Tragical cases represented in a Theatre produce, it is placed more in the Sense, than in the Soul itself, which at the same time injoyeth the satisfaction of thinking that she doth her duty in sympathizing with the afflicted. (129–30)

While the first sort of pity is the result of a sympathetic identification in which people imagine themselves undergoing someone else's hardships, this second sort of pity emerges from the *inability* to identify with the suffering of others, an inability that is equivalent to that generated by "Tragical cases represented in a Theatre."

As Charleton admits, this discussion of tragedy is a literal translation of a passage from *The Passions of the Mind* in which Descartes sets out to redefine the concept of greatness.[9] Prior to Descartes, there had been disagreement over whether greatness was a form of behavior or a state of mind.[10] The former approach encouraged charitable giving and heroic sacrifice, but also fostered a culture of competition that led to moments like Achilles' sulking petulance. The latter eliminated such destructive displays, but had the unfortunate effect of encouraging individuals to take so much satisfaction in their own virtue that they withdrew entirely from society. Each approach, in short, had its limitations, and so rather than confining himself to either, Descartes decided to combine the best of both.[11] Defining greatness as an internal self-sufficiency that led to an outward charity, Descartes replaced the traditional term for greatness, *magnanimitas*, with his own *générosité*:

> True generosity, which causes a person's self-esteem to be as great as it may legitimately be, has only two components. The first consists in his knowing that nothing truly belongs to him but this freedom to dispose his volitions, and that he ought to be praised or blamed for no other reason than using this freedom well or badly. The second consists in his feeling within himself a firm and constant resolution to use it well—that is, to never lack the will to undertake and carry out what he judges best. (*The Passions*, 3.153)

Because self-esteem is a private virtue, depending not on our social standing but on our free disposal of our own will, greatness originates not in heroic conflict, but in rational meditation. And yet, as the term *générosité* implies, this private reflection has major public consequences:

> Such people never have contempt for anyone. Although they often see that others do wrong in ways that show up their weakness, they are nevertheless more inclined to excuse than to blame them and to regard such wrong-doing as due rather to lack of knowledge than to a lack of a virtuous will. Just as they do not consider themselves much inferior to those who have greater wealth or honor, or even to those who have more intelligence, knowledge, or beauty, or generally to those who surpass them in some other perfections, equally they do not have much more esteem for themselves than for those whom they surpass. For all these things seem to them to be very unimportant, by contrast to the virtuous will for which alone they esteem themselves, and which

they suppose also to be present, or at least capable of being present, in every other person. (*The Passions*, 3.154)

When people ground their sense of self-worth entirely in their own free will, they are less inclined to judge others for their external attributes. Instead, they recognize that—regardless of differences in beauty, or intelligence, or wealth—everyone is capable of being equally worthy. What starts as a private satisfaction thus ends as a public generosity. Out of the self comes society.

It is to illustrate this ethical attitude that Descartes introduces his view of tragedy. Watching tragedy, he claims, makes us aware of an outside suffering without altering our awareness of our own autonomy. Tragedy, that is, provides the experience of generosity: a greatness of soul that allows us to feel concern for others while remaining fully detached. By offering the experience of tragedy as support for his new account of greatness, however, Descartes was guilty of something of a sleight of hand. For what he was proposing was not just a rethinking of greatness; it was also a rethinking of tragedy. Prior to *The Passions*, there were two dominant theories of the psychological effect of tragedy, the first originating in Aristotle and the second in Lucretius. Aristotle had argued in his *Poetics* that tragedy moved spectators to pity by encouraging them to imagine that the events on stage were actually happening to them. Tragedy thus encouraged a self-centered identification in which viewers were moved less by a concern for others than by a concern for themselves. As Hobbes bluntly put it: "Pity is imagination or fiction of future calamity to ourselves, proceeding from the sense of another man's calamity."[12] If this view of tragedy was egoistic, however, the alternative was more so. Laying the foundation for what would become the theory of *schadenfreude*,[13] Lucretius suggested that tragedy afforded spectators the satisfaction of watching the misery of others. Recognizing their own immunity from the disaster unfolding before them, audiences reveled at their own preservation. Descartes' description of tragedy leaves behind the egoism of both these previous accounts. In response to Aristotle, he suggests that a concern for others does not require a sense of personal endangerment. And in response to Lucretius, he suggests that it is possible to be detached without being callous. While Aristotle describes tragedy as a source of immersive pity, and while Lucretius describes it as a source of detached pleasure, Descartes takes one term from each, claiming the experience of tragedy as a detached pity.

This is precisely the experience that Dryden discovers in *Richard II*, where the audience feels concernment for Richard without partaking in his suffering. And indeed, this experience attracted Dryden for the same reason that it attracted Descartes. Descartes had written *The Passions* as a final attempt to establish a working basis for society; where his philosophical method and his science of optics had failed to overcome the mind's paranoid isolation and establish an ethical connection to the outside world, perhaps tragedy could succeed.[14] Dryden, meanwhile, was well aware of the relevance of Descartes' account of tragedy to the development of his own drama. Although Dryden's primary inspiration for the rational paranoia of his heroic plays was Hobbes, he recognized that Hobbes had himself come to this problem via Descartes' *cogito*.[15] The detached pity of Cartesian *générosité* was thus literally a tailor-made response to the problem of Dryden's heroic plays, a method of practicing tragedy that directly addressed the rational egoism of Almanzor. All that remained was to find a more precise illustration of how this practice worked, for neither Charleton nor Descartes had gone beyond the vague suggestion that all good tragedy stirred a detached pity. And so it was that Dryden turned to Shakespeare, translating his earlier intuition about the Bard's great soul into the more particular theory of greatness that he now celebrated in *Richard II*. In Shakespeare, Dryden imagined, was working evidence of the detached pity that could turn the mind's isolation into a social ethics. In Shakespeare was a way to escape the problem of Almanzor's prison.

Yet even here, the escape was far from accomplished. For having uncovered the detached pity of *Richard II*, Dryden found himself at a loss for further examples—hardly surprising given that Shakespeare's concerns were entirely different from the post-Cartesian problem that Dryden was now attributing to him.[16] And so rather than simply celebrating Shakespeare, Dryden discovered that he had to rewrite him, bringing his imagined original in line with his own actual progression. This project began with *All for Love* (1677), Dryden's reworking of *Antony and Cleopatra*. In the play's opening scene—which Dryden claims to prefer to anything that he has written "in this kind" (*Works*, 13.19)—Ventidius watches from afar while Antony is caught up in an elaborate fancy in which he has "turn'd wild, a Commoner of Nature; / Of all forsaken, and forsaking all" (1.1.232–33).[17] Ventidius has previously expressed his disdain for Antony's nervous collapse, and

yet as Antony continues in this vein, imagining himself growing
moss alongside some blasted oak, Ventidius is overcome with pity
(1.1.243). Even so, Dryden is careful to emphasize that this pity
does not imply a consonance of perspective. Rather, it involves the
same remove that we feel at the suffering of Richard II. The climax of the scene occurs when Ventidius is moved by Antony's fantasy to cry out, "Methinks I fancy / My self there" (1.1.240–41).
In his "Apology for Heroic Poetry," Dryden had commented on
Cowley's use of "methought" in the middle of a simile, suggesting that it "mollified" the reader's emotional response by revealing that the image was not grounds for full "belief."[18] The use of
the term in *All for Love* achieves the same effect. Conscious that
he is nearly immersed in another's perspective, Ventidius alerts
the audience to their own remove from the situation, so that even
as they can sense Antony's suffering, they do not participate in it
themselves.

Having introduced his audience to this detached pity, Dryden
then hinges the action of his play upon the inability of Antony himself to practice it. For the first four acts, the Roman commander
finds himself struggling to imagine greatness as anything other than
a competitive dominance. This struggle begins in the opening act
when Antony is dragged from his dejection by Ventidius' reminders
of his soldierly past. Although Antony is slow to respond and never
seems to rid himself of his desire to be with Cleopatra, he at last
reaffirms his dedication to martial glory: "Though, Heav'n knows,
I love / beyond Life, Conquest, Empire; all, but honor: / But I
will leave her" (1.423–25). Love may trump the material trappings
of victory, but honor remains a necessary good. Ventidius' reaction
is immediate: "You breath / Another Soul: your looks are more
Divine; / You speak a Heroe, and you move a God" (1.435–37).
This praise for his newly great soul inspires Antony into a bout of
heroic fancy. Dreaming of smashing enemy formations while the
foremost of his own men lag behind, Antony commits himself to
the comparative logic of honor. He is not great alone. He is great in
contrast to the ignominy of others.

Antony persists in this mode through the beginning of the
next act. After reviewing his troops, he builds himself up further
by sneering at Octavius, and when Cleopatra wanders into view,
he similarly attempts to domineer over her: "I will be justify'd in
all I do / To late Posterity" (2.251–52). Ventidius greets this display enthusiastically, noting "I like this well: he shows Authority"

(2.256). But a few moments later Antony's performance is abruptly deflated by Cleopatra, who begins by assailing his newfound logic of greatness:

> 'twill please my Lord
> To ruine me, and therefore I'll be guilty.
> But, could I once have thought it would have pleas'd you,
> That you would pry, with narrow searching eyes
> Into all my faults, severe to my destruction,
> And watching all advantages with care,
> That serve to make me wretched? Speak, my Lord,
> For I end here. Though I deserve this usage,
> Was it like you to give it?
>
> (2.332–40)

Cleopatra's intention here is to move Antony to pity. She couples her self-deprecation with a critique of his cold authority, replacing Ventidius' "you move a god" with a comment on her lover's "narrow, searching eyes." Although Antony's bullying has left him with a grand sense of self-worth, Cleopatra suggests that it has in fact made him as narrow-souled as the writers that Dryden himself disdains.

The queen follows this critique of Antony's meanness by presenting herself as an example of generosity. Extending a letter in which Octavius promises her terrific wealth, Cleopatra declares, "I have refus'd a Kingdom; / That's a Trifle: / For I could part with life; with any thing, / But onely you" (2.402–5). The effect on Antony is immediate. Vowing that he would prefer apocalypse to losing Cleopatra, he embraces her with the cry: "My Eyes, my Soul, my all!" (2.428). Desperately, Ventidius steps into the breech to demand, "And what's this Toy / in balance with your fortune, Honour, Fame?" Antony, though, has made his choice: "What is't, Ventidius? It out-weighs 'em all" (2.428–30). Even so, the shift in Antony's values is not as great as it might appear. By responding to Octavius' letter with the remark "My Queen's not only Innocent, but Loves me," he reveals that he is driven not just by pity for his lover; he is also motivated by the glee of triumphing over a rival (2.432). His behavior is still tied to a culture of competitive masculinity, so that he responds with disinterest when uncertain about Cleopatra's inclinations and with wild exaltation when believing her won. Although he no longer feels the need to impress Ventidius, Antony has hardly acquired the self-sufficiency required for generosity. His self-worth continues to depend upon others.

Antony's difficulties continue in the third act, when he is caught off-guard by Octavia's offer to make peace between him and Caesar. At first, Antony reacts violently against this proposal, fearing that it will cost him his honor by making him seem indebted to either his enemy or his wife. Again, his actions are driven by his concern over public semblances, but he finds himself suddenly blush when he learns that Octavia has pled nobly for his honor and asked nothing in return. As Dollabella notes, this shame stems from Antony's realization that he has been "out-done in Generosity" (3.310), and Antony acknowledges to Octavia that he "must praise / The greatness of [her] Soul" (3.313–14). Here he makes the connection between generosity and greatness that Cleopatra had earlier drawn, and after struggling for a few moments against his feelings, he confesses at last that he finds "a secret yielding in [his] Soul" (3.336). Still, he cannot quite give himself over to this new emotion: "Pity pleads for Octavia; / But does it not plead more for Cleopatra?" (3.338–39). Unable to get over his attachment to Cleopatra, he makes pity itself into a competition.

Finally though, Antony is able to cast off the competitive mind-set attached to a heroic model of greatness. After hearing that his Egyptian queen has killed herself, he falls on his own sword, only to be approached by a still-living Cleopatra. As is often pointed out, Dryden does not follow Shakespeare in making Cleopatra the author of the false report that causes Antony to kill himself. Instead, he assigns blame to Alexas. While this alteration may make things clearer to the audience, however, Antony has no way of knowing who is ultimately responsible. Instead, he must take Cleopatra's word that the blame lies with Alexas. Moreover, he must also believe her claim that she now intends to kill herself. In response to her insistences, he says,

> Enough: my life's not long enough for more.
> Thou say'st thou wilt come after: I believe thee;
> For I can now believe whate'er thou say'st,
> That we may part more kindly.
>
> (5.381–84)

Antony admits that it does not matter whether Cleopatra's oaths are genuine or not, for all that concerns him is his own desire to part kindly. He is able to devise a peace that is dependent only upon himself, and so instead of demanding more promises, he allows Cleopatra

to do as she will. As in *The Passions,* moreover, the result of this
extreme detachment is not paranoia, but generosity. After Cleopatra
swears to follow Antony in death, he responds,

> But grieve not, while thou stayst
> My last disastrous times:
> Think we have had a clear and glorious day;
> And Heav'n did kindly to delay the storm
> Just till our close of ev'ning.
>
> (5.387–91)

In these gentle lines, Antony reveals his continuing interest in
Cleopatra's happiness. His intellectual remove has not divorced him
from others, but allowed a noble generosity, and his closing metaphor neatly captures this newfound sense of completeness, pairing an
awareness of an encroaching storm with a consciousness of an inner
satisfaction that no outside force can disrupt. Like Descartes' tragic
spectator, Antony is at once concerned and immune.

With this moment, Dryden separates himself completely from
Shakespeare's *Antony and Cleopatra.* Although both plays center
on the conflict between public and private greatness, Shakespeare's
avoids pity, moving instead between lyric romance and dark irony.[19]
It then draws to a close with Octavius' smug claim that the lovers'
"story is / No less in pity than his glory which / Brought them to
be lamented" (5.2.361–63). For Shakespeare's Octavius, the world
is composed of winners and of losers, making an aloof pity for the
vanquished a suitable prologue for his own glorious triumph. In
contrast, *All for Love* offers a practice of pity that eschews this competitive view of greatness. Antony is triumphant in defeat, finding in his dying fall an alternative to both the introverted retreat
and the extroverted heroism that had marked his earlier behavior.
Instead, he discovers a greatness that takes others into account but
does not depend upon them, that is grounded in the self but does
not devolve into solipsism. Following Descartes' own progression,
he discovers generosity.

Despite the grand ambitions of *All for Love,* however, Dryden
was not entirely satisfied with the result, feeling that the inclusion of
Octavia had damaged the audience's ability to pity the lovers:

> I had not enough consider'd, that the compassion she mov'd to herself
> and children, was destructive to that which I reserv'd for Antony and
> Cleopatra, whose mutual love being founded upon vice, must lessen

the favor of the audience to them, when Virtue and Innocence were
oppress'd by it. (*Works*, 13.10–11)

Because the behavior of Antony and Cleopatra inflicts real harm,
Dryden admits, it is difficult not to feel ambivalent toward them.
Whatever the merits of *All for Love*, it had thus failed to communicate
the full experience of generosity, and to remedy this fault, Dryden
undertook another revision of Shakespeare: *Troilus and Cressida*
(1679). Produced roughly a year after *All for Love*, it comes far closer
to being a copy of the original. Dryden lifts not only most of the plot,
but also a slew of poetic images from his source. Yet the faithfulness
of Dryden's version makes his alterations all the more evident, and his
revisions of the ending and of Cressida yield a completely different
experience of tragedy.[20] The dark cynicism of Shakespeare's original
prompted one early twentieth-century critic to dub it "the work of a
man whose soul is poisoned with filth."[21] Other readers of the time
were not inclined to disagree, and although recent interpretations
have seen a more positive spirit at work in the play, there remains a
general consensus that the play is difficult and discomfiting, forcing
the audience to come to grips with a war gone sour. Whatever noble
intentions once existed at Troy have given way to a vista of waste and
dissipation. Even moments that pass for optimism are quickly and
savagely deflated. Ulysses' grand speech on the cosmic chain of order
is exposed as a mask for a cynical willingness to subvert hierarchy
in pursuit of immediate political ends.[22] Troilus' defense of Helen
runs afoul of his own misadventures with Cressida. And finally, after
Hector is slain trying to steal the armor off a dead Greek, Pandarus
oozes onto stage to deliver the play's syphilitic moral: "Good traders
in the flesh…if you cannot weep, yet give some groans, / Though
not for me, yet for your aching bones" (5.10.46–50).

So inconclusive is this ending, so lacking in any sense of purpose
or possibility, that Dryden seems to have thought that Shakespeare
had run out of energy and left the play unfinished: "For the Play
it self, the Author seems to have begun it with some fire; the
Characters of Pandarus and Thersites, are promising enough; but
as if he grew weary of his task, after an Entrance or two, he lets 'em
fall: and the latter part of the Tragedy is nothing but a confusion of
Drums and Trumpets, Excursions and Alarms" (*Works*, 13.226). In
"finishing" Shakespeare's play, Dryden made thousands of changes,
from altering individual words, to rearranging scenes, to adding and
removing characters, to introducing a completely new ending. These
changes have not struck scholars as particularly remarkable; instead,

they have simply seemed evidence for Dryden's investment in the neoclassical standards of decorum, linguistic clarity, and poetic justice.[23] If this is the case, though, it seems odd that Dryden's conclusion is so remiss at satisfying neoclassical ideals. After Cressida dies blameless of any wrongdoing, the play ends when a group of Greeks congregate loosely on stage to offer a series of sardonic perspectives on the value of the war and the institutions it maintains. In effect, Dryden not only preserves the disorganized cynicism of his source, but increases the horror by making Cressida's death seem even more unjust.

Yet even though Dryden's play does not fulfill the prescriptions of neoclassical decorum, it does offer a way out of the numbing despair of Shakespeare's original. Encouraging its audience to pity a world that has no claim on them, Dryden's revision fosters generosity. This project begins in a scene that has no precedent in Shakespeare's play: a debate between Hector and Troilus over Cressida's fate. After Hector extracts a promise from his brother to control his temper, he clumsily tries to soften Troilus' pain by dispensing bad news in stages. Hector's oblique approach, however, only increases Troilus' anxiety, prompting him to moan: "It comes like thunder grumbling in a cloud, / Before the dreadfull break: if here it fall, / The subtile flame will lick up all my blood, / And in a moment turn my heart to ashes" (3.2.270–73). Hector, though, remains oblivious to the failure of his strategy, and when he finally tells Troilus that Cressida must be turned over to the Greeks, he boasts: "Because I knew 'twas harsh, I wou'd not tell; / Not all at once; but by degrees and glimpses / I let it in, lest it might rush upon you / And quite o'repower your Soul" (3.2.275–78). Troilus is stunned by this revelation—so stunned that he refuses to part with Cressida. Hector then tries to bully Troilus with reason, insisting that he must do it not only out of civic duty, but to preserve his honor. This use of reason for coercive purposes is a common strategy in Dryden's tragedies, going all the way back to the attempt in *The Indian Emperour* to convert Montezuma on the rack. As always, it proves fruitless. Troilus insists that love outweighs honor and then demands to know why Hector is not insisting on the return of Helen if he is truly so interested in the good of Troy. At this point, all attempts at communication break down. Hector calls Troilus "a boy" and Cressida "common" (3.2.338; 356). Meanwhile, Troilus defies his brother by laughing at him.

Suddenly, though, when the men are at their most incensed, Troilus is moved to shame by Hector's admission that he still considers him a friend. When Troilus presses his brother to see if this can really be the case, Hector answers, "I blame thee not: / I know thou lov'st; and what can love not do! ... I pity thee, indeed I pity thee" (3.3.414–18). In Dryden's earlier heroic plays, such an offer of pity would almost certainly be rebuffed, for as characters such as Montezuma and Cortez see it, only the base and vulnerable are pitied. The pity that moves Hector, however, is not a gesture of dominance. It is a sign of a generosity that recognizes others' right to self-determination. So it is that Hector's pity leads him to proclaim: "I feel it for thee: Let me go to Priam, / I'le break this treaty off; or let me fight; / I'le be thy champion" (3.2.428–30). In pitying Troilus, Hector thus shows no contempt, but offers to put himself at his brother's service. Similarly moved, Troilus relents and surrenders Cressida. Where reason has failed, a generous pity succeeds.

As warming as this moment is, however, it reveals a flaw in Hector and Troilus' relationship that will soon undo their accord. Lost amid their genial agreement to hand over Cressida is any consideration of what Cressida might want, exposing a tacit misogyny that compromises their newfound generosity. Misogyny is by its very nature incompatible with generosity—to elevate one sex over another is to participate in the comparative logic that the generous reject—and the practical consequences of Hector and Troilus' sexism are illustrated at the outset of act 5, when Andromache reveals to Hector that she has had a terrible premonition of his death. Hector initially refuses to acknowledge her fears, asking her to consider his honor and fame, but he at last relents, saying to his wife: "Therefore to thee, and not to fear of fate, / Which once must come to all, give I this day" (5.1.95–96). At this very moment Troilus appears, and when he finds that Hector has listened to his wife's counsel, mocks him for his cowardice before "superstition ... the worst of fear ... [either] that or fondness of a wife, / (The more unpardonable ill)" (5.1.132–34). Troilus thus fails to discover the same pity for his brother that his brother has earlier shown for him, sneering at Hector for his irrational and even effeminate decision. Stung, Hector abandons both his wife and his selfless generosity, instead reassuming the competitive model of greatness that leads shortly to his death: "I'le through and through 'em, ev'n their hindmost ranks, / Till I have found that large-siz'd boasting fool / Who dare presume my life is his gift" (5.1.160–62).[24]

If Troilus fails to learn from his brother's example toward him, however, there is one character who provides a lasting example of generosity: Cressida. Dryden's "complete overturning of Cressida's reputation" has been claimed by previous scholars as the centerpiece of a clarified spectrum of heroic virtue that spans from Hector's courage to Ulysses' honest wisdom.[25] And yet what is really remarkable about Cressida is not that she works in concert with the men around her, but that her generosity provides an alternative to the competitive ethos of the heroic code. The climax of Dryden's play occurs at the end of the fifth act when an enraged Troilus, convinced that Diomede has stolen Cressida's heart, looms over his rival, threatening to kill him. The audience knows that Troilus is mistaken. Cressida has not been unfaithful; rather, she has been following her father's directive to placate Diomede in order to preserve both of their lives. Now, however, she is placed in an even more difficult position. Once again following her father's advice, she intercedes for Diomede's life, fearing that if he is killed, she and her father will be enslaved by the Greeks.

Troilus takes Cressida's defense of Diomede as final proof of her inconstancy. Despite her protests, he prefers to listen to the taunts of Diomede, who undermines the Trojan's confidence with a series of well-placed digs: "There, take her Trojan; thou deserv'st her best; / You good, kind natur'd, well-believing fools / Are treasures to a woman" (5.2.229–31). Troilus' need to seem dominant over other men prompts him to react violently to this jeer, treating Cressida to a torrent of abuse: "Now hells blewest flames / Receive her quick; with all her crimes upon her. / Let her sink spotted down. Let the dark host / Make room, and point, and hisse at her, as she goes. / Let the most branded Ghosts of all her Sex / Rejoyce, and cry, *Here comes a blacker fiend*! / Let her—" (5.2.250–56). Here, in its rawest form, is the comparative logic that sustains heroic greatness. Unable to detach his personal sense of honor from his relationship to Diomede, Troilus is also incapable of denigrating Cressida without relating her behavior to a host of loose women.

Cressida responds to this abuse by announcing:

> Enough, my Lord; you've said enough:
> This faithlesse, perjur'd, hated Cressida,
> Shall be no more the subject of your Curses:
> Some few hours hence, and grief had done your work;
> But then your eyes had miss'd the Satisfaction
> Which thus I give you.
>
> (5.2.256–61)

With this, Cressida stabs herself. In the same manner that Hector
sacrifices his own interest in order to be Troilus' champion, so too
does Cressida show generosity by placing her lover's wishes ahead of
her own. He wishes her dead, and she obliges. Troilus' response to
this event is divided:

> She's gone for ever, and she blest me dying!
> Cou'd she have curs'd me worse? She dy'd for me;
> And like a woman, I lament for her:
> Distraction pulls me several ways at once,
> Here pity calls me to weep out my eyes;
> Despair then turns me back upon myself.
> (5.2.281–86)

Though Troilus feels a pang of sorrow for Cressida, his focus is on
himself. After toying with the idea that Cressida's generosity was just
a means to torment him, he finds himself caught in a conflict between
pity and self-involved despair. In the end, self-involvement triumphs.
Unwilling to accept his role in this disaster, Troilus turns on Diomede:
"Smilst thou Traitor? Thou instruct'st me best / And turn'st my just
revenge to punish thee" (5.2.288–89). Not to be outdone, Diomede
crows that victory is already his: "I triumph in thy vain credulity, /
Which levels thy despairing state to mine" (5.2.291–92). And the
Greek is right. He has succeeded in ruining Troilus. Unable to see
beyond the logic of heroic greatness, the Trojan warrior has allowed
himself to get dragged into a competition in which there can be no
winners.

And no winners there are. Over the ensuing melee, the Trojan
forces are attacked from both sides and wiped out in a confusion of
killing. At this point, the Greek high-command appears to comment on the destruction. Achilles boasts that—as he previously
avenged Patroclus by killing Hector—so too has he now "reveng'd"
Diomede by killing Troilus (5.2.313). Ajax responds bluntly:
"Reveng'd it basely: / For Troilus fell by multitudes opprest; / And
so fell Hector, but 'tis vain to talk" (5.2.313–15). So disillusioned
that he cannot bring himself to comment further, Ajax sums up
the general sense of weariness that has come to permeate the play.
Trying to salvage a sense of victory from this malaise, Ulysses hur-
riedly launches into what one scholar has referred to as a "radiant
address" on the rights of kings, and yet if anything, this speech only
heightens the cynical tone of the ending.[26] The same man whose
speech on order began the play now brings things to a close by

simply repeating his earlier theme. No new answers have emerged to quiet the doubts raised over the course of the play. Instead, the uncertainties of the war are once again glossed over and ignored by the Greeks' master rhetorician. Far from ridding Shakespeare's play of its oppressive atmosphere, Dryden preserves the unsettled tone that he found repugnant in the original.

But though Dryden concludes on the same note as Shakespeare, the effect of his ending is very different. In Shakespeare's play, the only alternative to despair is the ghoulish irony modeled by Pandarus. Dryden's version presents a more social choice. Cressida's death hangs over these closing moments—less than fifty lines separate her suicide from the end of the play—and the opportunity extended to the audience is to imitate her generosity. Rather than condemning Troilus and the other self-involved warriors who crowd the stage, we can follow Cressida and pity them. In doing so, we separate ourselves from the paranoid egoism and competitive strife embodied in the heroic culture of the Trojan War, regretting an unnecessary suffering from which we are ourselves immune. To pity characters like Troilus is not to identify with them. Indeed, quite the reverse. It is to be concerned for their misfortune while feeling safely insulated from it. Cressida's passing, in effect, shows that the problem that leads Almanzor into his antisocial aggression (and that still triggers this effect in Troilus) can be experienced differently. Instead of being a spur to judgment, it can be an opportunity to practice generosity.

Dryden's motivation for providing this opportunity was simply his desire to escape the particular dilemma of his own stagecraft: the gnawing sense that his foray into skepticism had trapped him into promoting the boorish behavior of characters like Almanzor. But when put in the context of Dewey's evolutionary ethics, it has implications beyond Dryden's artistic development. As we have seen, Dewey's pragmatic response to Darwin opens the possibility that art can be a tool for fashioning progressive society in a world of natural selection. Because art can engage our emotions, our senses, and our other sources of bodily experience, it can make physical problems vivid and immanent, allowing us to practice these problems firsthand. Moreover, by dealing in a specific category of physical problems—ethical problems—art carries us to the threshold of our selves, to the point at which our individual survival intersects with the lives of others. Based on our own private experience, there is no way for us to resolve the problem of allocating food, or of when to forgive, or of how to react to death. Instead, since the remedies to ethical problems depend upon the experience of others, we must open ourselves to outside perspectives, engaging in a practical pluralism. By communicating ethical problems, art thus enlarges the cooperative problem-solving of science, introducing pluralism into walks of life that have seen the example of science as irrelevant or antithetical to their own practice. Encouraging our society to be practically plural through and through, it turns the model of scientific inquiry into the basis of society itself.

This Deweyian vision of the power of art is broad and ambitious, but in *Hamlet, Macbeth*, and the other tragedies discussed in chapters 1 and 2, we saw evidence for its basic plausibility. Using a variety of innovative aesthetic techniques to communicate different experiences of wrestling with death, these tragedies not only foster a practical pluralism, but check the development of religious ideologies that prey upon our fear of mortality. Like Hamlet, we are eased out of our dangerous desire to have answers about not-being and are instead encouraged to take advantage of the social possibilities of practicing death as an ongoing concern, transforming the favorite goad of prophets into an opportunity for progressive politics. But even as *Hamlet* and *Macbeth* promote a problem-based pluralism, they cannot by themselves substantiate the capacity of art to meet one crucial requirement of Dewey's evolutionary ethics: the need to change and develop "as now this, now that, problem [is] uppermost."[27] In a world driven by the changing tides of natural selection, ethical problems too are in flux. Even seemingly constant problems such as death wax and wane in their relative importance, and new problems continually present themselves. If art is to function properly as a source of progressive society, it thus must be adaptive, fitting itself to new problems without sacrificing the practice of cooperative problem-solving. Art, in short, must preserve ethical pluralism through change.

Its capacity to do so is demonstrated by Dryden's *Troilus*. By using the problem that drives the heroic judgments of *The Indian Emperour* to encourage a very different ethical response, the example of Cressida's generosity demonstrates that seventeenth-century tragedy was able to maintain the practice of organic pluralism through the upheavals of the age. Integrating continuity with change, it achieved what Dewey identifies as the core characteristic of an evolutionary ethics: "growth." In Dewey's technical definition, growth is the use of "active capacities to readjust activity to meet new conditions."[28] As its name implies, growth thus involves adaptive change. And yet as Dewey also notes, this readjustment is not without its deeper continuities: "Continuity of growth not atomism is thus the alternative to fixity of principles and aims" (245).[29] While directionless change would seem a recipe for ruin, the pressures of natural selection have not shattered life into atoms, but produced the organic progress we call evolution:

> The ethical import of the doctrine of evolution is enormous... for evolution means continuity of change; and the fact that change may take the form of present growth of complexity and interaction. Significant stages in change are found not in access of fixity of attainment but in those crises in which a seeming fixity of habits gives way to a release of capacities that have not previously functioned: in times that is of readjustment and redirection... The doctrine of progress is not yet bankrupt. The bankruptcy of the notion of fixed goods to be attained and stably possessed may possibly be the means of turning the mind of man to a tenable theory of progress—to attention to present troubles and possibilities.[30]

Seen as an extension of life in a Darwinist cosmos, ethics operates as neither a set of fixed principles nor a forced march to nowhere. Rather, it functions as "a tenable theory of progress"—"tenable" because it abandons the "bankrupt" idea of progress as a journey into some more perfect state. In place of such impossible teleology, it roots progress in our "present troubles and possibilities," that is, in our search for functions that can help us endure the shifting conditions of the moment. Ethics is thus progressive in the sense that it maintains practices that work and jettisons ones that do not, giving human conduct both the continuity and the flexibility of other forms of biological life. Just as a living organism inherits a complex series of faculties from its ancestors, but survives not simply on the strength of these inheritances, but also on the new functions it has acquired through mutation, so too does ethics function by joining the successes of the past to the possibilities of the present. It is in this sense, then, that Dryden's plays participate in a progressive ethics. Rather than moving toward a more perfect form or fundamentally reinventing tragedy each time a new concern emerges, they pair continuity with change, integrating an ongoing commitment to functional diversity with a recognition of the need to adapt to new problems. Like life itself, they grow.

By showing that art can be a source of ethical growth, the preceding study of *Troilus* would seem like the natural place to stop this book. After all, we have now found in seventeenth-century tragedy the very thing that Dewey predicted: a practical method for reconciling our human need for intentional life with the profound nonintentionality of material existence. The turnings of the world may have no ultimate end, but by encouraging ethical growth, problem-based art can generate a living purpose. However, by using seventeenth-century tragedy as their evidence of growth, the preceding chapters have raised one last pressing question: what exactly is it that we mean by an "intentional" ethics? After all, growth is not a human invention. It is a natural force that originates from the blind workings of evolution. Growth thus does not require human intention, and indeed, the ethics outlined over the preceding chapters has much about it that seems distinctly unintentional. Unlike Dewey, Shakespeare and Dryden did not consciously set out to author an adaptive practice rooted in "present troubles and possibilities." Rather, these playwrights treated present troubles as though they were permanent ones, a myopia that leads Dryden to his impossible reading of Shakespeare as a proponent of Cartesian pity. Furthermore, although Shakespeare's varied corpus implies an interest in plural possibilities, Dryden's critical writings suggest that he saw his later works as an improvement on his earlier ones. He did not intend the experience of *The Indian Emperour* to coexist with that of *All for Love*, but expected the latter to supplant the former. That the subsequent performance histories of these plays overlapped was not his wish. To the extent that seventeenth-century tragedy grew to include new problems and new pluralities, this development thus cannot be credited entirely to the intent of its authors. Instead, the intricate function of seventeenth-century tragedy, like the intricate function of the human bodies that wrote it, was shaped by physical pressures that inhered more broadly in the environment. What the previous chapters have offered as an intentional ethics seems on closer inspection to be not so intentional after all.

This apparent contradiction, moreover, is one that extends beyond the particular case-studies of the preceding chapters, reaching deep into the critical practice that inspired this book. One of the major reasons that pragmatism fell out of favor in the mid-twentieth century is that it was suspected of an elaborate tautology that confounded the intentional with the not. For since the focus of pragmatism is what works, and since what works is evident only in retrospect, then isn't pragmatism an after-the-fact justification marauding as an intentional guide? This is the same concern that led Darwin to his own acquiescent naturalism, and it continues to remain a pervasive feature of biological approaches to culture. Perhaps the most famous example of such approaches is memetics: Richard Dawkins' proposal that culture is driven by a process of blind selection in which "memes" (the cultural analogue of genes) mutate and replicate, passing themselves onto subsequent generations or quietly going extinct. If memetics is correct, then human life is nonintentional all the way through, and although Dawkins' hypothesis has not won widespread assent, most contemporary biologists agree that there is likely something preconditioned about our appreciation for artworks like *Hamlet*. After all, since art is a constant property of human life, as omnipresent as child-rearing and other behaviors with a known genetic basis, then it seems probable that our enjoyment of certain art-functions has been genetically hardwired through natural selection. While it may be in the power of authors to write whatever they like, artworks will thus only be celebrated and preserved if they meet the standard instilled in audiences by nature. And so in the end, human culture seems highly constrained, even dictated, by an outside force. What we see as intentional is from the vantage of nature decidedly not.

This tension is easily misinterpreted as a version of the old problem of free will—where before it was god, or fate, or matter and motion that raised questions about the scope of human agency, now it is the mechanism of natural selection that stirs irresolvable conjecture over Nature versus Nurture.[31] But in fact, the difficulty raised by the biological pragmatism of this book is less an entrance to the carousel of metaphysical speculation than an invitation to a more narrow and practical concern. For to establish nature as the working standard for ethics is not to delve into the theoretical mystery of first causes, but more practically to ask whether there is any purpose in intentionally promoting particular forms of art. After all, if nature is the standard against which life is judged, then should we not trust it entirely as our guide? Instead of actively using art to communicate new problem-based practices, should we not just accept that nature is the source of human life and that our own intentions, however important they may seem to us, are in the end of no particular account? In effect, though the past chapters of this book have aimed to achieve an intentional ethics, have they not inadvertently arrived at the opposite practice: the acquiescent naturalism that seems the inevitable fate of any Darwinist approach to human life?

This concern, I will argue over the following and final two chapters of this book, is misplaced. For in fact, the example of seventeenth-century tragedy suggests that problem-based art is not only a useful aid for human life, but one that must be protected from the blind turnings of nature. From a pragmatic perspective, in effect, it is not simply that art should be intentional. Our relationship to art should be intentional as well. To see why this is so, I will break down acquiescent naturalism into its two possible practical applications, each of which intersects with seventeenth-century tragedy in a different way. The first (and less extreme) is to position art as a return to nature, while the second (and more rigorous) is to dismiss all attempts to shape the future direction of art, trusting in the action of nature alone. In effect, the former version of acquiescent naturalism urges an intentional search for nonintentional art, while the latter adopts a strictly laissez-faire stance that treats both art and our relationship to it as nonintentional. I will outline the practical limitations of this latter version in chapter 7, but first I will address the difficulties of the former, using chapter 6 to explore the most historically influential effort to treat seventeenth-century tragedy as a return to nature: Romanticism. As I will show, Romanticism is compatible in theory with a Darwinist ethics. Yet as I will also show, in practice, it is not. For in encouraging us to think of ourselves as extensions of nature, Romanticism constrains life, limiting the possibilities for growth.

Chapter 6

King Lear and the Endurance of Tragedy

When *King Lear* was published in Nicolas Rowe's 1710 edition of *The Works of William Shakespeare*, it was with the warning that its disregard for poetic justice had ruined its tragic effect.[1] For the next hundred years, audiences agreed,[2] but in the nineteenth century, the play's critical fortunes slowly reversed. Schlegel defended Cordelia's death as a moral necessity, Keats celebrated its "close relationship with Beauty & Truth," Coleridge insisted that it was grounded on the "moral verities," Edmund Dowden saw it as the "supreme fact" of moral life, and Lamb and Hazlitt called it "sublime."[3] Yet at the same time as *Lear* was gaining a reputation as Shakespeare's most ethical tragedy, it was also becoming notorious as his least playable one. Though revived by William Macready in 1834, it was never as popular as *Hamlet*, *Othello*, or *Macbeth*. Lamb declared it unactable, and Hazlitt thoroughly agreed. *Lear* may no longer have been seen as an immoral play, but neither was it seen as good theater.

Behind this double-edged assessment of *Lear* was a new approach to the good life: Romantic naturalism. "Nature" was a term much debated by Romantics, but it served a common function in their various philosophies, allowing them to shake free from the constraining structures of conventional morality. Nature was a release from Anglican dogma, from Lockean social contracts, from Kantian reason, and from any other artificial structure that imposed itself upon human existence. It was a return to spirit, to love, to feeling, but most of all, to the origin of being, to the great spring that fed life in the present. And so it was that Romanticism caught *Lear* in a bind. A tragedy without gods or ghosts, but only storms and curses, it seemed a distinctly naturalist work. Indeed, the word "nature" is itself invoked nearly three dozen times (more than in any other Shakespeare play), and Romantic critics delighted in noting that the disasters of the play could all be traced to crimes against nature: filial ingratitude, a love of ceremony, a fear of nakedness. And yet no matter how well *Lear* illustrated the effects of unnatural behaviors, the difficulty for Romantic critics was that even the most naturalistic of plays was still a work of art. This fact might be glossed over on the page, but in performance, the play's artificiality was painfully exposed.[4] For Romantics, *Lear* was thus a contradiction, a work that tried to recover nature by forsaking it.

Romantic naturalism is no longer as dominant as it once was, yet it has remained an important influence on ethics. Many important twentieth-century theories of the good life—from Freud's critique of repression, to Wittgenstein's discussions of the pleasure of ordinary language, to Adorno's neo-Marxist meditations on disenchantment—have been associated with the Romantic drive for a return to authentic nature, and popular interest in an explicitly Romantic approach to seventeenth-century tragedy is such that the best-selling critic on *Lear* is currently Harold Bloom. In light of the Darwinist ethics outlined over the previous chapters, moreover, Romanticism is important because it directly challenges the particular interpretation of Darwinism set forth by pragmatism. For Romantics, nature is not a blind and inhuman force. Rather, it is a source of love and human society. And while this view of nature has been rejected by many post-Romantic thinkers as naïve, the recent discovery by neuroscientists and other biologists that humans have hardwired social emotions suggests that the Romantics were not so far off after all. Though our emotions may not plug us into an eternal order of nature, they do seem to connect us to the social behaviors that allowed our ancient ancestors to survive. This in turn raises the possibility that there could be an evolutionary advantage to treating tragedy not as a source of new problem-based practices, but as a means to return us to our original nature. If this version of naturalism were correct, ethics would be intentional in only the narrowest of senses. Although our relationship to art would be intentional—we would still need to seek out and appreciate appropriately naturalist art—the effect of art would be to return us to a nonintentional state, restoring a natural condition obscured by cultural artifice, philosophical speculation, and the like. Far from having a progressive function in an evolutionary ethics, tragedy would thus have a conservative one, neutralizing the unwelcome consequences of our intentionality. As I will show over the following pages, however, this approach to seventeenth-century tragedy has a major practical drawback: its celebration of our original self flatters us into ignoring our present shortcomings, stripping us of the ambition to grow. In effect, while Romantic naturalism is theoretically viable, it is not practically so. For by encouraging us to focus on our past success, it threatens our future development.

Although Bloom is the contemporary critic most responsible for popularizing a Romantic approach to seventeenth-century tragedy, a more useful introduction can be found in the work of Stanley Cavell.[5] Where Bloom has frequently been accused of perpetuating the complacent humanism of nineteenth-century Romanticism, Cavell's background as a moral philosopher leads him to an extremely rigorous account of tragedy that bears little resemblance to Bloom's genially old-fashioned stylings. Cavell's interest in seventeenth-century tragedy, moreover, cannot be dismissed as the work of a philosopher dabbling in literature, for his essay on *Lear* appears in his earliest book and continues to form the foundation of his ethical project.[6] This attention to *Lear* reflects an investment in what Cavell terms the problem of skepticism. Of this problem, he remarks: "I do not...confine the term to philosophers who wind up denying that we can ever know; I apply it to any view which takes the existence of the world to be a problem of knowledge."[7] For Cavell, skeptics are thus not simply those rogue individuals who deny that we can know that the world (and other minds) certainly exist. Their ranks also include the many philosophers—most prominently Descartes—who search for an epistemology that can definitively convince the doubter.[8] In Cavell's view, this search constitutes a form of madness, for the solution to our doubt is not to try to think our way out of rationally induced solipsism. Rather, it is to participate in the natural processes of life. This participation can take many forms, but the one that interests Cavell the most is language-games. Following Wittgenstein, he argues that language-games are made possible by our acceptance of a set of rules (in his terminology, "a grammar") that lies permanently beyond our rational comprehension. Because we neither make the rules of a language game, nor can ever fully uncover them, these rules are evidence of a social framework that exists beyond the capacity of individual minds to invent or even know. By reading, or writing, or conversing with others, we thus submit to a "form of life" that is larger than ourselves. Although reason will always entertain the possibility that we have imagined everything beyond our own consciousness, our language-games prove that we are not alone.

Because of Cavell's focus on this function of language-games, it is sometimes assumed that he conceives of his own project entirely as a refutation of skepticism.[9] Cavell is not interested, however, in dispensing with skepticism as quickly as possible.[10] Rather, he wants to explore its appeal, intellectual and emotional. For he believes that if we are to purge skepticism's destructive influence, we must grasp why it takes root in the first place. It is over the course of this exploration that Cavell becomes interested in the opening scene of *Lear*. In this scene, Lear calls together his three daughters and asks them to profess their love for him. As a reward, he promises them his kingdom. His eldest two daughters comply, but his favorite and youngest daughter, Cordelia, refuses, claiming that she has reserved her love for her husband. Hearing this, Lear is thrown into a fury, and he banishes her. For this tantrum, Lear is condemned by his older daughters (and by many subsequent interpreters) as a fool, but Cavell sees something more complex at work: an anticipation of Descartes' skeptical desire to lay claim to a certainty that originates entirely within his own perspective. Put in the terminology of Cavell's ordinary-language philosophy, the ritualized ceremony through which Lear attempts to secure his daughters' love is an attempt to create a private language. When Cordelia frustrates this aim by revealing that language-games cannot be played alone, the old king loses his temper, giving vent to a rage that reveals his primitive desire to be thoroughly self-reliant.

This rage, according to Cavell, demonstrates the enormous appeal of skepticism. So strong is the king's desire to be independent that it leads him to banish the daughter he cares most deeply about. Indeed, Cavell suggests that Lear ultimately banishes Cordelia *because* he cares so deeply about her, for it is just such emotional attachment that the old king fears. Even as Cavell believes that *Lear* illustrates the strong pull of skepticism, however, he also thinks that the play can help to cure this sickness. To begin with, *Lear* illustrates that the inevitable end of skepticism is tragedy. To deny the claim that others make upon us is to lose them, a loss that is literalized in Lear's case when his daughter dies.[11] This point, moreover, is reinforced by the experience of play-watching itself. For to watch a play is to witness events in which we do not participate. If we wanted to, of course, we could interrupt the performance, saving

Cordelia. But instead, we sit still in our seats, allowing ourselves to be held in check by the conventions of theater-going. Like the old king, we thus allow our Cartesian detachment from the world to rob us of Cordelia's company. And so like him, we are punished by having our detachment ratified into actual bereavement.

The shock of this loss, Cavell believes, can heal us of the artificial condition of modernity. For just like *Lear*, our daily lives are filled with tragedy that we watch with detachment, convincing ourselves that it is not happening to us, that it is not our business, that there is nothing we should do:

> No death is more mysterious or portentous than others; because every death which is not the fruit of a long life is now unaccounted for, since we cannot or will not account for it: not just because taking local examples, we no longer know why a society may put its own people to death for breaking its rules, nor when it may intervene with death in a foreign place, nor because highway deaths need not happen, not because the pollution of our air and water has become deliberate, nor because poverty has become inflicted—but because we do not know our position with respect to such things. We are present at these events, and no one is present without making something happen; everything which is happening is happening to me, and I do not know what is happening.[12]

Like spectators at a play, we are so conditioned to be passive witnesses that we deny our own agency, ignoring the moral claim that other lives have upon us. Indeed, our detachment is so strong that we no longer can imagine any alternative—what else could we be but spectators to a life that is not happening to us? When we watch *Lear*, however, we realize that there is no physical, actual force that keeps us in our seats; we stay there because we have allowed long custom to assume the aura of inevitability. Wrapping ourselves in a skeptical bubble that conditions us not to intervene in the suffering of others, we have come to inhabit a tragedy of our own making. This is not reason, but madness, and by showing us this, Shakespeare's play encourages us to step out of our seats and embrace the present. Shaking us out of our skepticism, *Lear* allows us to grasp a reality that was always already there.

In taking this view of *Lear*, Cavell adapts an idea of therapy that originates in the work of Wittgenstein and Freud. In his later writings, Wittgenstein argued that philosophy does not generate new knowledge, for it contains neither theories nor explanations.[13] Rather, philosophy helps us play with our current ideas until we

discover how to arrange them in such a way that our questions and
anxieties disappear, leaving us with a feeling of clarity and well-
being. This attitude toward philosophy has parallels to psychoanalysis, and despite Wittgenstein's objections to Freud's theory of mind,
Cavell takes advantage of this resonance in developing his own theory of reading:

> I imagine that [a] credible psychological model of [reading] will have
> to be psychoanalytic in character, yet psychoanalytic interpretations of
> texts have seemed typically to tell us something we more or less already
> knew, to leave us pretty much where we were before we read. It ought
> to help us see that from the point of view of psychoanalytic therapy
> the situation of reading has typically been turned around, that it is not
> first of all the text that is subject to interpretation, but we in the gaze
> or hearing of the text.[14]

To read a text is to undergo psychoanalytic therapy, to literally be the
patient of the text, so that it is we and not the text that is interpreted.[15]
Cavell continues: "The goal of the encounter is not consummation
but freedom. Freedom from what, to do what? In the picture of psychoanalytic therapy, casting ourselves as its patient, its sufferer...the
goal is freedom from the person of the author" (52–53). In short,
Cavell views literature in the same way that Wittgenstein views philosophy and Freud views analysis. The ultimate goal of literature is to
free us from its author, rendering itself unnecessary, and this freeing,
Cavell claims, is precisely what *Lear* accomplishes. Although most of
us are able to refrain from physically interrupting the performance of
Shakespeare's play, we nevertheless leave the theater with a desire to
reconnect with life. We will not just sit and watch, allowing tragedy
to unfold before us. We will intervene. The art of *Lear* thus undoes
the artificial sense of detachment bred by modern skepticism, and as
artifice deconstructs itself, we are returned to nature.

Like other Romantic readings of tragedy, Cavell's interpretation
thus culminates in a return to nature. And like other Romantics,
Cavell sees this return as inherently ethical because he views nature
as the entity that binds all life together into "love."[16] At the same
time as Cavell provides a classically Romantic reading, moreover,
he appears to insulate himself against the critique typically leveled against Romantic approaches to seventeenth-century tragedy: that they encourage us to root our understanding of nature
too deeply in ourselves. Coleridge famously remarked, "I have a
smack of Hamlet myself," and though this self-referential approach

has led Romanticism to be widely viewed over the past century as uncritical, Bloom has doggedly maintained it as the centerpiece of his interpretation of seventeenth-century tragedy: "Insofar as we ourselves value, and deplore, our own personalities, we are the heirs of [Shakespeare's characters]."[17] Indeed, Bloom not only uses his observations of his own personality as his standard for judging plays like *Lear*, but indulges in direct quotations of his own work ("to appropriate from myself…"), quite literally offering himself as the authority for his own claims (4). This tending into self-love is the major reason that Romanticism has come to be seen as unethical—it is the source of Hegel's racial hierarchies, Wordsworth's nationalism, Wagner's anti-semitism, and other similarly dim moments. And so it is that Cavell's work seems especially appealing. For his work offers the hope that a Romantic ethics can be rooted not in one's own self-regard, but in one's regard for others.

In fact, however, Cavell's Romanticism is not as different from Bloom's as it initially appears. The crucial moment in Cavell's reading is his interpretation of Cordelia's death, for it is in this moment, Cavell suggests, that Lear is at last able to recognize the destructive effects of his own self-love:

> The cause of tragedy is that we would rather murder the world than permit it to expose us to change. Our threat is that this has become a common option; our tragedy is that it does not seem to us that we are taking it…It is the enormity of this plain fact which accompanies the overthrow of Lear's mind, and we honor him for it.[18]

According to Cavell, Cordelia's death thus prompts Lear to realize his monstrous egoism. The old king has done everything to avoid the claims of his daughter's love, even telling himself that she is the one avoiding his love, that she is the one who will not "change" for him. But in her death, the foolishness of this becomes clear, and the old king relents. At last, he changes. Admitting the claim that other people make upon him, he forfeits himself.

Cavell's reading of this moment is elegant and compelling, but it is also intensely self-referential. To begin with, by framing Cordelia's death as a comment on Cartesian skepticism, Cavell enlists the play in the service of a cause that could not possibly have concerned a pre-Cartesian writer like Shakespeare.[19] Severing *Lear* from its origins, Cavell assimilates it into his own personal quandary. By repositioning *Lear* in this way, moreover, Cavell overlooks the fact that the old king has not changed as much as he himself would like.

Certainly, the Lear who hunches over his daughter's corpse insisting that she will awaken—"This feather stirs, she lives!"—is in one sense very far removed from the old man who banished his daughter (5.3.266). No longer is his sole concern his own well-being, for now he is able to connect his well-being to the well-being of others. But in another sense, Lear's condition has not changed. No less than his ceremonial abdication or his invocations of the gods, his belief that Cordelia will rise is a product of his mistaken belief that his private reasons carry an absolute authority. When he demands of his daughter's body, "Why should a dog, a horse, a rat, have life, / And thou no breath at all?" he is still clinging fast to his own logic of life, to his personal sense of what is reasonable (5.3.307–8). So it is that when Kent and Edgar kneel to comfort him, he snaps: "A plague upon you, murderers, traitors all! / I might have sav'd her, now she's gone for ever!" (5.3.270–71). Cavell praises Lear in this moment for taking responsibility for Cordelia's death,[20] but really the king seems to be doing just the reverse, blaming others for interrupting the ritual through which he would somehow have resurrected his daughter. Like his curses, this moment reveals Lear in the midst of a self-delusion that isolates him from those who would help him, and his dying moments are spent indulging in the fantasy that Cordelia's body has life: "Look on her! Look her lips, / Look there, look there!" (5.3.311–12). As much as Cavell wants to see Lear shake off his egoism, the old king persists in his false reasons.

Indeed, in this moment, it is not Lear who finds Cavell's ethic of love, but Cavell who slips into Lear's ethos of self-concern. In response to Lear's failed efforts to revive his daughter, Cavell announces, "In Cordelia's death there is hope, because it shows the gods more just—more than we had hoped or wished... Cordelia's death means that *every* falsehood, every refusal of acknowledgement, will be tracked down...there is absolute justice."[21] Just as Lear seeks comfort in the belief that his daughter's life must be more valuable than that of an animal, Cavell takes solace in the thought that Cordelia's death proves the existence of "absolute justice." But despite being dressed in the language of universalism, this is a fundamentally egocentric conclusion. For it is *not* just for Cordelia to die. She is the victim of Lear's crime, not the perpetrator. To suggest that there is absolute justice in her death is thus to reduce her to a symbol—she is not a real person who has her own claim to justice, but a cipher whose significance lies entirely in what she means to her father. In effect, like Lear, Cavell avoids the claim that Cordelia makes upon his own interpretation of the world. He fails to acknowledge her, instead treating her as an extension of his own perspective.

This tendency of Romanticism to lead to moral self-absorption is what led Dewey to abandon it. As he notes, in turning back toward some originary authentic, Romantics pull out of the world and into themselves, losing the present, losing their connection to others.[22] The method of Romanticism, in effect, is at odds with its values, and because Dewey shared these values, he wanted a more effective practice for achieving them. In pragmatism's emphasis on problem-solving, he found it. An investment in shared problems not only connects us to the here and now of our physical existence; it also offers a practical source of community, binding us together in a mutual search for relief. Problems thus provide what Romanticism promises: a presentness that joins us to other lives. And indeed, when the ending of *Lear* is read from the vantage of Dewey's problem-based ethics, it functions as a far more effective source of the qualities that Cavell associates with ethical practice. The first step in this approach is to accept that *Lear* should not be read as an engagement with Cartesian skepticism. Instead, it should be approached from the perspective of the pre-Cartesian problem that troubles Hamlet and Macbeth: the indeterminacy of our future state. In the final scene of *Lear*, this very perspective is expressed by Kent, who upon witnessing Lear's helpless attempts to revive Cordelia, asks: "Is this the promis'd end?" (5.3.264). Here is the same doubt that accompanies Hamlet's mortal wound and that strikes Macbeth when he learns the secret of MacDuff's birth. Here is a doubt that lays bare the inability of human reason to distinguish the riddle from its solution, to tell whether the logic of life has at last unfurled itself or remains twisted still. This doubt opposes Lear's egoistic conviction, and it has an immediately social end. No sooner has Kent asked his question than it is picked up by Edgar: "Or image of that horror?" (5.3.265). Like Kent, Edgar cannot grasp the ultimate meaning of Cordelia's death, struggling to fathom whether it reveals the intrusion of the future on the present, or some mystery yet to be unraveled, or nothing at all. Where Lear is certain that he could have saved his daughter, Kent and Edgar thus discover the same uncertain sense of their tomorrow. The old king dies alone, but Kent and Edgar doubt together.

This shared doubt offers a very different window into nature than the one offered by Romanticism. As we have seen, Romantics view nature as an intrinsic good, whether because it was set up that way by some benevolent force, or because (from a Darwinist revision of Romanticism) it is the form of life that has allowed our survival to this point. In contrast, pragmatism views nature not just as the source of our current existence, but as the possible cause of our future extinction. For nature has neither long-term plans nor lasting affections. It is directionless, inhuman, and will extinguish us as readily as it created us. While the Romantic finds ecstasy and eternity in recovering the nature of life, the pragmatist therefore discovers a difficult and endless "labor."[23] To recover the way of things from artifice and human dream is not to dig down to a benevolent order beneath. It is to unearth the blind violence that we have tried so pathetically to tame with indulgent philosophies and comfortable customs, to feel the storm that gives Lear such contempt for his fine robes. From this perspective, the baubles that we fashion to block out nature are not the problem. They are simply a buckling repair, a quick fix that has bred in us the delusion of permanent safety. The real problem is nature itself. And so the answer cannot be to do away with artifice, to tear off our clothes and stand naked with Lear—after all, artifice is the only shield our poor bodies have against the rain. Rather, the answer is to improve on the labors of the past, to replace ruined fashions with new art, to develop a more durable style of life. The task we inherit from nature, in short, is not a going back. It is the need to build a new tomorrow.

This sense of the task ahead is the final experience of *Lear*. In the destruction of Cordelia, Kent and Edgar find what Dewey calls our "potential doom of disaster and death," and when Lear's passing stuns Edgar into silence and leaves Kent with only the energy to prophecy his own demise, it falls to Albany to deliver the play's grim conclusion:

> The weight of this sad time we must obey,
> Speak what we feel, not what we ought to say:
> The oldest hath borne most; we that are young
> Shall never see so much, nor live so long.
>   (5.3.324–27)

Surrounded by the bodies of the dead, Albany discovers Lear's disgust at artifice. It is a time to "speak what we feel, not what we ought." With this reminder of the nature of things comes a suddenly diminished sense of the present: "We that are young / Shall never see so much, nor live so long." Life is less significant now, its possibilities literally stunted. Yet in this realization is not the utter despair that crushes Lear. For Albany, like Kent and Edgar, recognizes the problem as a common one. In the tradition of Malcolm and Fortinbras, who close *Macbeth* and *Hamlet* by reminding their listeners that tragedy joins them together, so too does Albany speak in commonalities: "We must obey...what we feel...we that are young..." With this sense of a common tomorrow, moreover, comes the sense of an active tomorrow. Determined to preserve the coming time, no matter how diminished it might be, Albany installs Kent and Edgar as the leaders of a recovery—"you twain, / Rule in this kingdom, and the gor'd state sustain"—and while Kent brushes aside this request, the hope for a human-fashioned future endures in the form of Albany's final lines (5.3.320–21). For where Lear's final sentences wobble between prose and blank verse, syllables sprawling over, syntax struggling with metrics, Albany's are perfect couplets. Like the rhymes with which Malcolm promises to build a better Scotland, or those with which Hamlet announces his plot to catch the conscience of the king, they are a gentle reminder of the worth of artifice, of the power of plans and plays to address the problems of the present.

By suggesting that there can be a practical place for artifice in human life, this reading of *Lear* suggests that there can also be a practical place for tragedy in ethics. Like any work of art, *Lear* evinces the possibilities of human ingenuity. Its plots, its characters, and its aesthetic techniques are all evidence that nature can serve as the inspiration to build something new, to create words and worlds and deeds that have their origins in our experience of life, but are not purely determined by it. Moreover, because the focus of *Lear* is the frailty of our past responses to the unending violence of natural existence, its continued commitment to craft is particularly encouraging. It does not quail under the horrors of the inhuman cosmos it describes; instead, it responds with new inventions. The commitment that *Lear* makes to promoting an active art is not, of course, absolute proof that such art is possible. Yet from the vantage of a practice-based ethics, it is practical to assume so. If this assumption is wrong, nothing has been lost, for there was nothing to be gained. But if it is right, it ensures that we do not waste the opportunity that life provides. Within a practice-based ethics, in short, hope becomes practical, and this is why—even after the death of Cordelia has ruined idealism— hope can cling to the final lines of *Lear*. There may be no perfect nature to return to, but we can still push artfully ahead.

Even as *Lear* answers the challenge of Romantic naturalism, however, it does not address the more rigorous naturalist claim that there is no use in seventeenth-century tragedy at all. For it is no longer the seventeenth century. New methods of ethics have emerged, and since it is these methods that are surviving the pressures of the present, have they not proved themselves the most effective source of ethical practice? Why then should we go back? Though it may be in our power to revive the ways of seventeenth-century tragedy, to do so is as good a use of our time as attempting to revive the dodo. It had its place in nature, and now it has its place no more. Like Romanticism, this laissez-faire naturalism is theoretically consistent with Darwinism, and no less a pragmatist than Dewey himself seems to incline toward it at moments in *Art as Experience*. In the following chapter, I will therefore explore its practical consequences by tracing the historical decline of the problem-based ethics of seventeenth-century tragedy. As I will show, this ethics was replaced by a method that—while theoretically ingenious—is less practically suited to coping with the pressures of a Darwinist cosmos. Far from offering a warming lesson on the inevitable wisdom of selection pressures, the subsequent history of seventeenth-century tragedy thus provides a warning. When we trust these pressures to determine ethics, we place our lives at the mercy of the horror that *Lear* discovers: a world that has no care for us.

Chapter 7

The Progress of Ethics

I doubt not, but from self-evident Propositions, by necessary Consequences, as incontestable as those in Mathematicks, the measures of right and wrong might be made out.[1]
—John Locke, *An Essay Concerning Human Understanding* (1690)

With this optimistic claim, Locke joined a long tradition of philosophers who were confident that the standards of human conduct could be derived without practice or experiment. Since at least the time of Plato, philosophers had believed that the mind could discover "the measures of right and wrong" by relying entirely on its own private logic, deriving laws of behavior as perfect and incontestable as the laws of geometry. Indeed, it was for this reason that philosophers had so long regarded the moral purchase of tragedy with concern. Tragedy, after all, was not built in a regular fashion out of first principles. Instead, it had tumbled its way into being, born out of the accidents of physical circumstance, the sudden inspirations of poets, and the strange enthusiasms of audiences. In an ideal world, there would be no need for tragedy, and although tragedy had established itself in this world by playing upon the more primitive parts of human nature, its actions needed to be guided by the firm hand of philosophy. And so Plato banned tragedies that included depictions of vice; Aristotle deductively proved that certain tragic plots were more morally suitable than others; and the Stoics looked forward to a time when tragedy would be purged of the taint of *pathos*. Two millennia prior to Locke, philosophers were thus already so certain that right and wrong could be speculatively deduced that they did not hesitate to overrule what generations of practice had established as an effective source of social conduct.

But though Locke's mathematical morality was not entirely original, it did add something distinctly new. This invention was the tabula rasa, and as I will show over the following pages, it provided a powerful new justification for subordinating tragedy to philosophy. Indeed, this justification proved so powerful that it not only convinced Locke's own followers, but passed into the hands of his critics, surviving long after many of the particulars of Locke's moral philosophy had fallen away. The tabula rasa, in short, was a success, apparent proof that philosophers had been right to suppose that their abstract speculations provided a better foundation for ethics than the physical practices of tragedy. And yet, as I will also show, there is reason to doubt that the historical durability of Locke's invention is evidence of its ethical utility. For while the tabula rasa is compelling in theory, it has proven less so in execution: not only does it retain the very difficulties that Locke set out to fix, but it introduces new ones that he did not anticipate. Read this way, the tabula rasa stands less as proof of the prescience of philosophy than as evidence that the processes of history—like the processes of natural selection—do not automatically preserve the most effective forms of ethical practice. It is evidence, in effect, of the danger of allowing a rigorously laissez-faire naturalism to form the foundation of ethics. We may owe our original existence to the unguided turnings of nature, but we would do well to place our future in more intentional hands, for life can lead us down blind alleys from which art must help us to escape.

The inspiration for Locke's great success came to him during a moment of failure:

> Five or six Friends meeting at my Chamber, and discoursing on a Subject very remote from this, found themselves quickly at a stand, by the Difficulties that rose on every side. After we had a while puzzled our selves, without coming any nearer a Resolution of those Doubts which perplexed us, it came into my Thoughts, that we took a wrong course; and that, before we set ourselves upon Enquiries of that Nature, it was necessary to examine our own Abilities, and see, what Objects our Understandings were, or were not fitted to deal with.[2]

Struggling to resolve his doubt, Locke suddenly realized that the issue was the doubt itself. Because he and his friends had set their sights on resolving a particular problem, they had got off on the wrong foot. Allowing themselves to be guided not by what the mind was capable of doing, but by what they wanted it to do, they had begun their efforts at objective inquiry with a subjective bias. Locke therefore counseled his friends to start over from scratch. Before they addressed their particular concerns about truth, or happiness, or the good, they needed a general method of inquiry that reflected their own powers of understanding. Their accounting of life, in short, should begin with an accounting of themselves, and to ensure that this really was a fresh start, Locke urged his friends to return their minds to their original state of ignorance. The search for enlightenment must begin not with a specific problem, but with total blankness.

As Locke took pains to establish in the opening portions of his essay, this blankness was the most extreme form of doubt possible, more extreme than any that had been imagined by previous philosophers. For though other philosophers had used skepticism to clear the mind, none of them had ever proposed that the mind could be cleansed of all its contents. Even Descartes, the most famous recent advocate of beginning philosophy with extreme doubt, had imposed a practical limit on the effects of skepticism, declaring that nothing could purge the mind of its innate ideas. Rather than emptying the mind, Cartesian doubt simply cleared away rootless opinions, revealing the solid foundation underneath. Against this restricted view of skepticism, Locke denied that "there are in the Understanding certain *innate Principles*; some primary Notions...Characters, as it were stamped upon the Mind of Man" (1.1.1). There was nothing, in short, permanently inscribed in the mind, and so there was nothing to stop it from being completely emptied.

Locke was so successful in separating himself from Descartes that the tabula rasa was often misunderstood in the nineteenth and early twentieth centuries as a direct reversal of *The Meditations*. Where Descartes was a rationalist, the argument went, Locke was the father of empiricism, a philosopher who rooted knowledge not in the mind, but in the senses. As a great deal of recent scholarship has shown, however, Locke's account of the tabula rasa led him and his followers to a very different understanding of empiricism than the one embraced by modern experimental science.[3] For Locke's extreme doubt did not just discount innate ideas; it also embraced the concerns that previous skeptical thinkers had raised about the reliability of the senses. Locke therefore rejected sensory experience as a reliable foundation for moral truth, ranking it below both intuitive and demonstrative knowledge.[4] Instead, he rooted morality in a different form of experience: the mind's observation of its own free activity. This observation, he believed, would reveal the eternal laws of human cognition, making it a sure foundation for his "Mathematick" method (4.3.18). To the extent that Locke embraced empiricism, it was thus a phenomenological empiricism, one that gave license to philosophers to retreat into their minds to reconstitute ethics anew. The tabula rasa was in every sense a fresh beginning, a blankness that did not just make possible a new future, but washed away the public problems that had grounded ethical practice in the past. Locke had promised to rid ethics of its problems, and with his invention, he literally made good.

If the tabula rasa was successful in displacing a problem-based approach to ethics, however, it was significantly less proficient at eliminating what Locke saw as the shortcomings of this earlier method. Locke had two practical concerns about problem-based ethics. First, by allowing ethics to exist as a hodge-podge of local responses to local concerns, it fragmented human society into different spheres of practice. And second, by eliminating a universal method for responding to moral doubt, it seemed to suggest that the only certain way to secure final agreement was brute force— "fire and sword."[5] So it was that Locke justified his new approach by claiming that it would eliminate both concerns: substituting a universal-starting point for the endless individual questions that had initiated inquiry in the past, the tabula rasa would offer a means for unifying ethics without resorting to coercion. In theory, this made utter sense; and yet in practice, Locke's reform failed to make good on his promises. To begin with, it did little to promote consensus. Although liberalism grew to include a broad collection of thinkers from Smith and Kant to de Tocqueville and Mill, these thinkers found themselves deeply divided on matters such as the role of government, the rights of individuals, and even the nature of freedom. At the heart of this disagreement was the growing sense that one person's version of liberty was an infringement on another's actual autonomy. Classical liberalism became notorious for imposing itself—Locke himself supported not only colonialism, but capital punishment—and yet when social liberals attempted to eliminate this autocratic bent by promoting practices such as economic leveling and pure democracy, they were accused by their more libertarian brethren of depriving individuals of their freedom to property and of inviting a mob rule that threatened the rights of minorities.[6] What Locke envisioned as a clear path to free society thus turned out in practice to be highly partial indeed.

The subsequent history of the tabula rasa in the hands of radical philosophers, moreover, did nothing to rid ethics of disunity. Nietzsche initiated radical ethics by summoning up Kant's vision of the logical consequence of the tabula rasa: the skeptic's denial of "space, time, and causality" and all other *aeternae veritates.*[7] Stripped of these external standards of proof and possessing nothing more than the disconnected impressions of his own consciousness, Nietzsche found that he could make sense of life only by imposing his will, a process that he dubbed "affirmation" (*Bejahung*). The resulting logic had only the authority of the mind that willed it, but since this authority was the only conceivable rejoinder to the tabula rasa, it was the only possible foundation for ethics.[8] This private judgment seemed to spell the end of Locke's dream of free society, and yet Nietzsche provocatively claimed the reverse. For if the ethical life was an ongoing cycle of skeptical critique and moral affirmation, then the past centuries of philosophical disagreement over the nature of liberty were not proof of the uselessness of grounding ethics in total doubt. Rather, they were evidence of the active ethos that characterized a free existence. What seemed the failure of a progressive ethics was in fact the sign of its success.[9] The victory that Nietzsche wrested from defeat was, however, a qualified one. For by shifting the criteria for a successful ethics, Nietzsche also eliminated one of the two practical reasons for the tabula rasa. After all, if Nietzsche was correct in claiming that ethics was fundamentally non-normative, then the pluralism that had bothered Locke about practice-based ethics was no longer a reason for dismissing it. Now, the only remaining practical justification for the tabula rasa was that it eliminated coercion from ethics, making behavior a matter of free choice. And yet here too, Nietzsche's reform did not so much establish the practical value of the tabula rasa as call it into question. Following Nietzsche, radical thinkers began to suspect that the method of skepticism that they had adopted from liberal moral philosophy had in fact adopted them. As Foucault observed in one of his late essays, the more that radical thinkers struggled to free themselves from the "manner of philosophizing" established by liberal humanists like Locke, the more they found themselves engaging in it.[10] For when radicals set out to question the assumptions of liberal humanism, they did so by shedding their inherited cultural assumptions and returning themselves to a state of autonomous blankness. In effect, they precisely repeated the move that Locke himself had made in the *Essay.* In attempting to resist, they had actually complied, so that what seemed like active skepticism was in fact a form of accidental submission. Radical ethics, Foucault declared, had been the victim of "blackmail."[11]

Foucault's discovery of this latent coercion, moreover, did little to alleviate its practical effects. His provisional response was to suggest that ethics should disown Locke and Kant's method in favor of a "critique of ourselves" that transitioned to an "experimental" attitude.[12] But far from distinguishing Foucault from Enlightenment liberals, this new strategy mirrored Locke's method of beginning ethics with an active critique of his own consciousness that transitioned into an "experiment in himself."[13] Foucault's solution to being blackmailed, in short, was not to develop a radical new foundation for ethics. Rather, it was to adopt Nietzsche's strategy of affirmation, claiming Locke's manner of philosophizing as his own. From the vantage of a purely speculative philosophy, this strategy may be valid, but on a practical level, it is the functional equivalent of a shackled man claiming that he has chosen his indenture. It does nothing to alter the dynamic that has constrained the options for radical ethics, and it reveals that Foucault was right to suspect that there was something inherently coercive about Locke's method. The tabula rasa, after all, was not simply an attempt to set the mind free; it was also an attempt to unify ethics by homogenizing the vast diversity of human concerns into a transcendent state of doubt. In both classical and social liberalism, this homogenization is masked somewhat by the fact that its practitioners soon leave total doubt behind in order to take up the labor of building a new ethics. But in radicalism, its constrictive effect is plainly evident. Since radicals root autonomy in an ethos of questioning, their response to any infringement on their freedom is active skepticism, and the more they turn in this direction, the more they converge on the same disembodied, departicularized, doubt. In effect, the tabula rasa not only establishes a universal starting-point for ethics, but channels dissent down a single path, funneling all ethical activity toward the same outcome. What seems a source of active individuality turns out to be a predetermined end.

Although Locke hypothesized that the tabula rasa would rid ethics of the fragmentation and coercion that characterized problem-based practice, its physical effect thus suggests otherwise. Liberalism has been fraught with unwelcome divisions, while radicalism has been hampered by unwanted influence. Moreover, the tabula rasa has not only failed to distinguish itself positively from a practice-based ethics; it has also eliminated the most useful feature of this older approach. As we have seen over the previous six chapters, the problem-based ethics developed in seventeenth-century tragedy serves a practical purpose: organic pluralism. Although the problems raised in these tragedies encourage a diversity of response—a diversity actively encouraged by the plays themselves—they also establish a strong basis for voluntary community. To share a problem is to have a reason to collaborate, a reason to put aside personal differences for a common good. Furthermore, to share a problem is to have a common standard for adjudicating differences, for if this problem is alleviated by a particular approach, then the approach is instrumentally valid. In short, a problem-based approach to ethics may not be perfect—how after all could any practice be?—but it serves a pragmatic purpose. Alerting people to a shared difficulty, it gives them a reason to work together, a method to conduct this work, and a standard for judging the results. All of this utility was necessarily purged from ethics by the tabula rasa, its place taken by the circular hostilities of speculative concerns. What Locke offered as a moral improvement has instead turned out to be a social impoverishment.

Had Locke's tabula rasa simply been an experiment in speculative ethics, this loss would be of no great concern. The fallout would have been confined to the aery castles of philosophy, and the physical world would have gone on unchanged. One of the central claims of pragmatism, however, is that the wayward musings of the mind often detract from physical life. Like Hamlet's brooding turn, vain speculation can cause physical hurt to ourselves and others by distracting our care from more practical pursuits, and so it has been with Locke's reform. For this reform has not only fueled centuries of clashing political idealism; it has also led to the physical dismantling of a more practical alternative: seventeenth-century tragedy.[14] In rejecting the problem-based ethics that preceded him, Locke necessarily also rejected tragedy. The longevity of tragedy gave it no standing in Locke's account, for his autonomous method held cultural authority in distrust. Nor did the logic of tragedy hold any appeal. Public performances had no place within Locke's introspective epistemology, and so he blanked out theater entirely, making no mention of it in his writing. His heirs, moreover, went further—for where Locke had simply ignored tragedy, subsequent advocates of the tabula rasa appropriated it, breaking it from its original seat and fixing it as an ornament in their own speculative philosophies. Following the example of Adam Smith, British liberals frequently invoked *Hamlet* as an expression of their own moral views,[15] and by the mid-nineteenth century, they had declared the play an ideal means to export an "emancipating rationality" to India and the other colonies of the empire.[16] At the end of the century, Nietzsche then claimed *Hamlet* as a partner in a radical ethics by suggesting that the prince's disgust at contemporary morality embodied the skeptical freedom that had characterized the Enlightenment before it ossified into positivism, Romanticism, and other strange faiths. And in the early twentieth century, the skeptical blankness that Locke had used to free himself from history was adapted by a new wave of formalists to liberate literature from biography, an approach that allowed John Crowe Ransom to claim in *The New Criticism* that the verse of *Hamlet*, like a "democratic state," was rich with endless voices.[17] The play that had begun as part of a practice-based ethics was thus used to promote a speculative ideal of liberty, and in our own time, this approach has provided a foundation for poststructuralists and postcolonialists, new historicists and cultural materialists, liberal humanists and formal pluralists to claim seventeenth-century tragedy as a source of critical thinking, active doubt, interpretive diversity, and other instances of the freedom that the tabula rasa installs as the basis of the good life.[18] So it is that students of tragedy now learn to debate the ethical value of *Hamlet* by reading it through the phenomenological investigations of Locke and Kant, Mills and Nietzsche, Derrida and Foucault. Once a rival to philosophy, tragedy has been pressed into the role of courtier.

By treating plays like *Hamlet* as an extension of speculative ethics, this critical turn has not just cost tragedy its independence; it has also cost us its practical benefit. Instead of serving as a source of organic pluralism, *Hamlet* has become another tabula rasa: a site of circular antagonisms. Perhaps most famously, there is the example of New Historicism, which emerged in the late twentieth century as an effort to incorporate seventeenth-century tragedy into a radical ethics. As Stephen Greenblatt writes at the end of *Renaissance Self-Fashioning*: "In all my texts and documents, there were, so far as I could tell, no moments of pure, unfettered subjectivity; indeed, the human subject itself began to seem remarkably unfree, the ideological product of the relations of power in a particular society."[19] Read through the lens of radical philosophy, seventeenth-century tragedy thus leads back to the old chestnut of free will, inspiring Greenblatt to a speculative meditation on the distastefulness of determinism: "[Yet] all of the sixteenth-century Englishmen I have written about here do in fact cling to the human subject and to self-fashioning. How could they do otherwise? What was—or, for that matter, is-the alternative?" (256–57). With this pivot from the past to the present, Greenblatt interrogates his own autonomy, a move that allows him to close with the declaration: "I want to bear witness at the close to my own overwhelming need to sustain the illusion that I am the principle maker of my own identity" (257). Like Foucault, Greenblatt borrows Nietzsche's strategy of *Bejahung*, affirming himself.

For all of the theoretical elegance of this conclusion, however, its practical effect is precisely the same as Locke's original innovation: an ethics that champions freedom but compels agreement. To begin with, there is the matter of Greenblatt's maneuver itself. Greenblatt does not credit Nietzsche or anyone else for his strategy of affirmation; instead, like Foucault when he adopts Locke's "experiment in oneself" as though it were his own invention, Greenblatt remains silent about his inheritance to "sustain the illusion" of his own identity. Just as Greenblatt echoes Foucault's predicament, moreover, so too have Greenblatt's readers echoed his. After *Renaissance Self-Fashioning* was published, it was quickly criticized by other radicals, most prominently by Jonathan Dollimore. In *Radical Tragedy*, Dollimore notes that he shares Greenblatt's belief that "Jacobean tragedy anticipates, and is therefore usefully explored in relation to, a central tenet of [Foucault's] analysis, namely that the essentialist concept of 'man' mystifies and obscures the real historical conditions in which the actual identity of people is rooted."[20] Even so, Dollimore disapproves of Greenblatt's conviction that "to abandon the illusion that we make our identity is 'to abandon the craving for freedom'" (181). This, in Dollimore's view, is not an ethical stance but an abnegation of moral responsibility. As an alternative, he posits: "But perhaps the reverse is true, by abandoning the fiction we may embrace freedom and in and through the '*affirmation* [which] *determines the noncentre otherwise than as loss of the centre*'" (181). Dollimore thus pits Derrida's ideal of affirmation against Greenblatt's Foucauldian ethics—and yet far from establishing a clear alternative to *Renaissance Self-Fashioning*, this turn to Derrida reveals that Dollimore has found no alternative at all. Greenblatt, as we have seen, commits himself to an ethos of affirmation that he recovers with Foucault's help from Nietzsche. And while Dollimore gives Derrida credit for his own ideal of affirmation, the above-quoted passage comes from the section of "Structure, Sign, and Play" where Derrida aligns his own ethos with "Nietzschean *affirmation.*"[21] In effect, rather than establishing a different form of ethical practice, Dollimore arrives at the one that Greenblatt had already established.[22] The only difference is that it now carries a different name. Imitating Greenblatt's appropriation of Foucault—which itself imitates Foucault's appropriation of Locke—Dollimore thus reveals the claustrophobic catch of a blank-slate approach to ethics. Since it is our differences from others that make us free, and since it is freedom that makes us ethical, Dollimore is bound by his own standard of ethics to force a distinction between himself and Greenblatt. He must establish his originality or lose his self-worth. In the process, Dollimore precisely reverses Hamlet's hard-won epiphany. Where Shakespeare's prince learns to abandon his speculative definition of self, Dollimore acts like Hamlet when he critiques Horatio in the opening act, alienating a friend in order to theorize his own individuality. And so it is that the tabula rasa reverses the practical effect of seventeenth-century tragedy in general. By purging the mind of all pressures past, it transforms a source of organic pluralism into a site of fraught likeness, encouraging readers of *Hamlet* to dispute their shared identity.

Read this way, Locke's reform stands as a parable on the danger of allowing nature to run its course. Against what laissez-faire naturalism suggests, the march of time has not produced a more effective approach to seventeenth-century tragedy. Instead, it has allowed a useful practice to be displaced by an unfulfilled promise. And really, this turn of events should come as no surprise. After all, natural selection is rooted in luck and short-term advantage. It does not work for the long run nor does it have the awareness to hold onto good stock through a chance downturn; in a careless instant, it will wipe out a thousand vital futures. The particular downturn suffered by seventeenth-century tragedy, moreover, is a familiar one. As the long tradition of philosophy reveals, the mind often gets caught up in its own mental landscape, abandoning the working good in pursuit of an impossible perfection. Puzzling over free will, the true meaning of liberty, and other metaphysical mysteries, the tool comes to fancy itself the architect, metastasizing from problem solver into superfluous predicament. Our intellectual nature, in short, can often lead us into trouble, and given the uncertain progress this implies, the historical record can be more than a graveyard of failures. It can also be a library of possibilities, a storing-house of useful practices that were interrupted by the wilful impulses of idealism. Seen this way, the problem-based ethics of seventeenth-century tragedy is something other than an evolutionary dead end. It is a social tool that met an untimely demise, and so far from encouraging us to passively accept nature, the success of the tabula rasa urges us to actively reverse it. It may no longer be the seventeenth century, but plays like *Hamlet* show us there is value in returning.

Yet while the history of Locke's reform encourages us to look back to the practice of seventeenth-century tragedy, it also suggests that we should not revive this practice entirely as it was. For if the problem-based ethics associated with *Hamlet* was truly an efficient mechanism for manufacturing and managing diversity, it would have survived Locke's challenge better than it did. This ethics, in short, did not work as well in practice as in theory, and a glance at Dewey's *Ethics* explains why. As Dewey points out, since problem-based ethics emerged out of practice, the understanding of its logical consequences lagged behind its physical development. It was not until the late nineteenth century, when American pragmatism first emerged, that a systematic effort was made to mount ethics upon a basis of pragmatic pluralism. Prior to this, a few thinkers, perhaps most notably Machiavelli,[23] had ventured down this road. Yet the overwhelming tendency in ethics was moral idealism, for even when philosophers admitted the importance of chance and fortune and other signs of nonintentional life, they continued to believe that the intricacies of human biology stood as evidence for some form of intentional design. Only with Darwin was human life permanently severed from any fixed *telos*, and so it was not until centuries after *Hamlet* was written that problem-based ethics could be freed of its idealist trappings and a consistent pragmatism could take root. Seen this way, the lesson of the tabula rasa is not that the problem-based ethics of seventeenth-century tragedy should be reconstituted entirely in its original form. Rather, the lesson is that this ethics should be approached from the vantage of modern pragmatism. Revealing the diverse practices of seventeenth-century tragedy as contributors to the same organic process, pragmatism forecloses Locke's critique: far from being a threat to community, the variousness of seventeenth-century tragedy is in fact a source of strength. And so with pragmatism, we do not reclaim seventeenth-century as history left it. Instead, we reclaim it as it only now can be.

Where Romanticism urges us to recover nature as it was and a laissez-faire naturalism urges us to accept nature as it is, pragmatism thus recommends a more intentional approach. Rather than asking us to commit ourselves entirely to either our original nature or our current state, it suggests an experimental integration of the two, one that takes advantage of our experience to sift and combine the best practices from history, using the benefits of hindsight to move forward without sacrificing the good in what we had. Inherent in this joining of past and present is the view that tragedies like *Hamlet* do not mark the final end of ethics, but stand only as useful points of inspiration. Although my focus in this book has been tightly fixed on the tragedy of the seventeenth century, I noted in the first chapter that my selection of subject matter was made for practical purposes. Like Darwin's finches, plays like *Hamlet* are useful because of the evidence they offer for a broader hypothesis. These plays show that art can be useful at communicating ethical problems; that this communication can serve as an organic source of functional variety; and that this functional variety can have an instrumental purpose in a world that is always changing. Beyond this, moreover, they have illustrated some of the practical qualities that can help art function in this manner: a focus on problems as problems; a flexibility of form; and a communal setting. Nevertheless, their usefulness in showing what art has accomplished should not restrict the possibilities for what art *could* do. Instead, just as *The Indian Emperour* adapted the problem-based mechanism of *Hamlet* to the concerns of its own time, so too do these plays urge us to adapt art to the ethical problems of today. For to adapt this way is to learn from past practices without being confined by their limits. It is to find the inspiration for an evolutionary ethics not just in the products of nature, but in the possibilities for growth.

Conclusion

This marks the end of what I referred to in the preface as an "unlikely experiment." I hope that, along the way, it has come to appear somewhat less unlikely. Though it seems incredible that art could provide the missing link in a scientific ethics, seventeenth-century tragedy suggests that it can. For try as it might, science cannot lend intention to life. The narrow purpose of its experimental method is to uncover the way that nature works, laying bare the turnings of physics and the biochemical processes of life. Science, that is to say, is designed to discover the world as it is, not as it could be, to tell us what we are, not what we might become. Moreover, by diminishing our uncertainty, science also necessarily diminishes our room to maneuver. The more we learn about the cosmos, the more it seems one great machine that spins on quantum gears; the more we learn about our brains, the more we seem a clockwork of desires. To embrace science is thus to be led into naturalism, and to accept naturalism is to see ourselves as products of our environment. And so it is that science catches itself in a practical bind. Although it has secured its place in human life with promises of power, it seems to take back more than it could possibly give.

In response to this difficulty, the advocates of science have often tried to repaint naturalism as a purposeful way of life. For example, there is perfectionism, the claim that we should intentionally anticipate nature, becoming the superhumans of eugenics and positivism, technological transhumanism and scientific hedonism. Or there is Romanticism, the claim that we should intentionally return to nature, using our knowledge of life to reconnect to our original source. But whatever plausibility these approaches might once have had, it has long since been extinguished by Darwin. To accept Darwin's theory is to accept that there is no perfection in nature, either in the future or in the past, making it impossible to build a better human or to restore a more authentic state. Natural selection, in short, makes explicit the old laissez-faire fatalism of naturalism: since nature has no intentions, to embrace it is to relinquish our own.[1] In restoring coherence to naturalism, however, Darwinism does little to improve the prospects for a scientific ethics. Rather, it ruins them in another way. Because we are fitted with intentional brains, we cannot live without direction. And indeed, as we saw in chapter 7, the irony of taking a laissez-faire approach to life is that it leads inevitably to the very opposite of scientific practice, for our minds are naturally inclined to run into idealism. This is why, despite the ubiquity of science, our culture is still thick with peculiar faiths and utopian dreams. We need purpose and we need progress, and since science cannot provide, we have sought satisfaction elsewhere, wandering back to the glittering idols of spiritualism and speculation, recovering our old intentions, and with them, our old justifications for bigotry and self-importance. Science has carried us to an inhuman place, and we have rebelled against it.

This shortcoming of science is what makes pragmatism useful. For really, pragmatism is nothing more than a method for enlarging the practices of science into the basis of progressive life. By encouraging an interest in problems—particularly ethical problems that link our survival to the survival of others—pragmatism expands the cooperative problem-solving of scientific inquiry into the foundation of democratic community, promoting a culture of pluralism, active questioning, and experiment. Out of naturalism comes intentional society. And yet, there is a practical problem with pragmatism. It has been around for a century, more or less, and although it has had some modest successes, it has not established scientific practice as a working alternative to ethical idealism. Science remains understood—even by most of its own practitioners—in far more limited terms. Instead of being seen as the foundation for a whole new way of living, it is viewed as a tool that must be guided by philosophy or faith or some other external source of the good. Science, that is, may make progress possible, but as for how we should progress—well, we must look outside science for that. The persistence of this attitude is the failure of pragmatism, and the failure is very near a lethal one. Idealists may take comfort in the knowledge that this world is not ready yet for their ideas, but when a pragmatist fails, there is no better world to retreat to. A pragmatism that does not succeed in practice is no pragmatism at all.

As I have tried to show over the preceding pages, however, this failure admits of a possible remedy: art. Using its foothold in our feelings and our fancy, art can guide us physically into problem-solving, taking the grand project of pragmatism and making it work. This potential of art has long been recognized by pragmatists, but for various reasons, it has gone unrealized. Partly this is because Dewey and other early pragmatists inherited certain idealist prejudices from traditional aesthetics, and partly this is because many recent pragmatists have taken a relativistic turn, refusing to acknowledge that science is a more useful practice than any other. But mostly it has been because of the operating divide between the arts and the sciences. Artists have tended to suspect the sciences as absolutist and imperial, and scientists for their part have tended to suspect the arts as squishy and indulgent. Even when respect exists, moreover, it has not led to an organic interdependence of purpose. Artists do not suppose that they need science to survive, nor do scientists suppose that they need art. Rather, each group believes themselves to be fundamentally independent of the other. And so it is that the possibilities for a progressive ethics rooted in science but elaborated by art have grown dim. Science has kept to its corridors, allowed to describe life but barred from prescribing it. And art has endured a reputation as a brilliant but impractical pursuit.

As the preceding pages have shown, this relationship can be transformed. For in the example of seventeenth-century tragedy, we have physical evidence that art can extend the problem-based practice of science, giving us a progressive, purposeful ethics that rids us of the misdirections of the old morality. We do not need deities when we can invent weird sisters. We do not need stories of heaven when we can tell tales of Danish ghosts. We do not need strange utopias when we can author Cressida's Troy. Seen through these inventions, the harsh difficulties of our physical existence are less impossible to behold. With *Faustus*, we can look into the horror of death, acknowledging that the *telos* of it all must remain forever hid; and with *The Indian Emperour*, we can look into the shock of unending struggle, accepting that we are part of a violence that will rage as long as there is life to wage it. These are the problems of our world, and they are so hard that they have often driven us into idealism, praying to one inhuman force to save us from another. But seventeenth-century tragedy offers another solution, one that does not surrender us to the wanton rules of gods and ideologies, but works with our humanity, fitting itself to our story-brains, our senses and imaginations, our flesh and blood. In place of an impossible perfection, it offers us a physical practice that establishes a plural ethics, adaptive and communal, continuous through change. In place of paradise, it offers life.

Yet if the preceding discussion of tragedy has diminished the unlikeliness of the experiment proposed at the beginning of this book, it cannot put an end to the experiment itself. As an exercise in natural history, the previous chapters do not prove anything: not that seventeenth-century tragedy functions in the ways that I hypothesize, not that art and science can achieve an organic interdependence, not that problem-based art can encourage progressive society. They only open the possibility that these things are so, inviting us to test the hypothesis further. Part of this test can be conducted by switching from the observational method of natural history to the more empirical methods of modern biology, running experiments that determine whether devices like riddling speech and incomplete metaphors work as their authors imagined them. But practically speaking, art is too subtle and fluid a thing to be fully digested by the tools and assays of biologists. And so though empirical science may prove a useful aid, much of the test must be run by artists and audiences in the more uncertain laboratories of life. This is the experiment that gave us life and has kept us living, and in our dark tomorrows, this will be the experiment that decides whether we have run our course or will keep progressing still. For an evolutionary ethics to succeed, it thus requires scientists to invest confidence in a way of life that cannot be reduced to their own laboratory practice. Just as artists must trust that science is the most effective means of problem-solving, so must scientists trust that art is the most effective means of enlarging this practice into society. Such trust is the precondition of organic pluralism, the mutual dependence of function that sustains our individual bodies and that fuels progressive growth. And in an inhuman world, blind, accidental, and uncertain, it can also be an instrument for something more. Giving us purpose, tolerance, and hope, it can be the means of our humanity.

Notes

Preface

1. *The Life and Letters of Charles Darwin*, ed. Francis Darwin (New York: D. Appleton, 1887), 2 vols., 2.44.
2. "From the perspective of Christian theology, biological evolution and creation are by no means mutually exclusive." Giuseppe Tanzella-Nitti, Vatican Press Office, February 10, 2009, promoting the conference: *Biological Evolution: Facts and Theories—A Critical Appraisal 150 Years after "The Origin of Species,"* Pontifical Gregorian University, Rome, March 3–7, 2009. In the same press release, Saverio Forestiero remarks that "biological evolution . . . is assumed and discussed as a fact beyond all reasonable doubt."
3. T.H. Huxley remarks: "The practice of that which is ethically best— what we call goodness or virtue—involves a course of conduct which, in all respects, is opposed to that which leads to success in the cosmic struggle for existence." Thomas Henry Huxley, "Evolution and Ethics" in *The Major Prose of Thomas Henry Huxley*, ed. Alan P. Barr (Athens: University of Georgia Press, 1997), 327. More modern evolutionary biologists like Stephen Jay Gould and Dawkins have agreed, claiming that the additional ingredient to morality is "humanism." See for example, Stephen Jay Gould, *The Richness of Life: The Essential Stephen Jay Gould*, ed. Steven Rose (New York, Norton, 2007), 543; Richard Dawkins, *The God Delusion* (New York: Houghton, Mifflin, Harcourt, 2006), 259–67; and Richard Dawkins, *The Selfish Gene* (Oxford: Oxford University Press, 1989), 200–201.
4. For example, through Kin Selection. The most famous instance of this is in insect colonies where the vast majority of individual organisms are sterile. For a general review of this topic, see Laurent Keller, ed., *Levels of Selection in Evolution* (Princeton, NJ: Princeton University Press, 1999). For a summary of more recent work, see jeff smith, J. David Van Dyken, and Peter C. Zee, "A Generalization of Hamilton's Rule for the Evolution of Microbial Cooperation," *Science* 328 (2010): 1700–1703.

5. E.g., Christopher Hitchens, *God Is Not Great: How Religion Poisons Everything* (New York: Twelve Books, 2007).

6. Blakey Vermeule, *Why Do We Care about Literary Characters?* (Baltimore: Johns Hopkins University Press, 2010); Alan Richardson, *The Neural Sublime: Cognitive Theories and Romantic Texts* (Baltimore: Johns Hopkins University Press, 2010); Lisa Zunshine, *Why We Read Fiction: Theory of Mind and the Novel* (Columbus: Ohio State University Press, 2006); Bruce McConachie and F. Elizabeth Hart, *Performance and Cognition: Theatre Studies after the Cognitive Turn* (New York: Routledge, 2006); Patrick Colm Hogan, *Cognitive Science, Literature, and the Arts: A Guide for Humanists* (New York: Routledge, 2003).

7. Brian Boyd, *On the Origin of Stories: Evolution, Cognition, and Fiction* (Cambridge, MA: Harvard University Press, 2009); William Flesch, *Comeuppance: Costly Signaling, Altruistic Punishment, and Other Biological Components of Fiction* (Cambridge, MA: Harvard University Press, 2007); Jonathan Gottschall and David Sloan Wilson, eds., *The Literary Animal: Evolution and the Nature of Narrative* (Evanston, IL: Northwestern University Press, 2005).

8. Jonathan Gottschall, *Literature, Science and a New Humanities* (New York: Palgrave Macmillan, 2008); Willie van Peer, Jèmeljan Hekemulder, and Sonia Zyngier, *Muses and Measures: Empirical Research Methods for the Humanities* (Cambridge: Cambridge Scholars, 2008); Bruce McConachie, "Falsifiable Theories for Theatre and Performance Studies," *Theatre Journal* 59 (2007): 553–77.

9. One brilliant exception is Suzanne Keen, *Empathy and the Novel* (Oxford: Oxford University Press, 2007), which urges literary critics to countenance the possibility that cognitive science may reveal novels to have no practical value at all.

10. For an excellent introduction, see the collection of essays in *Primates and Philosophers: How Morality Evolved*, ed. Stephen Macedo and Josiah Ober (Princeton, NJ: Princeton University Press, 2006).

11. P. S. Churchland, "The Impact of Neuroscience on Philosophy," *Neuron* 60 (2008): 409–11.

12. "[H]umans are the only species for whom tool use is a defining and universal characteristic." Scott H Johnson-Frey, "What's So Special about Human Tool Use?" *Neuron* 39 (2003): 201–4, 201.

13. James K. Rilling, "Neuroscientific Approaches and Applications within Anthropology," *Yearbook of Physical Anthropology* 137; S47 (2008): 2–32, 17.

14. Dietrich Stout and Thierry Chaminade, "Making Tools and Making Sense: Complex, Intentional Behaviour in Human Evolution," *Cambridge Archaeological Journal* 19 (2009): 85–96.

15. A century after the thirty-seven volumes of Epicurus' *Physics* had fallen out of circulation, Lucretius' poem was singled out by Jerome

in his *Apology against Rufinus* as one of a handful of antique works that remained widely and actively read.

Introduction: The Descent of Ethics

1. Charles Darwin, *The Descent of Man and Selection in Relation to Sex,* 2nd ed. (New York: D. Appleton, 1909), 112.
2. The term was coined by Darwin's cousin, Francis Galton, in response to *The Origin of Species.*
3. In direct response to Galton's work, Darwin argues, "If we were intentionally to neglect the weak and helpless, it could only be for a contingent benefit, with an overwhelming present evil" (136).
4. Charles Darwin, *The Descent of Man,* 139.
5. Thus he writes, "The more efficient causes of progress seem to consist of a good education during youth whilst the brain is impressible, and of a high standard of excellence, inculcated by the ablest and best men, embodied in the laws, customs and traditions of the nation, and enforced by public opinion. It should, however, be borne in mind, that the enforcement of public opinion depends on our appreciation of the approbation and disapprobation of others; and this appreciation is founded on our sympathy, which it can hardly be doubted was originally developed through natural selection" (146).
6. B. Seymour and R. Dolan, "Emotion, Decision Making, and the Amygdala" *Neuron* 58 (2008): 662–71; Ming Hsu, Cédric Anen, and Steven R. Quartz, "The Right and the Good: Distributive Justice and Neural Encoding of Equity and Efficiency," *Science* 320 (2008): 1092–95.
7. R. H. Thaler, "The Ultimatum Game," *Journal of Economic Perspectives,* 2 (1988): 195–206.
8. P. S. Churchland, "The Impact of Neuroscience on Philosophy," *Neuron* 60 (2008): 409–11.
9. A. R. Damasio, *Descartes' Error: Emotion, Reason, and the Human Brain* (New York: G.P. Putnam, 1994).
10. In addition to the empirical evidence (e.g., Damasio, *Descartes' Error*) that moral volition is emotional, this conclusion is supported by the principle of evolutionary conservation, which suggests that it is unlikely that humans would independently develop a volitional faculty in two separate regions of the brain.
11. J. Haidt, "The Emotional Dog and Its Rational Tail: A Social Intuitionist Approach to Moral Judgment," *Psychological Review* 108 (2001): 814–34.
12. "With highly civilised nations continued progress depends in a subordinate degree on natural selection; for such nations do not supplant and exterminate one another as do savage tribes. Nevertheless the more intelligent members within the same community will succeed

better in the long run than the inferior, and leave a more numerous progeny, and this is a form of natural selection." Charles Darwin, *The Descent of Man*, 145–46).

13. Daniel Dennet, *Darwin's Dangerous Idea: Evolution and the Meanings of Life* (New York: Simon and Schuster, 1996), 315.

14. Kim Sterelny, *Thought in a Hostile World: The Evolution of Human Cognition* (New York: Blackwell, 2003).

15. For a summary of Darwin's influence on James, especially in regard to ethics, see Ignas Skrupskelis, "Evolution and Pragmatism: An Unpublished Letter of William James," *Transactions of the Charles S. Peirce Society* 43 (2007): 745–52.

16. Mark Johnson, "Cognitive Science" in *A Companion to Pragmatism*, ed. John R. Shook and Joseph Margolis (London: Blackwell, 2006), 369–77. Johnson notes that William James and modern cognitive science take the same stance on issues such as functionalism, nonreductionism, and Darwinism.

17. John Dewey, *The Influence of Darwin on Philosophy and Other Essays* (New York: Henry Holt, 1910), 9–19.

18. John Dewey, *Art as Experience* (New York: Perigree, 2005), 26.

19. For Dewey, as for other pragmatists, problem solving involves practical problems, not speculative ones. For a discussion, see John Dewey, *Logic: The Theory of Inquiry* (New York: Henry Holt, 1938): "logical texts usually remark incidentally that reflection grows out of the presence of a problem and then proceed as if this fact had no further interest for the theory of reflection... But in every interaction that involves intelligent direction, the physical environment is part of a more inclusive social or cultural environment" (20).

20. John Dewey, *Freedom and Culture* (New York: Putnam, 1939), 81.

21. Dewey, *Art as Experience*, 298.

22. "The design of a painting or novel is the arrangement of its elements by means of which it becomes an expressive unity in direct perception" (121). Dewey mentions the concept of unity over two-dozen times in the treatise.

23. Over the twentieth century, this had the physical effect of making *Art as Experience* appear a work of pure—not practical—aesthetics, and it was claimed as an ally by movements like New Criticism—movements that celebrated variety and unity as intrinsic goods, not instrumental ones.

24. Richard Rorty, "Dewey Between Hegel and Darwin," in *Rorty & Pragmatism: The Philosopher Responds to His Critics*, ed. Herman Saatkamp Jr., (Nashville, TN: Vanderbilt University Press, 1995), 1–15, 12. Emphasis added.

25. Cornel West gives Darwin no place in his poetic politics; his only gesture to Darwin is the observation that C. S. Pierce was uncomfortable with him for "scientific and moral" reasons. Richard

Bernstein is able to claim "democracy as a *moral* ideal" by tracing Dewey's interest in Darwin to his background in Hegel, conflating Dewey's practical progressivism with a creative-radical idealism: "Creative—radical—democracy is still 'the task before us'" (58). Richard Shusterman installs Emerson's transcendentalism as the primary source of pragmatism's aesthetic naturalism and then connects both back to Kant, resubsuming pragmatism aesthetics into a tradition that celebrates the intrinsic (as opposed to the instrumental) worth of pluralism. Even Giles Gunn, who notes that "what Charles Darwin...undertook upon H. M. S. Beagle is no less a part of the humanities than what Marcel Proust undertook in the cork-lined room," follows Foucault in treating Darwin's writings as simply another example of "critical discourse." Cornel West, *The American Evasion of Philosophy*, (Madison: University of Wisconsin Press, 1989), 52. Richard Bernstein, "Dewey, Democracy: The Task Ahead" in *Post-Analytic Philosophy*, ed. John Rajchman and Cornel West (New York: Columbia University Press, 1985), 49, 53, 58. Richard Shusterman, *Pragmatist Aesthetics: Living Beauty, Rethinking Art* (Oxford: Blackwell, 1992); "Aesthetics" in Shook and Margolis, *A Companion to Pragmatism*, 352–60. Giles Gunn, *The Culture of Criticism and the Criticism of Culture* (New York: Oxford University Press, 1988), 121. Gunn also cites Rorty's view of Darwin as part of his critique of Rortyian neopragmatism in *Thinking across the American Grain: Ideology, Intellect, and the New Pragmatism* (Chicago: University of Chicago Press, 1992), 98.

26. See Johnson, "Cognitive Science" for discussion.
27. See for example, Eric MacGilvray, *Reconstructing Public Reason* (Cambridge, MA: Harvard University Press, 2004).
28. For a broad discussion of these skeptical developments, see Richard Popkin, *The History of Skepticism from Erasmus to Spinoza* (Berkeley: University of California Press, 1979).
29. John Dewey and James Hayden Tufts, *Ethics* (New York: Henry Holt, 1908), 224.
30. Philip Sidney, *An Apologie for Poesie* (London, 1595), F 4.
31. When the moral philosophers of the church raised profound ethical questions, as the medieval schoolmen did in their *quaestiones*, they were expected to answer them. For as Luther discovered when he attempted to force the clergy to admit the inscrutability of God's purpose, admission of ignorance on such fundamental matters crippled the basis of the church's moral authority. Outside the church, too, the expectation that knowledge was the goal of ethics proved so durable that even moral philosophers who questioned the possibility of certainty were typically associated by their followers with dogmatic stances. Montaigne's cultural relativism was taken as a validation of a Catholic tolerance, while Hobbes' claim that "God" denoted a power

beyond human comprehension was typically interpreted as an expression of atheism.

32. On the notion of the blank slate, C. S. Pierce remarks, "We cannot begin with complete doubt. We must begin with all the prejudices which we actually have when we enter upon the study of philosophy. These prejudices are not to be dispelled by a maxim, for they are things which it does not occur to us *can* be questioned." Charles S. Peirce, "Some Consequences of Four Capacities," *Journal of Speculative Philosophy* 2 (1868): 140–57, 140. For the perspective of contemporary cognitive science, see Steven Pinker, *The Blank Slate: The Modern Denial of Human Nature* (New York: Putnam, 2002). Pinker's core claim is that Locke's tabula rasa is incompatible with what practical experience teaches us about the function of the mind.

33. In this, my method will differ from radical critics who approach literature from the method of Foucault's critical "archaeology." Against these critics, I will treat theatrical performances not as cultural artifacts, but as parts of a living system, bound to it by the various organic associations that sustain life.

1   Faustus, Macbeth, and the Riddle of Tomorrow

1. Algernon Charles Swinburne, *The Poems of Algernon Charles Swinburne* (London: Chatto & Windus, 1905), 406.

2. H. G. Wells, *The Time Machine* (London, 1895), Epilogue.

3. Christopher Marlowe, *Doctor Faustus A- and B- Texts (1604, 1616)*, ed. David M. Bevington and Eric Rasmussen (Manchester: University of Manchester Press, 1993), 53–54.

4. For a summary of this criticism, see Angus Fletcher, "*Doctor Faustus* and the Lutheran Aesthetic," *English Literary Renaissance* 35 (2005): 187–209.

5. James observes that the problem of free will as "insoluble," noting: "we can thus ignore the free-will question." William James, *Psychology* (New York: Henry Holt, 1915), 456, 458.

6. For further discussion, see Angus Fletcher and Mike Benveniste, "Defending Pluralism: The Chicago School and the Case of *Tom Jones*," *New Literary History* 41 (2010): 653–67.

7. This is a direction in which pragmatism itself increasingly inclined over the twentieth century as its connection to Darwinism was severed and it became more and more associated with speculative philosophy. For example, as Sidney Hook writes in "Pragmatism and the Tragic Sense of Life," his presidential address to the American Philosophical Association in 1959: "Pragmatism, as I interpret it, is the theory and practice of enlarging human freedom in a precarious and tragic world by the arts of intelligent social control. It may be a lost cause. I do not know of a better one." Sidney Hook,

"Pragmatism and the Tragic Sense of Life" *Proceedings and Addresses of the American Philosophical Association* 33 (1959–60): 5–26, 26.

8. John Dewey critiques the "dissolving atomistic individualism of the liberal school" in *Liberalism and Social Action* (New York: Putnam, 1935), 38.

9. "Its distrust of science (and more generally, the search for testable hypotheses and cumulative objective knowledge) has left it, according to many accounts, mired in faddism, obscurantism, and parochialism." Steven Pinker, "Toward a Consilient Study of Literature," *Philosophy and Literature* 31 (2007): 162–178, 163.

10. All citations from *Faustus* are taken from Marlowe, *Doctor Faustus A- and B- Texts*. For summaries of the critical debate surrounding the authority of these two texts, see Richard Proudfoot, "Marlowe and the Editors," in *Constructing Christopher Marlowe*, ed. J. A. Downie and J. T. Parnell (Cambridge: Cambridge University Press, 2000), 41–54; and Marlowe, *Doctor Faustus A- and B-Texts*, 62–77. The B-text contains more spectacle and burlesque, and in general critics who read *Faustus* as a pure tragedy incline to the A-text, while critics who like to highlight the play's destabilizing satiric energy prefer the B-text. The reading offered in this chapter prefers neither text, relying on passages that occur in both and suggesting that the tragic mood is not diminished by the increased comedy of the B-text.

11. Theodore Spencer, *Death and Elizabethan Tragedy* (Cambridge, MA: Harvard University Press, 1936).

12. Michael Neill, *Issues of Death: Mortality and Identity in English Renaissance Tragedy* (Oxford: Oxford University Press, 1997); Robert Watson, *The Rest Is Silence: Death as Annihilation in English Renaissance Tragedy* (Berkeley: University of California Press, 1994); James Calderwood, *Shakespeare and the Denial of Death* (Amherst: University of Massachusetts Press, 1987).

13. G. M. Pinciss, "Marlowe's Cambridge Years and the Writing of *Doctor Faustus*," *SEL* 33 (1993): 249–64.

14. See Richard Marius, *Martin Luther: The Christian between God and Death* (Cambridge, MA: Harvard University Press, 1999), for discussion.

15. Martin Luther, *Luther's Works: American Edition*, ed. Jaroslav Pelikan and Helmut Lehman, 55 vols. (Philadelphia: Fortress Press, 1955–86), 31.69.

16. At moments, even Luther's belief in God seems in doubt. For treatment of Luther's fits of atheism, see Marius, *Martin Luther*. Marius remarks, "Luther's doubts were...swept along by one of the great recurring waves of skepticism in human history, doubts that God exists at all" (xiii). For the influence of Luther's iconoclasm, see Huston Diehl, *Staging Reform, Reforming the Stage: Protestantism and Popular Theatre in Early Modern England* (Ithaca, NY: Cornell

University Press, 1997), esp. 9–39; Paul White, *Theatre and Reformation* (Cambridge: Cambridge University Press, 1993); Ernest Gilman, *Iconoclasm and Poetry in the English Renaissance* (Chicago: University of Chicago Press, 1986).

17. In *The Babylonian Captivity of the Church* (1520) in *Luther's Works*, 36.11–126, 29, 35.

18. *Luther's Works*, 36.335.

19. In technical terms, where Catholics and Reform Protestants see an ontological dualism at work in the eucharist, Luther discovers an epistemological dualism—communion is not the meeting of two distinct substances (bread and Christ) but two distinct perspectives (the eyes of flesh and the heart of spirit).

20. "est actus imperfectus, semper partim acquisirus et partim acquirendus." In *Luthers Werke*, ed. J. F. K. Knaake et al., 72 vols. (Weimar: Verlag Hermann Böhlaus Nachfolger, 1883–2007), 4.362; *Luther's Works*, 11.494.

21. See especially Gerhard Ebeling, "Die Anfange von Luthers Hermeneutik," *Die Zeitschrift fur Theologie und Kirche* 48 (1951): 172–230. Ebeling is responding to proponents of a dialectical approach to Luther, especially Karl Holl, Karl Barth, and Friedrich Gogarten.

22. Luther declared that "every Christian, no matter how crude he may be, can comprehend in the eucharist the whole Christian doctrine." In *The Sacrament of the Body and Blood of Christ—Against the Fanatics* (1526) in *Luther's Works*, 11.335–61, 352.

23. Martin Luther, *A Commentarie upon the Fiftene Psalmes*, trans. Henry Bull (London, 1577), 29–30.

24. In addition to various translations of his commentaries, he authored a short letter of consolation that was rendered into English: *A right comfortable treatise containing sundrie pointes of consolation* (1578). In this work, Luther comforts the suffering by assuring them that it may be worse in the future: "It will not a little lighten every present evil, if thou turne thy mind to them that are to come...[especially] that which of all terrible things is sayd to be the greatest, namely death, shall most certainly come, and nothing is more uncertain than the power thereof" (6–8). There can be no avoiding the terrible uncertainty of death, so if nothing else, we should be thankful that we are still living. This darkling consolation struck a chord with English readers, and Luther's treatise went through three editions in as many years (1578, 1579, 1580).

25. Clifford Davidson, "Doctor Faustus of Wittenberg," *Studies in Philology* 59 (1962): 524–23; Pauline Honderich, "John Calvin and Doctor Faustus," *Modern Language Review* 68 (1973): 1–13.

26. T. McAlindon, "*Doctor Faustus*: The Predestination Theory," *English Studies* 76 (1995): 215–20.

27. That Faustus is currently in agony is revealed when the thought of conjuring spirits prompts him to blurt: "O this cheers my soul!" (A. 1.1.151; B. 1.1.143).

28. See the summaries of criticism in Suzan Last, "Marlowe's Literary Double Agency: *Doctor Faustus* as a Subversive Comedy of Error," *Renaissance and Reformation* 24 (2000): 23–44 and J. T. McNeely, "The Integrated Design of *Doctor Faustus*: An Essay in Iconoclasm," *Cahiers Elisabethains* 41 (1992): 1–16.

29. For example, *Luther: Letters of Spiritual Counsel*, ed. and trans. Theodore G. Tappert (Philadelphia, PA: Westminster Press, 1955), 85–87.

30. One of the earliest known remarks on the play is a sneer at its unreal stage machinery, and whether modern critics view the allegorical elements as a remnant of an older tradition, or an intentional object of parody, they are broadly agreed that these elements are less sophisticated than Faustus' descriptions of his mental strife. For some of the foundational accounts of this view, see Leo Kirschbaum, "Marlowe's *Faustus*: A Reconsideration," *Review of English Studies* 19 (1943): 225–41; Nicholas Brooke, "The Moral Tragedy of *Dr. Faustus*," *Cambridge Journal* 5 (1952): 662–87; Margaret Ann O'Brien, "Christian Belief in *Doctor Faustus*," *English Literary History* 37 (1970): 1–11.

31. For a good summary of recent work in this area, see David Steinmetz, "Divided by a Common Past: The Reshaping of the Christian Exegetical Tradition in the Sixteenth Century," *Journal of Medieval and Early Modern Studies* 27 (1997): 245–64.

32. Bruce Marshall "Faith and Reason Reconsidered: Aquinas and Luther on Deciding What is True," *The Thomist* 63 (1999): 1–48, 30.

33. *Luther's Works*, 36.34–35.

34. Philip Sidney, *An Apologie for Poesie* (London, 1595), F 4.

35. Prior to the battle of Tewkesbury, Richard is tormented by a succession of ghosts that howl: "Despair and die!" (5.3.126)—the same phrase that Faustus uses to castigate himself in his own final act: "Damn'd art thou, Faustus, damn'd; despair and die!" (A. 5.1.48).

36. Of Helen, Troilus remarks that her "price hath launch'd above a thousand ships" (2.2.81–82)—playing off Faustus' description of Helen as "the face that launched a thousand ships" (A. 5.1.90).

37. The parallels between Faustus and Macbeth have been evident from at least the mid-eighteenth century. For Macbeth's final soliloquy, David Garrick turned to Faustus: "My soul is clog'd with blood— / I cannot rise! I dare not ask for mercy— / It is too late, hell drags me down; I sink, / I sink,—my soul is lost for ever!" *Macbeth* 5.6.77–80 in *The Plays of David Garrick*, ed. Harry Pedicord and Frederick Bergman, 4 vols. (Carbondale: Southern Illinois University Press,

1981). For more recent discussions on the connection, see Kristian Smidt, "*Dr. Faustus* and *Macbeth*," *English Studies* 23 (1966): 235–48; Richard Waswo, "Damnation Protestant Style: Macbeth, Faustus, and Christian Tragedy," *Journal of Medieval and Renaissance Studies* 4 (1974): 63–99; James Nosworthy, "*Macbeth, Doctor Faustus*, and the Juggling Fiends," in J. C. Gray, ed., *Mirror Up to Shakespeare* (Toronto: University of Toronto Press, 1984), 208–22; K. Tentzeli von Rosador, " 'Supernatural Soliciting': Temptation and Imagination in *Doctor Faustus and Macbeth*," in E. A. J. Honigmann, ed., *Shakespeare and His Contemporaries* (Manchester: Manchester University Press, 1986), 42–59; Gillian Sharpe, "Damnation and Death in *Macbeth* and *Doctor Faustus*," *English Review* 8 (1997): 8–11.

38. For example, Helen Gardner, "Milton's Satan and the Theme of Damnation in Elizabethan Tragedy," in *A Reading of Paradise Lost* (Oxford: Oxford University Press, 1965), 99–120. Gardner's basic argument is that both *Macbeth* and *Faustus* portray "the deforming of a creature in its origins bright and good, by its own willed persistence in acts against its own nature." I will discuss the scholarship on *Macbeth* as an exploration of moral relativism below.

39. Except where noted otherwise, all citations from Shakespeare are taken from *The Riverside Shakespeare: The Complete Works, second edition*, ed. G. Blakemore Evans, et al. (New York: Houghton Mifflin, 2005).

40. The earliest formulations of this view are Wilbur Sanders, *The Dramatist and the Received Idea: Studies in the Plays of Marlowe and Shakespeare* (Cambridge: Cambridge University Press, 1968), 253–307 and Harry Berger, "The Early Scenes in *Macbeth*: Preface to a New Interpretation," rpt. in *Making Trifles of Terrors* (Stanford: Stanford University Press, 1997), 70–97. This view is now pervasive, but for some recent examples, see Stephen Greenblatt, "Shakespeare Bewitched," in *New Historical Literary Study*, ed. Jeffrey Cox and Larry Reynolds (Princeton, NJ: Princeton University Press, 1993), 108–35; Stephen Orgel, "Shakespeare and the Antic Round," *Shakespeare Survey* 52 (1999): 143–53; Alan Sinfield, "Macbeth: History, Ideology, and Intellectuals," *Critical Quarterly* 28 (1986): 63–77; and Graham Bradshaw, *Shakespeare's Skepticism* (Brighton: Harvester Press, 1987), 219–56.

41. G. Wilson Knight, "*Macbeth* and the Metaphysic of Evil," in *The Wheel of Fire* (Oxford: Oxford University Press, 1930), 154. Also see L. C. Knights, *How Many Children Had Lady Macbeth?* (Cambridge: Cambridge University Press, 1933); Caroline Spurgeon, *Shakespeare's Imagery and What It Tells Us* (Cambridge: Cambridge University Press, 1935); Cleanth Brooks, "The Naked Babe and the Cloak of Manliness," *The Well-Wrought Urn* (New York: Harcourt Brace, 1947), 22–49. For a discussion of the

pervasiveness of this view in recent criticism, see Carol Tufts, "Shakespeare's Conception of Moral Order in *Macbeth*," *Renascence* 50 (1998): 169–82, and for a recent example, see Jean Gooder, " 'Fixt Fate' and 'Free-will' in *Phedre* and *Macbeth*," *Cambridge Quarterly* 28 (1999): 214–31.

42. *Luther's Works*, 10.119; *Luther's Works*, 11.133.

43. *Luther's Works*, 11.548.

44. For some summaries of this material see Roger Abrahams, "A Riddling on St. Vincent," *Western Folklore* 42 (1983): 272–95; Thomas Burns, "Riddling: Occasion to Act," *Journal of American Folklore* 89 (1976): 139–65, 143.

45. A comb has teeth but cannot eat. A door is not a door when it is ajar. A towel gets wetter the more that it dries. For discussion of this cognitive aspect of riddles, see Robert A. Georges and Alan Dundes, "Toward a Structural Definition of the Riddle," *Journal of American Folklore* 76 (1963): 111–18; Ian Hamnett, "Ambiguity, Classification, and Change: The Function of Riddles," *Man* 2 (1967): 379–92; and Thomas Green and W. J. Pepicello, "The Riddle Process," *Journal of American Folklore* 97 (1984): 189–203.

46. Arnold van Gennep, *Rites of Passage* (Chicago: Chicago University Press, 1960).

47. This functional connection between rites and riddles was first proposed in Alan Dundes, "Texture, Text, and Context," *Southern Folklore Quarterly* 28 (1964): 251–65. The idea has subsequently been taken up and refined by numerous anthropologists. For a summary of recent work, see Don Handelman, "Traps of Transformation: Theoretical Convergences between Riddle and Ritual," in *Untying the Knot: On Riddles and Other Enigmatic Modes*, ed. Galit Hasan-Rakem and David Shulman (Oxford: Oxford University Press, 1996), 37–61.

48. See P. Gorfain, "Riddles and Reconciliation: Formal Unity in *All's Well that Ends Well*," *Journal of the Folklore Institute* 13 (1976): 263–81, for discussion.

49. John Donne, "Sermon on Job 19:26," in *The Sermons of John Donne*, ed. George Potter and Evelyn Simpson, 10 vols. (Berkeley: University of California Press, 1953–62), 3.91–113, 111.

50. For a discussion of the Protestant background of *Macbeth*, see Frank Huntley, "*Macbeth* and the Background of Jesuitical Equivocation," *PMLA* 79 (1964): 390–400.

51. See Marius, *Martin Luther*, 253, for discussion.

2 Partial Belief in *Julius Caesar* and *Hamlet*

1. While Titus stoically claims to feel nothing but honor at the death of his children, Constance is so discomposed by the loss of hers that she

rejects all efforts at philosophical consolation: "Fare you well. Had you such a loss as I, / I could give better comfort than you do" (*King John*, 3.4.99–100).

2. This was first suggested by J. Resch, "Zu Shakespeares *Julius Caesar*," *Archiv fur des Studium der Sprachen und Literaturen* 67 (1879): 446, and upheld by most of Shakespeare's editors in the first half of the twentieth century, including H. H. Furness, Harley Granville-Barker, E. K. Chambers, G. B. Harrison, and Dover Wilson. This argument was provided with additional support by typographical evidence adduced by Brents Stirling in "*Julius Caesar* in Revision" *Shakespeare Quarterly* 13 (1962): 188–205, and subsequently used to support the two revision theory by Fredson Bowers, "The Copy for Shakespeare's *Julius Caesar*," *South Atlantic Bulletin* 43 (1978): 23–36. Recent editors who have maintained the plausibility of this view include David Bevington, Frank Kermode, and Kenneth Muir.

3. This case was first made by Warren Smith, "The Duplicate Revelation of Portia's Death," *Shakespeare Quarterly* 4 (1953): 153–61. More recently, this claim has been argued by David Greene, "*Julius Caesar* and Its Source," *Salzburg Studies in English Literature* 86 (Salzburg: Institut fur Anglistik und Amerikanistik, 1979), 97; Thomas Clayton, "'Should Brutus Never Taste of Portia's Death but Once?': Text and Performance in *Julius Caesar*," *SEL* 23 (1983): 237–58. The case for a single version has been aided by the convincing refutation of Stirling and Bowers' typographical evidence in John Jowett, "Ligature Shortage and Speech-prefix Variation in *Julius Caesar*," *Library* 6 (1984): 244–53.

4. For summary, Geoffrey Miles, *Shakespeare and the Constant Romans* (Oxford: Clarendon Press, 1996), 145.

5. See Letizia Panizza, "Stoic Psychotherapy in the Middles Ages and Renaissance: Petrarch's *De remediis*," in *Atoms, Pneuma, and Tranquility: Epicurean and Stoic Themes in European Thought*, ed. Margaret Osler (Cambridge: Cambridge University Press, 1991), 39–65; and George McClure, *Sorrow and Consolation in Italian Humanism* (Princeton, NJ: Princeton University Press, 1991), 46–72.

6. Cicero, *Tusculan Disputations* (Cambridge, MA: Harvard University Press, 1989), 3.11.24–25. "Est igitur causa omnis in opinione nec vero aegritudinis solum sed etiam reliquarum omnium perturbationum...id autem est, ut is, qui doleat, opportere opinetur se dolere." The Latin word *perturbatio* is Cicero's rendering of the Greek *pathos*. For specific treatment of this passage from *Tusculans*, see Riccardo Miceli, "La Classificazione stoica delle passioni nelle 'Tusculanae' di Cicerone," *Sophia* 3 (1935): 181–86 and Marcia Calish, *Stoicism in Classical Latin Literature* (Leiden: E. J. Brill, 1990), 126–51. For an excellent treatment of Cicero's views of mourning, see Stephen

White, "Cicero and the Therapists," in *Cicero the Philosopher*, ed. J. G. F. Powell (Oxford: Clarendon Press, 1995), 219–46.

7. Consolation to Marcia, 7.1.

8. The term "neo-Stoicism" has a wide range of connotations, for it is used in general parlance to refer to the many distinct philosophical positions that have roots in the writings of the ancient Stoa. In this chapter, I do not intend it to be associated with anything other than the texts of Cicero, Seneca, and Plutarch that I discuss.

9. Plutarch, "A Letter of Condolence to Apollonius," in *Moralia*, trans. Frank Babbitt, 14 vols. (Cambridge, MA: Harvard University Press, 1924), vol. 2, pp. 105–213, *106c*. In Plutarch's neo-Stoic philosophy, *dócan* has a range of meaning from unsubstantiated opinion to a philosophical judgment, a range that, as I discuss below, is crucial to his view of mind.

10. "The instances of distress I have cited are not intended to delight the wicked, but to help the mourner believe that he should bear the burdens which many others have calmly shouldered." "Enumeratio exemplorum, non ut animum malevolorum oblectet, ad fertur, sed ut ille, qui maeret, ferendum sibi id censeat, quod videat multos moderate et tranquille tulisse" (*Tusc.* 3.60).

11. "Praemeditatio futurorum malorum lenit eorum adventum, quae venientia longe ante videris" (*Tusc.* 3.29).

12. "Et mihi quidem videtur idem fere accidere iis, qui ante meditantur, quod iis, quibus medetur dies, nisi quod ratio quaedam sanat illos, hos ipsa natura" (*Tusc.* 3.58).

13. "Quod ratio debuerat, usus docet minora esse ea, quae sint visa maiora" (*Tusc.* 3.54).

14. Panizza, "Stoic Psychotherapy in the Middles Ages," 56.

15. Brian Vickers, "Shakespearean Consolations," *Proceedings of the British Academy* 82 (1993): 219–84, esp. 245–47. For additional studies on the influence of the Stoic consolation upon Shakespeare, see Benjamin Boyce, "The Stoic *Consolatio* and Shakespeare," *PMLA* 64 (1949): 771–80; Rolf Soellner, "Shakespeare and the Consolatio" *Notes and Queries* 199 (1954):108–9; John Tison, "Shakespeare's *Consolatio* for Exile," *Modern Language Quarterly* 21 (1960): 142–57.

16. Miles, *Shakespeare and the Constant Romans*, 143.

17. Cicero's *De Officiis* was widely available in Nicholas Grimald's translation, *Marcus Tullius Ciceroes the bokes of duties* (London, 1556). For treatment of the dissemination of *De Officiis* in fifteenth- and early sixteenth-century England, see *The Renaissance English Text Society's facsimile of Grimald's translation*, ed. Gerald O'Gorman (Washington: The Folger Shakespeare Library, 1990), 13–15.

18. For a good thumbnail sketch of Cicero's philosophy, see J. G. F. Powell, "Introduction: Cicero's Philosophical Works and Their

Background," in Powell, *Cicero the Philosopher*, 1–35. Also see E. V. Arnold, *Roman Stoicism* (Cambridge: Cambridge University Press, 1911); A. E. Douglas, "Cicero the Philosopher" in *Cicero*, ed. T. A. Dorey (London, 1965), 135–170; J. Glucker, "Cicero's Philosophical Affiliations," in *The Question of "Eclecticism": Studies in Later Greek Philosophy*, ed. J. M. Dillon and A. A. Long (Berkeley: University of California Press, 1988), 34–69; Woldemar Gorler, "Silencing the Toublemaker: *De Legibus 1.39* and the Continuity of Cicero's Skepticism," in Powell, *Cicero the Philosopher*, 85–113.

19. John Dolman, *Those fyve questions, which Mark Tullye Cicero, disputed in his manor of Tusculanum* (London, 1561), 60–61.

20. The precise form of Brutus' remark can be seen to reinforce this neo-Stoic view that action precedes understanding. Using an anaphoristic structure, it creates the feeling of a belated coming into knowledge. Taken by itself, the first phrase of this remark—"the eye sees not itself but by reflection"—indicates that we achieve self-knowledge by reflecting on ourselves, that is, by introspection. The second clause— "by some other things"—rewrites the meaning of the first clause, however, by introducing another sense of the word "reflection." Now instead of being a synonym for meditation, it suggests an external activity, a casting back of images between surfaces. The first phrase is thus both necessary and insufficient to Brutus' meaning. Although it contains an essential part of the simile, its signification needs to be clarified by the introduction of the second phrase. Meanwhile, though the second phrase elucidates the first, it is dependent upon this phrase for its own meaning, and in fact even borrows its structure. The overall feeling of this passage is thus of a rough initial stab at meaning that permits Brutus' eventual articulation of his point. Just as we come to know our capabilities only by acting in the absence of self-knowledge, so too does Brutus' simile arrive at its full meaning only after hazarding an incomplete initial formulation.

21. This view derived from the treatment of "belief" and "faith" as synonyms from the fourteenth century onward, and although belief came gradually over the seventeenth century to have a meaning closer to that of opinion, it was still typically used in the early part of the century to suggest the full certainty of faith. Consider, for example, William Tyndale's rendering of Matthew 17:20–23: "Then came the disciples to Jesus secretly and sayde: Why could not we cast him [i.e., Satan] out? Jesus sayd unto them: Because of youre unbelefe. For I say veryly unto you: If you had faythe as a grayne of mustard seed, ye should saye unto this mountayne, remove hence to yonder place, and he shuld remove." Here belief and faith are clear synonyms, an agreement of meaning that is especially significant in light of the fact that this passage is concerned to describe the totalness of even the tiniest amount of faith. Moreover, while modern editions of the

Bible tend to replace the term "unbelief" with "little faith," eliminating the equation of faith and belief, the King James Version leaves Tyndale's translation intact, suggesting that the two terms continued to be interchangeable into the early seventeenth century. So too, when Francis Bacon was looking for a term to describe the complete acceptance of truth, he bypassed both "knowledge" and "faith" and instead selected "belief," arguing that "truth, which only doth judge itself, teacheth that...the knowledge of truth, which is the presence of it, and the belief of truth, which is the enjoying of it, is the sovereign good of human nature." Francis Bacon, "Of Truth" in *The Essays or Counsels Civil and Moral* (London, 1625).

22. For treatment of this issue, see Lorraine Daston, "Probability and Evidence," in *The Cambridge History of Seventeenth-Century Philosophy*, ed. Daniel Garber and Michael Ayers (Cambridge: Cambridge University Press, 1998), 1108–44.

23. For examples of Shakespeare's use of "belief" before 1599, see *King John* (1594–96), where Constance declares, "Let belief and life encounter so / As doth the fury of two desperate men, / Which in the very meeting fall, and die," (3.1.31–33); and Falstaff in *The Merry Wives of Windsor* (1597): "I was three or four times in the thought they were not fairies, and yet the guiltiness of my mind, the sudden surprise of my powers, drove the grossness of the foppery into a received belief, in despite of the teeth of all rhyme and reason, that they were fairies" (5.5.121–26).

24. For the classic formulation of this claim, see Gordon Braden, *Renaissance Tragedy and the Senecan Tradition: Anger's Privilege* (New Haven, CT: Yale University Press, 1985). For a summary of criticism on the influence of Senecan tragedy upon Shakespeare, see Robert Miola, *Shakespeare and Classical Tragedy: The Influence of Seneca* (Oxford: Oxford University Press, 1992), 3–9.

25. Thomas Rosenmeyer, *Senecan Drama and Stoic Cosmology* (Berkeley: University of California Press, 1989).

26. This technique found its way into a number of Elizabethan tragedies. Hieronimo laments in *The Spanish Tragedy* that "the blust'ring winds, conspiring with my words, at my lament have moved the leafless trees, disrobed the meadows of their flowered green" (3.7.5–7). Similarly, in *Titus Andronicus*, Titus groans in response to the mutilation of Lavinia: "I am the sea. Hark how her sighs doth blow. She is the weeping welkin, I the earth" (3.1.226–27).

27. For a summary of critical views on the subject, see Mark Sacharoff, "Suicide and Brutus' Philosophy in *Julius Caesar*," *Journal of the History of Ideas* 33 (1972): 115–22, 115–16. Also see R. F. Fleissner, "The Philosophy in *Julius Caesar* Again," *Archiv fur das Studium der Neuren Sprachen und Literaturen* 222 (1985): 344–45, for a rebuttal of Sacharoff's piece.

28. My account is based largely upon Brad Inwood, "Rules and Reasoning in Stoic Ethics," in *Topics in Stoic Philosophy*, ed. Katerina Ierodiakonou (Oxford: Clarendon Press, 1999), 95–127; "Stoic Ethics" in *The Cambridge History of Hellenistic Philosophy* (Cambridge: Cambridge University Press, 2000); *Ethics and Action in Early Stoicism* (Oxford: Clarendon Press, 1985). But see also Julia Annas, *The Morality of Happiness* (Oxford: Clarendon Press, 1993), 84–108; Philip Mitsis, "Moral Rules and the Aims of Stoic Ethics," *Journal of Philosophy* 83 (1986): 556–59, and "Seneca on Reason, Rules, and Moral Development," in *Passions and Perceptions*, ed. J. Brunschwig and Martha Nussbaum (Cambridge: Cambridge University Press, 1993), 285–312; Gerard Watson, "The Natural Law and Stoicism," in *Problems in Stoicism*, ed. A. A. Long (London: Athlone Press, 1971), 216–38.

29. For discussion of Cato's suicide, see Miriam Griffin, "Philosophy, Cato, and Roman Suicide," *Greece and Rome* 33 (1986): 64–77; 192–202.

30. See Gilles Monsarrat, *Light from the Porch: Stoicism and English Renaissance Literature* (Paris: Didier, 1984), 135–47 for a review of the debate. Horatio is the only one of Shakespeare's characters that Monsarrat—who is more rigorous in his definition of Stoicism than any other critic—accepts as a genuine Stoic.

31. The play marks this neo-Stoic view of belief by allowing it to emerge against the backdrop of traditional sixteenth-century psychology. Before Horatio's transformation, belief is treated in the play as the absolute result of an irresistible external force. As Marcellus relates, Horatio "will not let belief take hold of him" without firm evidence, indicating that belief is both total and imposed (1.1.24). Only after Horatio abruptly reverses his views on the ghost does he admit that he does "in part believe" that the cock banishes evil spirits at Christmas by singing all night long. Like Cassius, Horatio is thus reminded of the partial nature of belief by an unsettling encounter with the supernatural, and this neo-Stoic perspective explains Horatio's peculiar remark that other strange occurrences have functioned as "prologue to the omen coming on" (1.1.123). Horatio's state of surprise has given way to the claim that the ghost was predicted by other portents, so that he displays the same belated anticipation that Brutus exhibits in response to Portia's death. Having recognized the commonplace nature of the ghost, Horatio imaginatively projects himself back in time to imagine other supernatural disturbances as "prologue" to the shock of encounter.

32. Horatio continues in this practical vein during his later account of the ghost. Although remarking to Hamlet that the encounter made Marcellus and Barnardo almost "to jelly with the act of fear," he omits any mention of his own terror (1.2.205). Instead, he concentrates on his evaluation of the ghost's form, rewriting his past behavior in the same manner that Brutus rewrites his response to Portia's suicide.

33. See for example, Katharine Eisaman Maus, *Inwardness and Theatre in the English Renaissance* (Chicago: University of Chicago Press, 1995), 1; Anne Ferry, *The "Inward" Language: Sonnets of Wyatt, Sidney, Shakespeare, Donne* (Chicago: University of Chicago Press, 1983), 6.

34. Paul Cefalu, "Damned Custom...Habits Devil": Shakespeare's *Hamlet*, Anti-Dualism, and the Early Modern Philosophy of Mind," *ELH* 67 (2000): 399–431, 403.

35. Seneca's *Thyestes*, for example, concerns a pair of royal brothers who strive to usurp each other from the throne. One of them finally settles upon what he claims is an unprecedented and totally individual course—feeding his brother his own children for dinner. The chorus, however, is unimpressed. Not only has this very thing happened before—Procne did exactly the same to Tereus—but human depravity has become so endemic that no deed, however ingeniously cruel, seems unusual anymore. A thousand years before *Hamlet*, in short, revenge tragedy had already given up on the idea that any murder was strange. Shakespeare was very familiar with *Thyestes*, likely through Jasper Heywood's translation, and it was a heavy influence on him as early as *Titus Andronicus* (ca. 1590).

36. M. H. Addington, "Shakespeare and Cicero," *Notes and Queries* 165 (1933): 116–18.

37. Dolman, *Those fyve questions*, 12.

38. Ibid., 112; 30.

39. Luke Wilson, "*Hamlet*, Hales vs Petit, and the Hysteresis of Action," *ELH* 60 (1993): 17–56.

40. *Hales vs. Petit* was known in Shakespeare's time because of its inclusion in Edmund Plowden's sixteenth-century *Commentaries*, a worked rooted in the claim that the common law revealed itself through practice. As Plowden puts it, "It is usage which proves what the law is" (1.485). Edmund Plowden, *The Commentaries, or Reports of Edmund Plowden*, 2 vols. (London, 1816). For discussions of Plowden, see L. W. Abbott, *Law Reporting in England, 1485–1585* (London, 1973), 198–239; J. W. Tubbs, *The Common Law Mind: Medieval and Early Modern Conceptions* (Baltimore: Johns Hopkins University Press, 2000), 110–28.

41. Roberta Morgan, "Some Stoic Lines in *Hamlet* and the Problem of Interpretation," *PQ* 20 (1941): 549–58.

42. James Sandford, trans., *The Manuell of Epictetus, translated out of Greeke into French and now into English* (London, 1567).

3   *Othello* and the Subject of Ocular Proof

1. William Congreve, *The Double-Dealer* (London, 1693), 4.5.42.

2. *Othello*, 3.3.365.

3. James Ogden, "Restoration Jocularity at Othello's Expense," *Notes and Queries* n.s. 39 (1992): 464.

4. *The London Stage, 1660–1800,* ed. George Stone, 5 vols. (Carbondale: Southern Illinois University Press, 1960–68).

5. Virginia Vaughn, "*Othello* in Restoration England" in *Othello: A Contextual History* (Cambridge: Cambridge University Press, 1994), 93–112.

6. This critical attitude and the recent attempt to rehabilitate Restoration tragedy are discussed in detail in the following chapter.

7. Leo Kirschbaum, "The Modern Othello," *ELH* 11 (1944): 283–96, 289. Kirschbaum's basic framework persists in subsequent New Critical readings, e.g., Maurianne S. Adams, "'Ocular Proof' in Othello and Its Source," *PMLA* 79 (1964): 234–41.

8. In the memorable phrase of one critic, the play is a critique of "ocularcentrism." James A Knapp, "'Ocular Proof': Archival Revelations and Aesthetic Response, *Poetics Today* 24 (2003): 695–727, 724. The notion that Othello "deconstructs" our modern (or as scholars sometimes call it, "Enlightenment") investment in visual authority is common in the scholarly literature on the play. For some representative examples see Terry Eagleton, *William Shakespeare* (London: Blackwell, 1986), 64–70; Kenneth Gross, "Slander and Skepticism in Othello," *ELH* 56 (1989): 819–52; Patricia Parker, "Othello and Hamlet: Dilation, Spying, and the "Secret Place" of Woman," *Representations* 44 (1993): 60–95, 67–68; Katharine Maus, *Inwardness and Theater in the English Renaissance* (Chicago: Chicago University Press, 1995), 104–27. These authors also often describe paranoia in explicitly post-Cartesian terms. Eagleton, for example, diagnoses Othello with "the classic condition of paranoia," remarking that "the closest thing to paranoia, Freud commented dryly, is philosophy" (65); Gross suggests that "the play forces us to question what it means in the largest sense to speak of or to accuse a devil, a demonic principle, how the idea of a devil enters into both our trust and our paranoia" (847), calling up Descartes' image of the deceiving devil; and Maus argues that "For Othello imagines he can see everything, that there is no difference between the way one knows oneself and the way one knows other people" (123), referencing Descartes' notion that the mind is transparent to itself.

9. According to Stanley Cavell, the key development of "modern philosophical thought" is Descartes' concern that the world presented to his eyes might be an illusion wrought by a malicious genie. Stanley Cavell, *Disowning Knowledge in Six Plays of Shakespeare* (Cambridge: Cambridge University Press, 1987), 126–27. Also see Millicent Bell, *Shakespeare's Tragic Skepticism* (New Haven, CT: Yale University Press, 2002). Bell argues that "the central utterance of the play is, certainly, Othello's anguished 'Be sure of it, give me the ocular proof'" (83).

10. Cavell is explicit on this point, wondering why we "assume that Shakespeare was incapable of going beyond what he read?" Stanley Cavell, "Reply to Four Chapter " in *Wittgenstein and Scepticism,* ed.

Denis McManus (London: Routledge, 2004), 278–91, 280. But this point is implicit in all the readings that treat *Othello* as an exploration of modern paranoia.

11. Blakemore Evans, ed., *Shakespearean Prompt-Books of the Seventeenth Century*, 8 vols. (Charlottesville: Bibliographical Society of the University of Virginia, 1961–), vol. 6.

12. Marvin Rosenberg, *The Masks of Othello* (Berkeley: University of California Press, 1961), 20–24; Gino Matteo, *Shakespeare's Othello: The Study and the Stage, 1604–1904* (Salzburg: Institute for English Language and Literature, 1974), 65–75.

13. Richard Popkin, *The History of Scepticism from Erasmus to Spinoza* (Berkeley: University of California Press, 1979).

14. For discussion, see E. M. Curley. *Descartes against the Skeptics* (Cambridge, MA: Harvard University Press, 1978). On the problem of skepticism, Descartes writes, "skeptical philosophy...is vigorously alive today, and almost all those who regard themselves as more intellectually gifted than others...take refuge in skepticism because they cannot see any alternative with greater claims to truth." *The Philosophical Writings of Descartes*, trans. John Cottingham, Rupert Stoothoff, and Dugald Murdoch, 3 vols. (Cambridge: Cambridge University Press, 1985), 2.374.

15. For discussion of the "Cartesian Circle," see James Van Cleve, "Foundationalism, Epistemic Principles, and the Cartesian Circle," in *Descartes*, ed. John Cottingham (Oxford: Oxford University Press, 1998), 101–31. For a recent defender of the Cartesian Circle, see Husain Sarkar, *Descartes' Cogito* (Cambridge: Cambridge University Press, 2003).

16. *The Philosophical Writings of Descartes*, trans. John Cottingham, Robert Stoothoff, and Dugald Murdoch, 3 vols. (Cambridge: Cambridge University Press, 1984), 2: 334–35.

17. For the influence of Descartes' skepticism on Hobbes, see Richard Tuck, "Hobbes and Descartes," in *Perspectives on Thomas Hobbes*, ed. G. A. J. Rogers and Alan Ryan (Oxford: Clarendon Press, 1988), 11–41.

18. Thomas Rymer, *A Short View of Tragedy* (London, 1692).

19. Robert Turner, "Heroic Passion in the Early Tragicomedies of Beaumont and Fletcher," *Medieval and Renaissance Drama* 13 (1983): 182–202; Peter Davison, "The Serious Concerns of *Philaster*," *ELH* 30 (1963): 1–15; *Philaster*, ed. Dora Ashe (Lincoln: University of Nebraska Press, 1974).

20. James Savage, "Beaumont and Fletcher's *Philaster* and Sidney's *Arcadia*," *ELH* 14 (1947): 194–206.

21. Francis Beaumont and John Fletcher, *Philaster, or Love lies a Bleeding* (London, 1622). Citations by act, scene, and page number, following the original.

22. Thomas Porter, *The Villain, a Tragedy* (London, 1663). Citations by act, scene, and page number.

23. For discussion, see J. P. Vander Motten, "Iago at Lincoln's Inn Fields: Thomas Porter's *The Villain* on the Early Restoration Stage," *SEL* 24 (1984): 415–28.

24. J. A. W. Gunn, "'Interest Will Not Lie': A Seventeenth-Century Political Maxim," *Journal of the History of Ideas* 29 (1968): 551–64.

25. Marchamont Nedham, *Interest Will not Lie or a View of England's True Interest* (London, 1659), 3.

26. Donald Frame, trans., *The Complete Essays of Montaigne* (Palo Alto: Stanford University Press, 1976), 447.

27. For a summary of work on Descartes' optics, see Neil Ribe, "Cartesian Optics and the Mastery of Nature," *Isis* 88 (1997): 42–61.

28. For an in-depth discussion of the relationship of Hobbes' work on optics to Descartes, see Tuck, "Hobbes and Descartes."

29. The full quote runs: "Give me but proof of it, ocular proof, that I may justify my dealing with him to the World!" *The Double-Dealer*, 4.5.42–43.

30. R. I. M. Dunbar, "Coevolution of Neocortical Size, Group Size and Language in Humans," *Behavioral and Brain Sciences* 16 (1993): 681–735. Although there has been debate over the precise number of other people that our neocortex can track, Dunbar's basic conclusions are broadly accepted by physical anthropologists.

4 *The Indian Emperour* and the Reason of New World Conflict

1. For a perceptive discussion of this problem, see Robert Newman, "Irony and the Problem of Tone in Dryden's *Aureng-Zebe*," *SEL* 10 (1970): 439–58.

2. *The Works of John Dryden*, ed. E. N Hooker, H. T Swedenberg, et al. (Berkeley: University of California Press, 1956–2000), 20 vols., 9.15. Hereafter cited in the text as "*Works*."

3. This approach was initiated by Phillip Harth, *Contexts of Dryden's Thought* (Chicago: University of Chicago Press, 1968). For an (often humorous) example of the disagreements that continued in the wake of Harth's work, see the related: William Empson, "Dryden's Apparent Scepticism," *Essays in Criticism* 20 (1970): 172–81; Robert Hume, "Dryden's Apparent Scepticism," *Essays in Criticism* 20 (1970): 492–95; William Empson, "Dryden's Apparent Scepticism," *Essays in Criticism* 21 (1971): 111–15; Earl Miner, "Dryden's Apparent Scepticism," *Essays in Criticism* 21 (1971): 410–11. More recent criticism has produced an increasingly fine-grained account of Dryden's skepticism. For example, Eric Jager, "Educating the Senses: Empiricism in Dryden's *King Arthur*," *Restoration* 11 (1987): 107–16; Helen Burke, "*Annus Mirabilis* and the Ideology of the

New Science," *English Literary History* 57 (1990): 307–34; Richard Kroll, *The Material Word: Literature and Culture in the Restoration and Early Eighteenth Century* (Baltimore: Johns Hopkins University Press, 1991); Steven Zwicker, "The Paradoxes of Tender Conscience," *English Literary History* 63 (1996): 851–69; Paul Hammond, *Dryden and the Traces of Classical Rome* (Oxford: Oxford University Press, 1999), 94.

4. In Allardyce Nicoll's assessment: "The age was debilitated: it was distinctly unheroic: and yet it was not so cynical as to throw over entirely the inculcation of heroism. To present, however, heroism in real-life plays would have raised too sharp a distinction between what was and what might have been, and accordingly in the heroic tragedy heroism is cast out of the world altogether...The heroic play is like a Tale of a Land of No-where" (*A History of Restoration Drama, 1660–1700* [Cambridge: Cambridge University Press, 1928], 79). For another lively example of this perspective, see D. W. Jefferson, "'All, all of a piece throughout': Thoughts on Dryden's Dramatic Poetry," in *Restoration Theatre*, ed. John Brown and Bernard Harris (New York: St. Martin's Press, 1965), 159–76. The first critic to argue that Dryden saw skepticism as an intellectual justification for pandering is Louis Bredvold, *The Intellectual Milieu of John Dryden* (Ann Arbor: University of Michigan Press, 1934).

5. On this view, the heroes of *The Indian Emperour* are not intended as actual people at all. Instead, they are quasi-allegorical figures whose interactions represent a philosophical struggle toward enlightenment. See for example, John Winterbottom, "The Development of the Hero in Dryden's Tragedies," *JEGP* 52 (1953): 161–73; Scott Osborn, "Heroical Love in Dryden's Heroic Drama," *PMLA* 73 (1958): 480–90; Jean Gagen, "Love and Honor in Dryden's Heroic Plays," *PMLA* 77 (1962): 208–20; Arthur Kirsch, *Dryden's Heroic Drama* (Princeton, NJ: Princeton University Press, 1965); Michael Alssid, *Dryden's Rhymed Heroic Plays* (Salzburg: Salzburg Studies in English Literature, 1974); Anne Barbeau, *The Intellectual Design of John Dryden's Heroic Plays* (New Haven, CT: Yale University Press, 1970); Douglas Canfield, "The Ideology of Restoration Tragicomedy," *ELH* 51 (1984): 447–64.

6. Four years after its initial run, it was still performed with enough regularity for Samuel Pepys to attend three different productions in six months. For the stage history of *The Indian Emperour*, see *The London Stage, 1660–1800, Part I*, ed. William Van Lennep (Carbondale: Southern Illinois University Press, 1965), 87. An index to the performances can be found on page ccxii.

7. Samuel Mintz, *The Hunting of Leviathan: Seventeenth-Century Reactions to the Materialism and Moral Philosophy of Thomas Hobbes* (Cambridge: Cambridge University Press, 1962).

8. Richard Tuck, "Grotius, Carneades, and Hobbes," *Grotiana* 4 (1983): 43–62; "The 'Modern' Theory of Natural Law," in *The Languages of Political Theory in Early Modern Europe*, ed. Anthony Pagden (Cambridge: Cambridge University Press, 1987), 99–119; "Optics and Sceptics: The Philosophical Foundations of Hobbes' Political Thought," in *Conscience and Casuistry in Early Modern Europe*, ed. Edmund Leites (Cambridge: Cambridge University Press, 1988), 235–63.

9. John Aubrey, *Brief Lives and Other Selected Writings*, ed. Anthony Powell (London: Cresset Press, 1949), 261.

10. See Louis Bredvold, "Dryden, Hobbes, and the Royal Society," *Modern Philology* 25 (1928): 417–38; Louis Teeter, "The Dramatic Use of Hobbes' Political Ideas," *English Literary History* 3 (1936): 140–69; Mildred Hartsock, "Dryden's Plays: A Study in Ideas," *Seventeenth Century Studies,* second series, ed. Robert Shafer (Princeton, NJ: Princeton University Press); Clarence Thorpe, *The Aesthetic Theory of Thomas Hobbes* (Ann Arbor: University of Michigan Press, 1940), 189–220; John Winterbottom, "The Place of Hobbesian Ideas in Dryden's Tragedies," *JEGP* 57 (1958): 665–83.

11. For discussion, see Bridget Orr, "Poetic Plate-Fleets and Universal Monarchy: The Heroic Plays and Empire in the Restoration," *Huntington Library Quarterly* 63 (2000): 71–97, and *Theatrical Voyages and Conquests: The Colonial Discourse of Restoration Drama,* unpublished dissertation (Cornell University, 1994); Blair Hoxby, "The Government of Trade: Commerce, Politics, and the Courtly Art of the Restoration, *ELH* 66 (1999): 591–627; Robert Markley, "Violence and Profits in the Restoration Stage," *Eighteenth Century Life* 22 (1998): 2–17.

12. William Davenant, *The Cruelty of the Spaniards in Peru* (London, 1658). Davenant's work is a strangely piecemeal affair. Between scenes depicting Spanish atrocities such as the roasting of an Indian over an open flame, it offers the leaping tricks of acrobats in ape-suits, and it concludes on a note of total fantasy when the English army arrives to liberate the oppressed people of Peru. A baffled contemporary described the performance as "Foppery . . . Two hours of I know not what."

13. Davenant, *Cruelty of the Spaniards,* song 6.

14. All citations are from *The Indian Emperour* from *Works* 9.1–112.

15. This interpretation of *Le Cid* was also held by Corneille's early critics, who objected to what they saw as the playwright's adoption of the same exclusionary ethos as his hero. As De Scudéry wrote in his 1637 *Observations,* "I believe myself obliged to show to the author of *Le Cid*—whose duty is to satisfy honor—that he is himself a citizen of a fine Republic and should not imagine himself able to become

Tyrant." De Scudéry, "Observations sur *Le Cid,*" in *La Querelle du Cid: Pièces et Pamphlets,* ed. Armand Gasté (Paris, 1898), 71–111. "Je v'avois cru que j'estois obligé, de faire voir à l'Autheur du CID, qu'il se doit contenter de l'honneur, d'estre Citoyen d'une si belle Republique, sans imaginer mal à propos, qu'il en peut devenir le Tiran" (110–11).

16. Laurence Gregario, "Their Mean Task: Women and the Classical Ideal in Corneille's Theatre," *Papers on French Seventeenth Century Literature* 51 (1999): 371–87; David Clarke, "Corneille's Differences with the Seventeenth-Century Doctrinaires over the Moral Authority of the Poet," *Modern Language Review* 80 (1985): 550–62.

17. "I feel a fierce combat, my love struggling against my honor ... Father, mistress, honor, love, illustrious dominion, sweet constraint." "Que je sens de rudes combats! / Contre mon propre honneur, mon amour s'intéresse...Père, maîtresse, honneur, amour, / Illustre tyrannie, adorable constrainte" (1.7.303–14; 301–12). I am using the text of the 1657 quarto, published by Augustin Courbé. The second set of line numbers are for the version of *Le Cid* in volume 3 of *Œuvres complètes,* ed. C. Marty-Laveaux, 12 vols. (Paris: Editions des Grands Ecrivains de la France, 1862–68).

18. "Et, tout honteux d'avoir tant balancé / Ne soyons plus en peine" (1.7.349–50; 347–48).

19. "A king learns prudence, and knows better causes in which to spill his subjects' blood." "Un Roi dont la prudence a de meilleurs objets / Est Meilleur ménager du sang de ses sujets" (2.6.597–98; 595–96). In placing this emphasis on "la prudence," the king aligns himself with an Aristotelian ethos more interested in developing a commonsense balancing of ethical considerations than in defining moral imperatives. For Aristotle, each virtue was not opposed to a single vice, but to two contrary vices, so that virtuous behavior involved achieving a balance between two extremes. Courage was the mean between cowardice and foolhardiness, honor between pride and undue modesty, and so forth. As the virtue of moderation, prudence was thus the source of all the other virtues. For a good introduction see Pierre Aubenque, *La Prudence chez Aristote* (Paris: Presses Universitaires de France, 1976). For a superb discussion of the influence of Aristotle's theory on Early Modern French thought, see Ullrich Langer, "La Prudence: De la Batelière Exemplaire à Montaigne Châtelain," in *Vertu du Discours, Discours de la Vertu: Littérature et Philosophie Morale au XVIe siècle en France* (Genève: Librairie Droz, 1999), 161–79.

20. Jean de la Bruyère, "Des Ouvrages de l'esprit" in *Caractères* (Paris, 1689). "*Le Cid* n'a eu qu'une voix pour lui à sa naissance, qui a été celle de l'admiration; il s'est vu plus fort que l'autorité et la politique qui ont tenté de le détruire; il a réuni en sa faveur des esprits toujours

partagés d'opinion et des sentiments, les grands et le peuple: ils s'accordent tous á le savoir de mémoire, et à prévenir au théâtre les acteurs qui le récitent" (31).

21. For Dryden's sources for this passage, see Dougald MacMillan, "The Sources of Dryden's *The Indian Emperour*," *Huntington Library Quarterly* 13 (1950): 355–70, 366.

22. For a useful introduction to Dryden's general views of metaphor, see Michael Gelber, *The Just and the Lively: The Literary Criticism of John Dryden* (Manchester: Manchester University Press, 1999).

23. From the Preface to *Annus Mirabilis* in *Works* 1.53.

24. This part of the process, as Dryden sees it, is peculiar to each individual. He aligns the judgment in his critical writings with "taste," and he frequently admits that what pleases one person will not please everybody.

25. *Works* 1.53. Dryden explains that the third and final stage of creation is "Elocution, or the Art of clothing and adorning that thought so found [by invention] and varied [by judgment]."

26. Christopher Marlowe, *The Jew of Malta* in *Christopher Marlowe: Doctor Faustus and Other Plays*, ed. David Bevington (New York: Oxford University Press, 1995).

5   Cartesian Generosity and the New Shakespeare

1. Almanzor lectures the current ruler of Granada: "I saw th' opprest, and thought it did belong / To a King's office to redress the wrong: / I brought that Succour which thou oughtst to bring, / and so, in Nature, am thy Subjects King" (1.1.218–21).

2. Even those rare moments when Almanzor takes an interest in others do nothing to ease this deep sense of isolation. After Abdalla attempts to prove his right to the crown to enlist Almanzor's aid, the latter remarks, "It is sufficient that you make the claim: / You wrong our friendship when your right you name. / When for myself I fight, I weigh the cause; / But friendship will admit no such Laws" (3.1.21–24). The man who announces grandly on his entrance, "My laws are made but only for my sake" happily extends his radical sovereignty to others, seeing willfulness not as a personal prerogative, but as a general right (1.1.214). This charitable attitude is hardly novel to the heroic tradition—the knights of romance are forever galloping off in the service of others—but there had always been the sense that some permanent standard (usually honor) was underlying the proceedings. In *The Adventure of Five Hours* (1662), one of the earliest examples of heroic action to hit the Restoration stage, Antonio's generous offer of aid to a friend is prefaced with the declaration: "Honor's my Standard... But you are such a Judge of Honor's Laws, / That 'twere Injurious to suspect your Cause" (5.3.192–95).

Antonio's confidence in his friends' ability to properly weigh the laws of honor is very different from Almanzor's total rejection of law. In the former case, the hero trusts that his friend ascribes to a similar chivalric code. In the latter, the hero is willing to trust his friend's anarchic self-determination.

3. As a contemporary noted sarcastically, heroes like Almanzor could not be "confin'd to the narrow walks of other mortals" but—like "Dramatick Planets"—were "images of *Excentric Virtue*, which was most beautifull when least regular." Richard Leigh, *The Censure of the Rota on Mr Driden's Conquest of Grenada* (Oxford, 1673), 2–3.

4. "Dedication to Aureng-Zebe" in *The Works of John Dryden*, gen. eds. E. N Hooker and H. T Swedenberg (Berkeley: University of California Press, 1956–2000), 20 vols., 12.153.

5. "If Shakespear be allow'd, as I think he must, to have made his Characters distinct, it will easily be infer'd that he understood the nature of the Passions: because it has been prov'd already, that confus'd passions make indistinguishable Characters" (*Works*, 13.244).

6. "If there be no manners appearing in the characters, no concernment for the persons can be rais'd: no pity or horror can be mov'd, but by vice and virtue, therefore without them, no person can have any business in the Play. If the inclinations be obscure, 'tis a sign the Poet is in the dark, and knows not what manner of man he presents to you; and consequently, you can have no Idea, or very imperfect, of that man: nor can judge what resolutions he ought to take; or what words or actions are proper for him" (*Works*, 13.237).

7. For summary, see Blakey Vermeule, *Why Do We Care about Literary Characters?* (Baltimore: Johns Hopkins University Press, 2010).

8. Walter Charleton, *A Natural History of the Passions* (London, 1674).

9. "Mais la Tristesse de cette Pitié n'est pas amère; et comme celle que causent les actions funestes qu'on voit représenter sur un théâtre, elle est plus dans l'extérieur et dans le sens, que dans l'intérieur de l'âme, laquelle a cependant la satisfaction de penser, qu'elle compatit avec des affligés." "This pity is not in the mind, but like that which is caused by the tragic actions of the theatre, is more in the exterior realm of the sense, than the interior of the mind (which nevertheless has the satisfaction of thinking that it sympathizes with the afflicted)." In *Oeuvres de Descartes*, ed. Charles Adam and Paul Tannery (Paris: J. Vrin, 1973–78), 11 vols, xi. For English translation, see "The Passions of the Soul," in *The Philosophical Writings of Descartes*, trans. John Cottingham, Rupert Stoothoff, and Dugald Murdoch, 3 vols. (Cambridge: Cambridge University Press, 1985), 1.325–404, 3.187.

10. See Helen Cullyer, *Greatness of Soul from Aristotle to Cicero: The Genealogy of a Virtue*, unpublished dissertation, Yale University, 1999; Howard Curzer, "A Great Philosopher's Not-So-Great Account of a Great Virtue: Aristotle's Treatment of Greatness of Soul," *Canadian*

Journal of Philosophy 20 (1990): 517–31; Howard J. Curzer, "Aristotle's Much Maligned *Megalopsychos*," *Australasian Journal of Philosophy* 69 (1991): 131–51; Neil Cooper, "Aristotle's Crowning Virtue," *Apeiron* 22 (1989): 191–205; R. A. Gauthier, *Magnanimité: L'idéal de la grandeur dans la philosophie païenne et dans la théologie chrétienne* (Paris, 1951). For a useful translation of this general background onto the drama of the seventeenth century, see Eugene Waith, *Ideas of Greatness: Heroic Drama in England* (London: Routledge, 1971).

11. "Following the vernacular, I have called this virtue *générosité* rather than magnanimity, a term used in the schools" (*Les Passions*, 3.161). See Susan James, *Passion and Action: The Emotions in Seventeenth-Century Philosophy* (Oxford: Clarendon Press, 1997) for a good introduction to Descartes' treatise.

12. *Elements of Law*, I. ix. 10.

13. *De Rerum Natura*, II.1–6. For discussion, see Clarence Thorpe, *The Aesthetic Theory of Thomas Hobbes* (Ann Arbor: University of Michigan Press, 1940), 143; Baxter Hathaway, "The Lucretian Return upon Ourselves in Eighteenth-Century Theories of Tragedy," *PMLA* 62 (1947): 672–89.

14. *Les Passions* was written for Princess Elisabeth of Bohemia, who had remarked in 1643 that nothing in the *Meditations* explained how the mind interacted with the body.

15. In *The State of Innocence*, Dryden's rewriting of *Paradise Lost*, Adam's initial moment of consciousness is the realization: "For that I am, / I know, because I think." Like Descartes, Adam thus begins in a state of doubt, only to find a measure of certainty in the method of the *cogito*: "I am... because I think." This Cartesian method of inquiry then leads Adam to the rationalist view of religion popularized by Hobbes and propounded by Montezuma and Almanzor: "I move, I see; I speak, discourse, and know / Though now I am, I was not always so. / Then that from which I was, must be before: / Whom as my Spring of Being, I adore."

16. Dryden's favored explanation for this contradiction was that there was something rough and unfinished about Shakespeare. Dryden liked to cite Shakespeare's language as evidence of a raw, but erratic, natural talent, and so it was that Dryden set out to refine and finish what Shakespeare had blindly unearthed.

17. All citations from *All for Love* taken from *Works*, 13.1–112.

18. *Works*, 12.92.

19. See for example A. C. Bradley's argument that the play does not belong among works like *Hamlet, Lear, Othello,* and *Macbeth* because it is too "half-hearted" and "ironical" to produce the "terrifying and overwhelming power" necessary for great tragedy. *Oxford Lectures on Poetry* (1909), 285, 290, 305.

20. See Sergio Rufini, "'To Make that Maxim Good': Dryden's Shakespeare," in *The European Tragedy of Troilus*, ed. Piero Boitani

(Oxford: Clarendon Press, 1989), 243–80, and Susan Owen, *Restoration Theatre and Crisis* (Oxford: Clarendon Press, 1996).

21. Agnes Mure Mackenzie, *The Women in Shakespeare's Plays* (New York: Doubleday, Page, and Company, 1924), 199.

22. For example, David Norbrook, "Rhetoric, Ideology and the Elizabethan World Picture," in *Renaissance Rhetoric*, ed. Peter Mack (1994), 140–64, 154–56; Robert Grundin, "The Soul of State: Ulyssean Irony in *Troilus and Cressida*," *Anglia* 93 (1975): 55–69; A. M. Potter," *Troilus and Cressida*: Deconstructing the Middle Ages," *Theoria* 72 (1988): 23–35, 33; William Elton, "Shakespeare's Ulysses and the Problem of Value," *Shakespeare Studies* 2 (1966): 95–111, 98–100.

23. See Sergio Rufini, " 'To Make that Maxim Good': Dryden's Shakespeare," in *The European Tragedy of Troilus*, ed. Piero Boitano (Oxford: Clarendon Press, 1989), 243–80, for summary.

24. See also Robin Sowerby, "The Last Parting of Hector and Andromache," in *John Dryden: Tercentenary Essays*, ed. Paul Hammond (Oxford: Oxford University Press, 2000), 240–63.

25. Rufini "To Make that Maxim Good," 247.

26. Ibid., 278.

27. John Dewey and James Hayden Tufts, *Ethics* (New York: Henry Holt, 1908), 224.

28. John Dewey, *Democracy and Education: An Introduction to the Philosophy of Education* (New York: Macmillan, 1916), 62.

29. John Dewey, *Human Nature and Conduct* (New York: Henry Holt, 1922), 245.

30. Ibid., 284–87.

31. Dawkins himself veers into speculative idealism in *The Selfish Gene*, remarking: "We have the power to defy the selfish genes of our birth and, if necessary, the selfish memes of our indoctrination. We can even discuss ways of deliberately cultivating and nurturing pure, dis- interested altruism—something that has no place in nature, some- thing that has never existed before in the whole history of the world. We are built as gene machines and cultured as meme machines, but we have the power to turn against our creators. We, alone on earth, can rebel against the tyranny of the selfish replicators." Richard Dawkins, *The Selfish Gene* (Oxford: Oxford University Press, 1989), 200–201. On this view, altruism—and, by extension, liberty—are both intrinsically good, ideals outside of nature.

6 *King Lear* and the Endurance of Tragedy

1. Charles Gildon, "The Art and Progress of the Stage in France, Rome and England," in *The Works of William Shakespeare*, ed. Nicholas Rowe, 7 vols. (London, 1709–10), 7.406.

2. The major indication being the preference for Nahum Tate's pious revision. Philip Hobsbaum, "*King Lear* in the Eighteenth Century," *Modern Language Review* 68 (1973): 494–506.
3. *The Letters of John Keats, 1814–1821,* 2 vols., ed. Hyder Edward Rollins (Cambridge: Harvard University Press, 1958), 1.192; Samuel Taylor Coleridge, *Coleridge's Criticism of Shakespeare: A Selection* (London: Athlone Press, 1989), 95; Edward Dowden, *Shakspere: A Critical Study of His Mind and Art* (London: Harper, 1918), 202; *Romantic Critical Essays,* ed. David Bromwich (Cambridge: Cambridge University Press, 1987), 66; *The Complete Works of William Hazlitt,* 21 vols., ed. P. P. Howe (London: J. M. Dent and Sons, 1930–34), 12.341, 342; 16.61, 63; 18.334, 335.
4. To see *Lear* acted was to lose its sublime insights into the nature of the human mind and to witness instead "an old man tottering about the stage." *Romantic Critical Essays,* 66.
5. On Cavell's Romanticism, see Richard Eldridge, *The Persistence of Romanticism* (Cambridge: Cambridge University Press, 2001) and William Desmond, "A Second *Primavera*: Cavell, German Philosophy, and Romanticism" in *Stanley Cavell,* ed. Richard Eldridge (Cambridge: Cambridge University Press, 2003), 143–71.
6. Stanley Cavell, *Must We Mean What We Say?* (New York: Charles Scribner's Sons, 1969), 267–53.
7. Stanley Cavell, *The Claim of Reason: Wittgenstein, Skepticism, Morality, and Tragedy* (Oxford: Oxford University Press, 1982), 46.
8. See James Conant, "On Bruns, On Cavell" *Critical Inquiry* 17 (1991): 616–34 for discussion. Conant is responding to Gerald Bruns, "Stanley Cavell's Shakespeare" *Critical Inquiry* 16 (1990): 612–32.
9. For example, Barry Stroud, "Reasonable Claims: Cavell and the Tradition" *Journal of Philosophy* 77 (1980): 731–44, 736. Also, *The Significance of Philosophical Skepticism* (Oxford: Clarendon Press, 1984), 258. See Eldridge, *Persistence of Romanticism,* 191, for discussion.
10. Indeed, he goes so far as to criticize the recent revival of American pragmatism for doing so. Stanley Cavell, "What's the Use of Calling Emerson a Pragmatist?" in *The Revival of Pragmatism,* ed. Morris Dickstein (Durham, NC: Duke University Press, 1998), 72–80, 78.
11. This claim is a version of the idea of poetic justice and will be discussed in this context below.
12. Stanley Cavell, *Disowning Knowledge in Six Plays of Shakespeare* (Cambridge: Cambridge University Press, 1987), 114–15.
13. Ludwig Wittgenstein, *Philosophical Investigations,* trans. G. E. M. Anscombe (Oxford: Blackwell, 1963).

14. Stanley Cavell, "The Politics of Interpretation" in *Themes Out of School: Effects and Causes* (San Francisco: North Point Press, 1984).

15. For a helpful discussion of Cavell's use of psychoanalysis, see Stephen Mulhall, *Stanley Cavell: Philosophy's Recounting of the Ordinary* (Oxford: Clarendon Press, 1994), 207–22.

16. Hence the title of his essay on *Lear*: "The Avoidance of Love." For more of Cavell's views on love, see *The Claim of Reason*, 359.

17. Harold Bloom, *Shakespeare: The Invention of the Human* (New York: Riverhead Trade, 1999), 4.

18. *Disowning Knowledge*, 122.

19. For example, Berel Lang, "Nothing Comes of All: Lear-Dying," *New Literary History* 9 (1978): 537–59, 541, and Anthony Palmer, "Skepticism and Tragedy: Crossing Shakespeare with Descartes" in *Wittgenstein and Scepticism*, ed. Denis McManus (London: Routledge, 2004), 260–77. For Cavell's response, see "Reply" in *Wittgenstein and Scepticism*, 278–91, 279–82.

20. Cavell writes of this moment: "Then the terrible knowledge is released: 'I might have saved her.' From the beginning, and through each moment until they are led to prison, he might have saved her, had he done what every love requires, put himself aside long enough to see through to her." *Disowning Knowledge*, 73.

21. *Disowning Knowledge*, 80.

22. He writes in *Experience and Nature*: "The road to freedom by escape into the inner life…was taken…by children, long before it was formulated in philosophical romanticism" (230).

23. Dewey writes of the difference: "Romanticism is an evangel in the garb of metaphysics. It sidesteps the painful, toilsome labor…which change sets us, by glorifying it for its own sake. Flux is made something to revere, something profoundly akin to what is best within ourselves, will and creative energy. It is not, as it is in experience, a call to effort, a challenge to investigation, a potential doom of disaster and death." *Experience and Nature*, 51.

7 The Progress of Ethics

1. John Locke, *An Essay Concerning Human Understanding*, ed. Peter H. Nidditch (Oxford: Clarendon Press, 1979), 4.3.18.

2. "The Epistle to the Reader," in John Locke, *An Essay*, 7.

3. For an introduction to recent work on Locke's *Essay*, see Vere Chappell, *Locke* (Oxford: Oxford University Press, 1998), esp. Michael Ayers, "The Foundations of Knowledge and the Logic of Substance," 24–47, Margaret Atherton, "Locke and the Issue over Innateness," 48–59, and Ruth Mattern, "Locke: 'Our Knowledge, which All Consists in Propositions,'" 226–41.

4. In Locke's view, "Truth properly belongs only to Propositions," and so knowledge can only be represented in statements such as "Honey is sweet" (4.5.2). Sense impressions, meanwhile, relay simple qualities such as "sweet" and "yellow" that by themselves constitute only one term of a proposition. Taken individually, then, sense impressions are not even candidates for knowledge. Moreover, while Locke allows that our sensory experiences train us to cluster certain qualities together, he ranks the propositions derived from such associations as the lowest form of knowledge (4.2.14).

5. "If anyone maintain that men ought to be compelled by fire and sword to profess certain doctrines...it cannot be doubted indeed but such a one is desirous to have a numerous assembly joined in the same profession with himself; but that he principally intends by those means to compose a truly Christian Church is altogether incredible." John Locke, "A Letter Concerning Toleration" in *Two Treatises of Government* and *A Letter Concerning Toleration*, ed. Ian Shapiro (New Haven, CT: Yale University Press, 2003), 211–54, 215, 216.

6. For a discussion of Locke's views on colonialism, see Barbara Arneil, *John Locke and America: The Defence of English Colonialism* (Oxford: Oxford University Press, 1996). For a carefully balanced examination of imperial liberalism, see Jennifer Pitts, *A Turn to Empire: The Rise of Imperial Liberalism in Britain and France* (Princeton, NJ: Princeton University Press, 2005).

7. "While this logic, based on *aeternae veritates* [eternal truths] which it did not consider open to objection, believed that all the riddles of the world could be recognized and resolved and had treated space, time, and causality as totally unconditional laws with the most universal validity, Kant showed how these really served only to raise mere appearance...to the complete and highest reality and to set it in place of the innermost and true essence of things and thus to make true knowledge of this essence impossible." Friedrich Nietzsche, *The Birth of Tragedy*, trans. Ronald Speirs (Cambridge: Cambridge University Press, 1999), 86.

8. "The *only* seeing is seeing from a perspective; the *only* knowledge, knowledge from a perspective." "Es giebt *nur* ein perspektivisches Sehen, *nur* ein perspektivisches 'Erkennen.'" *On the Genealogy of Morals, A Polemic* (*Zur Genealogie der Moral, Eine Streitschrift*, 1887), Essay 3, Section 12.

9. Nietzsche was not complimentary toward Locke, whom he abused in *Beyond Good and Evil*, nor did he acknowledge that Kant arrived at account of "the skeptic" through Locke via Hume. Nevertheless, Kant openly acknowledged his debt to Hume, and for Hume's debt to Locke, see David Owen, *Hume's Reason* (Oxford: Oxford University Press, 1999), 63. Richard Popkin has written eloquently

on the danger of oversimplifying Hume's thought by treating him as nothing other than the successor to Locke, but there is no question that Locke looms large in the opening sections of *An Enquiry*.

10. *The Foucault Reader*, ed. Paul Rabinow (New York: Pantheon, 1984), 43.

11. "This ethos implies, first, the refusal of what I like to call the 'blackmail' of the Enlightenment." *The Foucault Reader*, 42. Foucault credits Locke and his heirs not just for initiating "a certain manner of philosophizing," but "for linking the progress of truth and the history of liberty in a bond of direct relation ... a philosophical question that remains for us to consider" (42–43).

12. "The critical ontology of ourselves has to be considered not, certainly, as a theory, nor even as a permanent body of knowledge that is accumulating; it has to be conceived as an attitude, an ethos, a philosophical life in which the critique of what we are is at one and the same time the historical analysis of the limits that are imposed on us and an experiment with the possibility of going beyond them." *The Foucault Reader*, 50.

13. This phrase occurs repeatedly in the *Essay*, but see, for example, 2.14.4 and 4.7.4.

14. Richard Rorty observes that by establishing its own speculative method as "the foundation of culture," philosophy displaced the practices of the arts, "the unforced flowers of life." Of Locke's role in this transition, Rorty notes: "We owe the notion of 'a theory of knowledge' based on an understanding of 'mental processes' to the seventeenth century, and especially to Locke." Richard Rorty, *Philosophy and the Mirror of Nature* (Princeton, NJ: Princeton University Press, 1979), 163, 3. I follow many other pragmatists in dissenting from Rorty's neopragmatic response to the problem of speculative philosophy, but I accept his historical account of its origins.

15. Adam Smith, *The Theory of Moral Sentiments*, ed. Knud Haakonssen (Cambridge: Cambridge University Press, 2002), 295. Smith invokes Hamlet as an example of the ethical problem of pride.

16. Gauri Vishwanathan, *Masks of Conquest: Literary Study and British Rule in India* (New York: Columbia University Press, 1989). For an early pragmatic critique of Shakespearean liberalism, see Rudyard Kipling's sardonic portrait of an Indian Babu who credits his degree in surveying to the wisdom he distills from—of all things—a second-hand copy of *Lear*. Rudyard Kipling, *Kim* (Oxford: Oxford University Press, 1998), 162–63.

17. John Crowe Ransom, *The New Criticism* (Norfolk: New Directions, 1941), 43–44. Ransom is not talking particularly here of *Hamlet*, but of poetic language in general. Nevertheless, New Critical readings of *Hamlet* quickly became the norm of postwar criticism.

18. Radical scholarship has proved the most fruitful in this regard, and both New Historicism and Cultural Materialism will be discussed in some detail below, but for an example of the continuance of formal pluralism, see Graham Bradshaw, *Shakespeare's Scepticism* (Ithaca, NY: Cornell University Press, 1991), and for an example of the continuance of a liberal humanist Shakespeare, see Annabel Patterson, *Shakespeare and the Popular Voice* (New York: Blackwell, 1991) and Richard Levin, "On Defending Shakespeare, 'Liberal Humanism,' Transcendent Love, and Other Sacred Cows and Lost Causes," *Textual Practice* 7 (1993): 50–55.

19. Stephen Greenblatt, *Renaissance Self-Fashioning: From More to Shakespeare* (Chicago: University of Chicago Press, 1980), 256.

20. Jonathan Dollimore, *Radical Tragedy: Religion, Ideology, and Power in the Drama of Shakespeare and His Contemporaries* (Durham, NC: Duke University Press, 2004), 153.

21. "The Nietzschean *affirmation*, that is the joyous affirmation of the play of the world and of the innocence of becoming, the affirmation of a world of signs without fault, without truth, and without origin which is offered to an active interpretation." Jacques Derrida, *Writing and Difference*, trans. Alan Bass (Chicago: University of Chicago Press, 1978), 292.

22. This convergence becomes even more apparent in light of Greenblatt's later writings. In his work on *Lear*, Greenblatt describes his skepticism about subjectivity as a form of Schopenhauerian resignation, a label which would seem to confirm Dollimore's suspicion that Greenblatt is ultimately a pessimist about human agency ("Shakespeare and the Exorcists," in *Shakespeare and the Question of Theory*, ed. Patricia Parker and Geoffrey Hartman [New York: Routledge 1985], 163–87; and "The Cultivation of Anxiety: King Lear and His Heirs," in *Learning to Curse* [New York: Routledge, 1992], 80–98). By aligning himself with Schopenhauer, however, Greenblatt simply rehearses a move made in *The Birth of Tragedy*, where Nietzsche describes how Schopenhauer's ethics inspired him to calmly accept, without false hope or useless despair, the inconsequentiality of his own will in comparison to the will of the cosmos. Unlike Schopenhauer, of course, Nietzsche does not remain in a state of passive acceptance. Instead, the enormous forces pitted against him become the foil against which his commitment to affirming his own will becomes truly heroic. Likewise, Greenblatt makes it clear that the overwhelming power of the world-will has not stranded him in a state of passive resignation. Rather, it has set him free, allowing him to assert his own will, and he goes on to celebrate his doubt with such life-affirming terms as "liberating" (Stephen Greenblatt, "Shakespeare Bewitched," in *New Historical Literary Study*, ed. Jeffrey Cox and Larry Reynolds [Princeton, NJ: Princeton University Press, 1993], 108–35).

23. For further discussion, see Angus Fletcher, "The Comic Ethos of *Il Principe*," *Comparative Drama* 43 (2009): 293–315.

Conclusion

1. As Stephen Jay Gould puts it: "Science can supply information as input to a moral decision, but the ethical realm of "oughts" cannot be logically specified by the factual "is" of the natural world—the only aspect of reality that science can adjudicate." Stephen Jay Gould, *The Richness of Life: The Essential Stephen Jay Gould*, ed. Steven Rose (New York: Norton, 2007), 543.

Index

acquiescent naturalism. *See* laissez-faire naturalism
All for Love, 107–12
  and the problem of reason, 107
  as source of generosity, 107–8, 110–11
Antony and Cleopatra, 107, 111
Aristotle, 12, 41, 73, 82, 106, 173n19
art
  as ethical tool, xv–xvi, 9, 10, 117–18, 145, 149
  as experience, 9, 23, 28, 37–8, 51, 63–4, 95–8, 106–7, 117–18, 149–50
  as intentional, 124–5, 132–3
  relationship to science, xiv–xvi, 11–12, 149–50
  See also tragedy

Bacon, Francis, 73, 164n21
Beaumont, Francis
  Philaster, or Love Lies a Bleeding, 76–7
belief, 41–2, 44–9, 52–6, 62
  See also partial belief
Bernstein, Richard, 11, 155n25
biological criticism, xiv–xvi, 17, 152n9
blank slate. *See* tabula rasa
Bloom, Harold, 124–5, 129
Booth, Stephen, 33

Calvin, John, 7, 15, 23, 28–9
  ideological appropriation of Luther'spractice-based ethics, 29

Cartesianism. *See* Descartes, René
Catholic Church, xi, 15–17, 20–9, 43, 65, 90, 94, 151n2, 155n31, 158n19
  See also eucharist
Cavell, Stanley, 125–31, 168n9
  See also Romanticism
Charleton, Walter
  Natural History of the Passions, 104–6
Cicero, 14, 42–6, 49, 56, 62, 64, 162n6, 163n8,17,18
  De Officiis, 45, 163n17
  The Tusculan Disputations, 45–6, 56, 162n6, 163n17
cognitive science, xii, 3–4, 11, 13, 154n16, 156n32
  See also biological criticism
Coleridge, Samuel Taylor, 123, 128
communication. *See* art, as experience
Congreve, William
  The Double-Dealer, 67–8, 80–1, 170n29
Copernicus, 12, 83
Corneille, Pierre
  Le Cid, 93, 172n15
Cultural Materialism. *See* Dollimore, Jonathan; radical ethics
Cyrenaics, 42–3

Damasio, Antonio, 153n9,10
Darwin, Charles, xi–xiv, 1–6, 10–11, 13–14, 17–18, 23, 117, 119–22, 124, 132, 134, 145–8,

Darwin, Charles—*Continued*
153n2,3, 154n15,16,25,
156n7
Darwinism
as challenge to ethics, xi–xiii,
1–3, 147–8
as foundation of pragmatic ethics,
4, 148
practical benefit of, xiii
See also natural selection
Davenant, William, 89, 172n12
*The Cruelty of the Spaniards in
Peru*, 89
Dawkins, Richard, xi, 121, 151n3,
177n31
death, problem of, 18–38, 39–66,
149
biological function of, 19
as physical problem, 19
See also ethical problems;
tomorrow, problem of
deconstruction. *See* Derrida,
Jacques; radical ethics
democracy, xvi, 4, 7–8, 16, 138,
142, 148, 155n25
pragmatic definition of, 7–8
See also progressive society
Derrida, Jacques, 142–4
Descartes, René, 12, 14, 65, 68,
73–7, 80–2, 84, 102, 105–7,
111, 120, 125–9, 131, 137,
168n8,9, 169n14, 176n11,15
appropriation of skepticism, 73,
137
on the ethical function of
tragedy, 102, 104–6
failure of rational method, 74
interest in the ethical possibilities
of vision, 80–1
Meditations on First Philosophy,
74, 137
Optics, 81, 107
and practice-based ethics, 105–6,
111
redefinition of greatness as
generous pity, 105–6

See also generosity, practice of;
skepticism, as tool of practical
ethics
Dewey, John, 4–7, 9–10, 16–18, 65,
68, 87, 118–20, 131–2, 134,
145, 149, 154n19,22, 157n8,
179n23
Art as Experience, 11, 134
*The Influence of Darwin on
Philosophy*, 154n17
See also art; ethics; growth;
pragmatism
diversity. *See* organic pluralism
Doctor Faustus, 15–20, 23–32,
34, 36–8, 39–40, 64–5, 149,
157n10, 159n27,30,35–7,
160n38
and the problem of death, 17,
18–19, 23–6
as source of ethical practice, 18,
23, 25, 27–8, 29
Dollimore, Jonathan, 143–4
Dolman, John, 46, 56
Donne, John, 34–5
Dowden, Edmund, 123
dramatic tragedy. *See* tragedy
Dryden, John, 84–93, 96–9, 101–4,
107–15, 117–20, 171n4,
174n21,22,24,25, 176n15,16
Aureng-Zebe, 101–2
The Conquest of Granada, 72,
101–2, 107, 117
An Essay of Dramatic Poesy,
102–2
influence of Descartes, 107
influence of Hobbes, 87–92, 107
skepticism, 86–91, 98, 117, 170n3
views on metaphor, 96–7
See also *All for Love*; *The Indian
Emperour*; *Troilus and Cressida*
(Dryden)

English civil war, 67
cultural shift of, 74–5
effect on tragedy, 76–9, 86
ethical problem raised by, 83

Epictetus
    Enchiridion, 61
Erasmus, 82
ethical problems
    art as communicator of, 10
    death as model of, 19
    origins in physical experience, 19,
        82–3, 117
    as source of progressive society,
        10
    See also death, problem of; free
        will, as false problem; paranoia,
        problem of; reason, problem
        of; social relations, problem of;
        tomorrow, problem of
ethics
    art as source of, xiii, xv–xvi, 4,
        9–10, 117–18, 149–50
    biological definition of, xv–xvi,
        10, 19
    challenge posed by Darwinism,
        xi–xiii, 1–3, 147–8
    as innate, xvi, 2, 121, 124–5,
        132, 147–8
    as intentional, xiii, 120–2,
        124–5, 132–4, 136, 144–6,
        148–50
    as opposed to morality, xii,
        149–50
    origins in physical problems, xii,
        xv–xvi, 6–8, 10, 16, 19, 82–3,
        117
    pragmatism as method for, 3,
        4–10, 12–14, 117–19, 148
    as progressive, 3, 119
    science as model for, 6, 118, 148
    See also ethical problems; growth;
        organic pluralism; pragmatism
eucharist, 21–7, 29, 33–5, 158n19
eugenics, 1–3, 147, 153n2
experience
    art as communicator of, 9
    See also art

Fletcher, John, 103
    See also Beaumont, Francis

Foucault, Michel, 139–40, 142–4,
        155n25, 156n33, 181n11,12
free will, as false problem, 5, 16, 19,
        61, 121, 142, 144, 156n5
Freud, Sigmund, 124, 127–8, 168n8
functional diversity. *See* organic
        pluralism

Galton, Francis, 153n2,3
generosity, practice of, 102, 104–6,
        109–18
Gould, Stephen Jay, 151n3, 183n1
Greenblatt, Stephen, 33, 142–4,
        182n22
growth, 118–20, 146, 150
    pragmatic definition of, 118–19
Gunn, Giles, 11, 155n25

Hamlet, xi, xiii–xvi, 4, 9–10, 12–14,
        34, 38, 40, 51–65, 83, 86–7,
        98–9, 118, 121, 123, 128, 131,
        133, 141–2, 144–6, 167n35,
        181n15,17
    and problem of death, 53–7, 62
    as source of neo-Stoic practice,
        52–3, 57–9, 60–4
    "To be" soliloquy, 55–7
    See also neo-Stoicism
Hegel, Georg Wilhelm Friedrich,
        129, 155n25
heroism, logic of. *See* paranoia,
        problem of; reason, problem of
Hobbes, Thomas, 12, 14, 65, 75,
        78–9, 81–2, 84, 88
    account of religion, 87–8
    critique of reason, 87–8
    Leviathan, 75, 78, 87–92, 95,
        106–7, 155n31, 170n28,
        176n15
    on the practical value of
        judgment, 91–2
    and practice-based ethics, 75, 88,
        91–2
    See also judgment, practice
        of; reason, problem of; self-
        interest; skepticism

Homer
  The Iliad, 9–10, 105
Hook, Sidney, 156n7
humanism
  idealist definition of, 151n3
  pragmatic definition of, xii–xiii,
    148, 150
Hume, David, 13, 180n9
Huxley, T.H., 151n3

idealism, xii–xiii, 6–7, 20, 29–30,
    33, 48, 64, 133, 141–2, 144–5,
    148
  practical dangers of, 7, 64–5,
    141–2, 144
  source of, xii–xiii, 6–7, 144–5,
    148
  See also metaphysics
The Indian Emperour, 85–99
  and the problem of reason, 86–7,
    89–91, 93–6
  as source of judgment, 92–4,
    96–8
intentionality. *See* ethics

James, William, 3–5, 154n15,16,
    156n5
  The Principles of Psychology, 4,
    12
judgment, practice of, 91–3, 95–8,
    101–2, 117–18, 174n24,25
Julius Caesar, 39–53, 56–7, 62–5,
    162n3, 164n20,21, 166n31,32
  and the problem of death, 39–41,
    43–4, 48–51
  as source of neo-Stoic practice,
    39–40, 43–5, 47, 50–1
  See also neo-Stoicism

Kant, Immanuel, 13, 123, 138–40,
    142, 155n25, 180n7,9
Keen, Suzanne, 152n9
King Lear, 123–34
  appropriation by Romantics,
    123–31

as source of practical ethics,
    131–3
kin selection, xi–xii, 151n4

laissez-faire naturalism, 2, 6, 14,
    120–2, 134, 136, 144–5, 148
Las Casas, Bartolomé de
  The Tears of the Indians, 89
liberalism, 13–14, 16–17, 138–42,
    157n8, 180n6, 181n16,
    182n18
literary studies
  approach to pluralism, 16–17,
    144
  as species of philosophy, xv,
    13–14, 141–2
  See also biological criticism;
    liberalism; New Criticism; New
    Historicism; radical ethics;
    Romanticism
Locke, John, 13–14, 123,
    135–45, 156n32, 180n4,5,6,9,
    181n11,14
  attack on practical ethics, 13,
    135–8, 140–1
  failure of epistemological reforms,
    138–44
  See also tabula rasa
Lucretius, xvi, 106, 152n15
Luther, Martin, 12, 14, 20–9,
    33–5, 37–8, 64, 73–4,
    155n31, 157n16,
    158n19,21,22,24
  critique of allegory, 26–7
  discussion of riddles, 33–5
  lingering idealism of, 29
  and practice-based ethics, 20–3,
    25, 26
  views on death, 20, 22–3
  See also eucharist

Macbeth, 17–18, 30–8, 39–40, 46,
    50–2, 64–5, 67, 86–7, 98–9,
    118, 123, 131, 133, 149,
    159n37, 160n38

and the problem of tomorrow,
  30–3, 34–8
as source of ethical practice, 35,
  37–8
Machiavelli, Niccolò
  as precursor to pragmatic ethics,
  145
Marlowe, Christopher, 16–20, 23,
  25–8, 30–1, 33, 36–7, 97–8,
  157n10
  The Jew of Malta, 97–8
  Tamburlaine, 26
  See also *Doctor Faustus*
The Merchant of Venice, 34
metaphor, practice of, 96–7, 98,
  150
metaphysics, xiv–xv, 16–17, 19–20,
  23, 30, 43, 74, 121, 144,
  160n41, 179n23
  See also idealism
Mill, J.S., 13, 138, 142
Montaigne, Michel de, 73–4, 80–1,
  88, 155n31
  Essais, 77
moral philosophy. *See* ethics

narrative
  as core feature of human
  psychology, xii–xiii, 148
natural history
  as basis for pragmatism, 5
  as method for pragmatic
  aesthetics, 12, 14, 18, 150
naturalism, 2, 6, 14, 120–5, 134,
  136, 144–5, 147–8, 155n25
  See also laissez-faire naturalism;
  Romantic naturalism
natural selection, xi–xii, 1–5, 10–12,
  38, 117–19, 121, 136, 144,
  147, 153n5,12
  See also Darwinism
Nedham, Marchamont, 78
neo-Pragmatism
  abandonment of Darwinism, 11,
  149

See also Bernstein, Richard;
  Gunn, Giles; Rorty, Richard;
  Shusterman, Richard; West,
  Cornel
neo-Stoicism, 42–50, 52–3, 56–8,
  60–4, 163n8,9, 164n20,
  166n31
  Cassius' conversion to, 44–5, 47
  contrast with Caesar's Stoic
  idealism, 47–8
  example of Brutus, 43–4, 46–7,
  48–51
  example of Horatio, 52–3, 57,
  61, 63
  Hamlet's conversion to, 57–63
  origins in Stoic view of belief,
  41–2
  and practice-based ethics, 42–3,
  45–6, 63
  theatrical account of ethics,
  45–6, 50, 63
  See also Cicero; partial belief;
  Plutarch; premeditation;
  Seneca
New Criticism, 14, 16, 68, 142,
  154n23, 168n7, 181n17
New Historicism, 14, 142
Nietzsche, Friedrich, 13–14,
  139–40, 142–4, 180n7,9,
  182n21,22
  as initiator of radical ethics,
  13–14, 139–40

Oedipus, xiii, 16
organic pluralism, 5–8, 12, 118,
  141, 145, 146
  body as model for, 5
  as opposed to simple diversity,
  16–17, 144
  as potential relationship between
  science and art, 150
  problems as source of, 6
  relationship to art, 13, 18, 38,
  40, 52, 64–6, 84, 99, 118,
  141, 148–50

Othello, 66, 67–84, 86, 123
  as pre-existing the problem of
    paranoia, 68, 69–71, 83
  retellings of. *See* Beaumont,
    Francis; Porter, Thomas
  See also *Othello* (Restoration
    adaptation)
Othello (Restoration adaptation), 67,
    71–3, 75–6, 81, 84, 98
  modification to fit the problem of
    paranoia, 71–3, 81–3

paranoia, problem of, 68, 71–6,
    77–84, 86, 101, 116–17
  See also ethical problems; reason,
    problem of; social relations,
    problem of
partial belief, 44–5, 47, 49, 52
Petrarch
  De Remediis, 43
philosophy, speculative. *See* idealism
Pinker, Steven, 156n32, 157n9
pity. *See* generosity, practice of
Plato, 9, 41, 135
pluralism
  intrinsic versus instrumental
    value of, 16–17
  Locke's objection to, 13, 138
  in radical ethics, 139, 144
  See also organic pluralism
Plutarch, 42–3, 163n8,9
Popper, Karl, xiv
Porter, Thomas
  The Villain, 77–81
pragmatic aesthetics
  historical failure of, 4, 10–12,
    149
  method for reviving, 12
  See also natural history
pragmatism
  as extension of scientific problem-
    solving, 6, 118, 148
  historical failure of, 3–4, 10–12,
    148
  as justification for art, 9–10,
    117–18, 119–20, 149

  as method of ethics, 4–9
  origins of, 3–4
  as source of progressive society,
    5–9, 14, 117–19, 148
  See also Dewey, John; growth;
    James, William; neo-
    pragmatism; pragmatic
    aesthetics; problem-solving;
    progressive society; tool
premeditation, 42–5
problem-based
  art, 10–14, 18, 38, 64–5, 99,
    120–2, 150
  ethics, 12–13, 16, 22–3, 29–30,
    131, 134, 138, 140–1, 145
  pluralism, 6, 118
  practice, 29, 40, 87, 124, 140–1,
    146, 149
problem-solving, xiv–xvi, 6–13,
    16–17, 22–3, 118, 148, 150
progress, pragmatic definition of. *See*
    growth
progressive society, 3, 5–8, 10, 12,
    17, 40, 68, 87, 102, 117–19,
    148–50
  as alternative to liberalism and
    radical ethics, 14
  See also growth

radical ethics, 13–14, 16–17, 33,
    139–40, 142–3, 155n25,
    156n33, 182n18
  See also Dollimore, Jonathan;
    Greenblatt, Stephen; literary
    studies; Nietzsche, Friedrich
Ransom, J.C., 16, 142, 181n17
reason, problem of, 87–99, 101–17
  See also ethical problems;
    paranoia, problem of; social
    relations, problem of
Reformation, 12, 21, 83
religion. *See* idealism
Restoration drama, 67–73, 75, 77,
    81–4, 85–6, 98, 101, 168n6,
    174n2
Richard II, 103–4, 107–8

Richard III, 30
riddles, 33–7, 52, 64, 99, 131,
    161n45,47, 180n7
  anthropological view of, 34
  Luther's view of, 34–5
Romantic naturalism, 123–5, 134
Romanticism, 122, 123–33, 142,
    145–7, 179n22
  approach to tragedy, 123–4
  Cavell as example of, 125
  as Darwinism, 124–5, 132
  Dewey's rejection for
    pragmatism, 131
  ethics of, 123, 124, 128–9
  pragmatism as alternative to,
    131–3
Romeo and Juliet, 43
Rorty, Richard, 11, 155n25,
    181n14
Rymer, Thomas, 75–6

science (modern experimental),
    xiv–xvi, 2–4, 6–8, 10–12, 14,
    17, 68, 118, 137, 147–50
  as basis of pragmatism, 6, 118,
    148
  limits of, xiv–xvi, 147–8
  pragmatic justification for, xiv–xv
  as progressive, xv, 6, 118
  See also cognitive science
scientific method. *See* problem-
    solving
self-interest
  as ethical concept, 75, 78–9, 83
Seneca, 42–3, 53, 57, 163n8
seventeenth-century tragedy. *See*
    tragedy
Shakespeare, Hamnet, 39
Shakespeare, William, xiii, 9, 17, 30,
    33, 35, 38–43, 46–7, 51–2,
    63–6, 67–8, 71–2, 75–7, 80,
    83–4, 102–4, 107, 110–13,
    117, 120, 123–4, 127–9
  See also *Antony and Cleopatra*;
    Hamlet; *Julius Caesar*; *King
    Lear*; *Macbeth*; *Othello*;

    Richard II; *Richard III*; *Romeo
    and Juliet*; *The Merchant of
    Venice*
Shepard, Alan, xvi
Shusterman, Richard, 11, 155n25
Sidney, Philip, 12
  Apologie for Poesie, 28–30
Sinfield, Alan, 33
skepticism
  appropriated by speculative
    philosophy, 13, 125–8, 137,
    139–40, 142, 180n9
  as tool of practical ethics, 3, 43,
    73–4, 80, 82, 86–7, 88, 91,
    98, 117, 137, 155n28, 157n16,
    164n18, 169n14,17
  See also tabula rasa
Smith, Adam, 14, 138, 141
social relations, problem of, 82–3
  See also ethical problems;
    paranoia, problem of; reason,
    problem of
Sophocles
  Antigone, 9–10
  See also Oedipus
specialization, 5–6, 10
  See also organic pluralism
speculative philosophy. *See* idealism
Stoicism, 39, 41–2, 48, 61–2
  See also neo-Stoicism
story-telling. *See* art; narrative
Swinburne, A.C., 15–17, 30

tabula rasa, 13–14, 136–42, 144–5,
    156n32
tomorrow, problem of, 30–8, 44,
    47, 52–3, 60–2
  See also death; ethical problems
tool
  art as, xv–xvi, 5, 9, 10, 117–18,
    145, 149
  biological definition of, xvi,
    152n12
  democracy as, 8
  ideas as, 6–7, 8, 144
  language as, 5

tool—*Continued*
  literary criticism as, 14
  mind as, 5
  narrative as, xiii
  pluralism as, 8, 16
  problem-solving as, 16
tragedy, xi, xiii–xiv, 12–14, 16, 18,
    28–30, 38, 40, 64–6, 67–8,
    73, 77, 84, 87, 89, 99, 104–5,
    118–20, 122, 124–5, 128–9,
    134, 135–6, 141–2, 144–5,
    149–50
  appropriation by speculative
    philosophy, 13–14, 141–4
  decline of place in ethics. *See*
    Locke, John
  as practical example of problem-
    based art, xiii–xiv, 12–14,
    146
  See also *All for Love*; *Doctor
    Faustus*; *Hamlet*; *Julius
    Caesar*; *King Lear*; *Macbeth*;
    Othello; *The Indian Emperour*;
    Troilus and Cressida
Troilus and Cressida (Dryden),
    112–18
  and the problem of paranoia,
    116–17
  as source of generosity, 113–17
Troilus and Cressida (Shakespeare),
    30, 112, 117

utopianism. *See* idealism

Valla, Lorenzo, 82
Villiers, George
  The Rehearsal, 85–6

Wagner, Richard, 129
Wells, H.G., xvi, 15
West, Cornel, 11, 154n25
Wittgenstein, Ludwig, 124–5,
    127–8
Wordsworth, William, 129